T0320932

BRAIN BASED ENTERPRISES

Brain Based Enterprises offers a unique synthesis of intelligent thought fused with pragmatic and pithy insights on the art and discipline of leading enterprises, where intelligence, ideas and innovation are the currencies of Sustainable Coopetive Advantage (SCA).

From the first signs of intelligence through making axes and fire, we now have access to unprecedented powers of creation through the convergence of humanity and technology. Rapid and dramatic advances in our understanding of genomics, biotechnology, computing and robotics make it possible for us to create a better world or destroy what we have created. The author explores both sides of the Man-Machine dynamic so that you can choose wisely.

Expressed clearly and concisely, this book is essential for busy people seeking to inform and illuminate themselves with a rich mixture of pragmatism, inspiration and wisdom. Featuring numerous micro case-ettes from enterprises ranging from biotechnology to banking and bots, *Brain Based Enterprises* grounds the ideas for people seeking to make the most of the Fourth Industrial Revolution.

Peter Cook leads Human Dynamics and The Academy of Rock, a creativity and innovation consultancy. Blending business, science and music, the author's background is in developing life-saving drugs, including the first HIV/AIDS treatment and human insulin. He is the author of eight books and a writer for Sir Richard Branson's Virgin brand.

Brain Based Enterprises

Harmonising the Head, Heart and Soul of Business

PETER COOK

Routledge
Taylor & Francis Group

LONDON AND NEW YORK

First published 2018
by Routledge
2 Park Square, Milton Park, Abingdon, Oxon OX14 4RN

and by Routledge
711 Third Avenue, New York, NY 10017

Routledge is an imprint of the Taylor & Francis Group, an informa business

British Library Cataloguing-in-Publication Data
A catalogue record for this book is available from the British Library

Library of Congress Cataloging in Publication Data
Names: Cook, Peter, 1958- author.
Title: Brain based enterprises : harmonising the head, heart and soul of
    business / Peter Cook.
Description: Abingdon, Oxon ; New York, NY : Routledge, 2018. | Includes
    bibliographical references and index.
Identifiers: LCCN 2018003449 (print) | LCCN 2018005145 (ebook) |
    ISBN 9781315178356 (eBook) | ISBN 9781138036741 (hardback :
    alk. paper)
Subjects: LCSH: Creative ability in business. | Creative thinking. | Robotics. |
    Technological innovations.
Classification: LCC HD53 (ebook) | LCC HD53 .C663 2018 (print) |
    DDC 658.4/038—dc23
LC record available at https://lccn.loc.gov/2018003449

ISBN: 978-1-138-03674-1 (hbk)
ISBN: 978-1-315-17835-6 (ebk)

Typeset in Sabon
by Swales & Willis Ltd, Exeter, Devon, UK

Printed and bound in Great Britain by
TJ International Ltd, Padstow, Cornwall

For Alison, Thomas and James, the truly intelligent people of the Cooking Clan.

CONTENTS

ACKNOWLEDGEMENTS

Gracious thanks are due to these people who breathed life into this work:

Madeleina Kay who illuminated this book through rich pictures and illustrations. Madeleina is a talented artist, author and musician (www. albawhitewolf.com).

Christina Jansen, professional photographer to people as diverse as Muhammed Ali, Emma Thompson and Robert Plant, who took the photographs for this book (www.cjansenphotography.com).

Jennifer Sertl, author of *Strategy and the Soul*, for her insights into intelligence and 21st-century capabilities (www.jennifersertl.com).

Keiron Sparrowhawk of My Cognition for his insights into neuroscience and its practical applications for our wellbeing.

Matt Bonam and Neil MacKillop at Astra Zeneca for their insights into working in an integrated way with machines.

Peter Cheese, David D'Souza, Warren Howlett and Ruth Stuart at The Chartered Institute of Personnel and Development for their insights into the future of work.

Gareth Jones at The Chemistry Group for an inspirational view of HR fused with big data.

Simon Warren, Managing Director of CaseWare UK for his insights into how AI is affecting financial services (www.caseware.co.uk).

Greg Smith and Carl Bate at Arthur D. Little for their thoughts on Next Practice and using artificial intelligence and human ingenuity to improve our enterprises.

Steve Gorton, Silvia Impellezzeri and Dr Melinda Fouts, for their wise and incisive counsel and insights on wide-ranging matters associated with writing this book.

John Varney, The Centre for Management Creativity, for his insights into creativity and futures (www.high-trenhouse.co.uk).

Professor Adrian Furnham, who offers a continuing source of inspiration, provocation and friendship (www.adrianfurnham.com).

Dr Stephen Leybourne at Boston State University for his collaborations on improvisation and innovation.

The staff at the Virgin Lounge in London, Karen's Diner, South Eastern Railway and Five Steps Café for allowing me to use their venues as mobile office locations.

PROLOGUE

During a recent interview, I was asked what was the most significant innovation in the last 50 years. Apart from the fact that the question is almost impossible to answer, as it is the business equivalent of your all time favourite record, I felt compelled to try to give an answer. I was drawn to mention The Human Genome Project and Wikipedia. What characterises both of these innovations is that neither are physical products such as the steam engine, the wheel and the light bulb. Instead they are information-based products of an economy where 3 i's: intelligence, ideas and innovation are the currencies of sustainable progress. I have dubbed the application of the 3 i's to the world of work as the Brain Based Economy.

Of course we have always used our brains to solve problems, but we have also thoughtlessly plundered the world's natural resources in the last few centuries. We will have to think much more cleverly and systemically to address some of the problems we have created in the wake of our industrial revolution. For example, in the 21st century, it is predicted that we might face a rise in sea levels by up to 3 metres and we will face shortages of critical chemical elements. These are not the dystopian futures from environmental obsessives but inconvenient truths from the U.S. National Climate Assessment and The Royal Society of Chemistry. Our chemical addiction is due to our voracious appetite for rare elements, e.g. helium, which cools much of our everyday life, and rare earths, which enable much of our computing power. If we are to live long and prosper, we must rethink Professor Michael Porter's paradigm of 'Competitive Advantage' to include notions of cooperative behaviour and sustainability. More than ever we now need **SCA** (**S**ustainable **C**oopetive **A**dvantage).

In terms of my personal revolution in the BBE, I was born in late 1958, I grew up in the 1960s. It was the age of science fiction, *The Man from Uncle*, Uncle Sam, Soyuz, Apollo, the white light and white heat of science and technology, C.P. Snow, hippies, the first man on the moon, *Star Trek*, *Lost in Space*, *Space Oddity* and unbridled optimism about the future. I studied sciences with great wonder and believed that technology would solve all our problems and we would live a life of leisure. However, we were wrong, as computers largely have created more things for humans to be interested in, concerned about and to interrupt our lives at this point of their evolution. Perhaps we were just suffering from a little bit of 'premature evaluation' pumped up by the summer of love and an unquestioning belief in the appliance of science. However, we are now at a tipping point where computer power, automation and robotics offer us the possibility of realising these dreams if we get our marriage between man, woman and machine right. That said, much of what we have considered 'work' may well be outsourced to machines and all of us will need to up our game to remain relevant and worthwhile in the 21st century.

Whether we face a dystopian 'Mad Max' future or a utopian life of leisure in the Man-Machine age rather depends on our responses to the future. Klaus Schwab, founder of the World Economic Forum described the convergence of artificial intelligence, automation and machine learning as the 'Fourth Industrial Revolution'. PwC recently reported that artificial intelligence could add up to $15.7 trillion to the global economy by 2030. This is approximately the same as the combined output of China and India. At the same time KPMG reported that up to two-thirds of the US knowledge workforce might be affected by 2025. The Bank of England estimates that automation will eliminate 15 million jobs from the UK economy in the next 20 years – that is roughly 50% of all UK jobs. In China the number will reach some 77% according to the OECD. These losses are most likely to take place in jobs where there are few social elements. So, for example, if you are an undertaker, a hairdresser or a specialised care worker, you will likely still have your job, due to the high social element and individuality of your work. Equally, if you are a dentist, a doctor, a surgeon or an optician your job will be enhanced by technology, but the infinite variety of humans and, therefore, the high degree of personalisation will keep you in work. But, if you trade in knowledge, e.g. a financial analyst, a pay administrator or a market research analyst, most if not all of your current job will be done by machines. As computers begin to learn, so we must grasp the nettles of making ourselves truly brainy people, brainy teams and brainy enterprises.

Brain Based Enterprises offers a unique synthesis of intelligent thought fused with pragmatic and pithy insights on the art and discipline of leading enterprises, where intelligence, ideas and innovation are the currencies of SCA. From the first signs of intelligence through making axes and fire, we now have access to unprecedented powers of creation through the convergence of humanity and technology. Rapid and dramatic advances in our understanding of genomics, biotechnology, computing and robotics make it possible for us to create a better world or destroy what we have created. We explore both sides of the Man-Machine dynamic so that you can choose wisely.

Brain Based Enterprises is expressed clearly and concisely for busy people seeking to inform and illuminate themselves with a rich mixture of pragmatism, inspiration and wisdom. Featuring numerous micro case-ettes from enterprises ranging from biotechnology to banking and bots, *Brain Based Enterprises* grounds the ideas for people seeking to make the most of the Fourth Industrial Revolution.

Brain Based Enterprises addresses critical questions such as:

1. How shall we function in a world where man, woman and machine will have interchangeable and complementary functions?
2. How will we reorganise organisations to make best use of collective cybernetic and human intelligence?
3. What will human intelligence actually mean in a world where we are drowning in data? Instead, how shall we swim with information?
4. How shall we become more intelligent, individually, collectively and corporately?
5. What can and should governments do to encourage intelligent societies and communities?
6. How shall we lay to rest the problems, threats and legacy of the industrial era?
7. How shall we find sustainable resolutions to emerging world problems?
8. How will education need to change in order to continue to be relevant and effective?
9. What role can leaders play in stimulating an enterprise's corporate corpuscles and collective synapses? How can they engender climates, cultures and structures where intelligence, ideas and innovation are the norm?
10. How shall we change work before work changes us?

Brain Based Enterprises is divided into three 'dialogues'.

Dialogue I: Brainy people (personal intelligence)

We begin by examining four postures that will enable us as individuals to sink or swim in the Man-Machine age. The transition to an intelligent society is a VUCA problem. We examine ways to handle Volatile, Uncertain, Complex and Ambiguous issues that we must address in order to thrive in the Fourth Industrial Revolution. Our core tenet of a Brain Based Enterprise (BBE) relies on some new thinking about what constitutes intelligence and a rebalancing between conventional IQ, emotional (EQ) and spiritual (SQ) intelligence. Finally we look at seven core habits for a Brain Based Economy where man, woman and machine align their corporate corpuscles and collective synapses for a better world.

Dialogue II: Brainy teams (collective intelligence)

Intelligent teams need excellent leadership and management. Simply stated, leading brains in the Man-Machine age differs from managing brawn in the industrial era. We examine the differences and offer an agenda for Brain Based Leaders to lead diverse teams including members you have no formal control over if they are not on your payroll or watch. Implicit in the art of leadership is the need to use dialogue instead of discussion and to facilitate rather than tell people what to do. We look at the gentle art and discipline of dialogue and skilful facilitation, which make teams more intelligent and valuable. Individual intelligence is relatively simple, but how does a team make itself more intelligent through networking and leveraging its knowledge, expertise and experiences?

Dialogue III: Brainy enterprises (global intelligence)

In a world of continuous disruption, long-range planning and strategy are dead. Yet random improvisation is not a strategy for success. In a complex and occasionally chaotic world we need strategy that allows for responsiveness and agility. Here we explore the idea of strategic improvisation, learning from the business gurus and from masters of the art and discipline of improvisation in music. Ultimately a BBE rests on having people-management strategies and practices that liberate minds, bodies and souls. We look at how you can cultivate a culture that liberates the head, heart and soul of your enterprise. We also examine the influence of organisation structure on networked intelligence, drawing from the fields of biology, sociology, anthropology and mathematics to inform our thinking.

In writing this book, I bring three main pillars of my experience together: science, business and music. I have considerable practical experience of leading knowledge-based innovative enterprises in my formative career in pharmaceuticals, successfully bringing novel life-saving treatments to the world, such as human insulin and the first HIV/AIDS treatment, plus 25 years' diverse business consulting across many different sectors. This is supported by many years in academia, teaching business and leadership at MBA level, plus experience from the artistic dimension, as a writer and performer of music. I dub this blend of art, academia and industry 'pracademic': informed by information, but not a slave to the rhythm of data; creative but not merely romantic dreaming; rooted in what works, but also constantly questioning what works in an endless obsession to learn.

I am grateful as always to my wife, Alison, who has tirelessly made suggestions, critiqued and improved the book with her sharp and witty pragmatism in ways that no other strategic adviser or business consultant could ever come close to. My children Thomas and James have also helped in ways that they will never know. Bless them!

I am happy to indulge in conversations with others about how we shall approach the Man-Machine age. I can be contacted as follows:

Tel: + 44 (0) 7725 927585
e-mail: peter@humdyn.co.uk
Websites: www.humdyn.co.uk; www.academy-of-rock.co.uk

Peter Cook

DIALOGUE ONE

Brainy people
(personal intelligence)

CHAPTER 1

The Man-Machine paradox

It is 06.05 a.m. on 5 January 2030 . . . The day begins for Julie:

Julie wakes up at exactly the optimum time to maximise her sleep, wellbeing and energy, to a vibration in her neck from her embedded wellbeing monitor. Some ambient music fills the room, bathed in soft purple swirling lighting. The smell of freshly brewed coffee percolates upwards from the kitchen. These are things she chose in her psychological contract with Rover. In a few minutes, coffee, water and fruit slices are brought to her by Rover, her personal robotic assistant. It's time for Julie's early morning wellbeing session, led by her ever-faithful 24/7 digital guide, who has already ironed her underwear, run a bath, organised her bag for the day, checked her travel schedule, confirmed her appointments and so on.

Rover also monitored Julie's vital signs and adjusted her personal exercise routine around her expected physical activity during the day, to maximise her balance of mind, body and soul. Rover is, of course, a robot and makes rational decisions based on an aggregation of big data about what's best for Julie's work, life and play. However, Rover has also integrated humanity by taking on board Julie's own personal values within the decision-making algorithms that Rover uses.

We are seeing the earliest signs and signifiers of a world where man and machine have switched roles, with driverless trains, 3D printing, self-service shops, smart cities, smart homes, smartphones and drones. We can already measure our vital signs to improve our vitality and receive live updates on life-threatening conditions to help us live long and prosper. However, the transformation towards our love affair with machines is not exactly new. We perhaps began to notice the difference as long ago as 1822 with Charles Babbage's invention of the difference engine. Since that time, we have had the enigma machine, The Casio FX77 and many more devices that have enabled us to do ever more complex things. Many more things are still

to come in our enigmatic relationship with machines via The Internet of Things, which promises to have 50 billion devices connected to the Internet by 2020. Innovation consultancy Arthur D. Little report that any technology innovations that enhance people's time to spend on higher-level Maslow needs and that reduce or remove the need to focus on the lower level needs is a good innovation. We will increasingly have the ability to separate the things that satisfy us from the things that we have to do. It is entirely feasible that we will have time to enjoy those things in life that we do purely for their intrinsic value, such as arts and crafts. Perhaps, like Julie's example in 2030, we will use machines to clear the space and time for us to enjoy such things. Chartered Institute of Personnel and Development (CIPD) CEO Peter Cheese points out that we see the emergence of different economic models in some sectors, for example in agriculture and transportation. These shifts are driven by technology and geopolitics: "The departure of farm workers is driving the introduction of mechanisation. In transportation the UK currently has a shortage of lorry drivers but this is producing calls for automation rather than more lorry drivers".

The economist Larry Summers pointed out that, whereas the availability of capital used to enhance labour, it could now displace labour. One only has to look at the automotive industry to see a glimpse of the future for these other sectors in terms of how automation has affected jobs. As well as technology, geopolitics is driving change. For example, in construction, agriculture, health and hospitality, where there has been easy access to low-cost labour, there has been little incentive to look at automation, but this has now appeared on the agenda in the wake of an uprising of popularism across the western world. From coal mining to data mining we can envisage a number of future scenarios in our love/indifference/hate affair with man, woman, machines, robotics, artificial intelligence (AI) and official stupidity.

War of the Worlds

In this dystopian view, humans battle it out with machines and all lose the value of each others' contributions. Like the film of the same name, it is a zero sum game for all concerned or a nil-nil draw in football terms, with dramatic consequences for humanity, humility and technology alike. Despite this being a lose-lose game for all concerned, we humans love a little drama in our lives, so *War of the Worlds* is not a completely unlikely scenario, especially in some business sectors, where it can be seen as a battle for supremacy that will at least appeal to some alpha males and females.

Planet of the Apes

Humans decide to work without machines. This is an impoverished retro world in which humanity slides backwards overall. In football terms this is one-nil to the humans or an 'ignore' strategy. Although it sounds unlikely

HIGH

CONCERN FOR MACHINERY

ATTACK of The CLONES

The MAN -MACHINE

WAR of the WORLDS

PLANET of the APES

LOW

LOW

HIGH

CONCERN FOR HUMANITY

as a scenario, we already see attempts to ignore the march of automation in terms of the arguments about driverless trains in the UK and, to a lesser degree, road transport. Railways have the advantage of having rails so the destination and journey is already pre-set to some degree. There are also already examples of driverless trains, for example the Docklands Light Railway in London. As I write, we have experienced a series of lengthy strikes by the staff of Southern Rail over the gradual erosion of human presence on their trains. The argument revolved around whether the trains would continue to have an onboard member of staff, although it was presented as a health and safety issue to the general public in terms of who was responsible for shutting the doors. This is verging on a War of the Worlds strategy by the unions rather than an ignore strategy. It is, however, certain that technology will not go away from such occupations and the unions would do well to think about what humans can contribute to people's lives on transport systems rather than attempting to stop the onward march of technology.

Road transport is more difficult in some ways as the landscape is more random, with pedestrians, cyclists, obstacles and the lack of what railway people call a 'permanent way' on most roads. There are currently concerns about the idea of having convoys of lorries on our motorways with the trailing driverless vehicles connected by Bluetooth. As an aside, I can understand the concern over the connectivity, having travelled widely and been repeatedly told that conference centres have Bluetooth speakers for my music, which then cease to work in every place from Dublin to Dubrovnik. Until a technology can be shown to be fail-safe why not use a good old wire? Sure, it does not matter that much when the risk is not that your music will not play at a seminar, but it does if you might kill someone on a motorway. However, the wider point is that the technology will eventually be made to be fail-safe, so never mind my occasional blue language over Bluetooth! So, returning to the issue of driverless cars and lorries, recent research from You Gov bears witness to our *Planet of the Apes* scenario:

> 58% of people think that driverless cars are an interesting technology with merit. But they also think that humans will always drive vehicles.

> 19% believe driverless cars are safer than cars driven by humans, and that replacing all human-operated vehicles should be the goal.

> 13% believe driverless cars are a dangerous technology, prone to accidents and hacking. They believe that widespread implementation would leave millions jobless. As such, they believe that we should rein in the implementation of automated vehicles. It is not clear from the research just who 'we' are however, manufacturers, politicians, consumers, etc. Within this 13% is the *Planet of the Apes* outlook on life.

This outlook is mirrored in views about convoys of lorries connected by Bluetooth, with 64% believing that this development would make roads more dangerous and with 46% believing that it would kill an entire industry. While technology marches on, we can see in this example what Twiss said, that technology is always impeded by social evolution. When evolution is actually perceived as a threat, we can see how there may be a rocky road to implementation.

We have seen a less belligerent form of *Planet of the Apes* in the return to various crafts, where human ingenuity and the personal touch are seen as more valuable/authentic than machine efficiency. Such nostalgia can co-exist with the efficiencies that can come from machines where people are prepared to pay a premium price for handmade products and services from craft beer to craft work.

Attack of the Clones

Machines not only augment human function, they mainly replace it, but without the human systems in place for us to enjoy the leisure time that this creates. We live easy yet unfulfilled lives as a result. In football terms this is one-nil to the machines as they replace entire jobs once performed by humans. Some observers have predicted that the technological singularity will signal the end of the human era around 2040, as superintelligence advances at exponential rates. We have not exactly been attacked by clones up till this point except in the movies, but just notice the quiet revolutions in areas that we take for granted. Your switchboard operator is digital, your lift operator is electric and some receptionists are now electronic. The *Attack of the Clones* scenario seems fairly unlikely, yet we already see how automation can de-skill jobs, such as car manufacture and agriculture if the people doing them do not step up to new levels to profit from augmentation. The choice is in our hands. All that needs to happen for this to become reality is for humans to decide to recline in their sofas and watch the world go by.

As Winston Churchill might have said in *Attack of the Clones*,

> "We will fight them with our synapses. We will fight them with our neurones. We shall never reprogram".

The Man (Woman) Machine

We work in an integrated way with machines, using them for what they do best and deploying human skills when they are of greatest advantage. As a result we live easier, more fulfilled lives. The epilogue I wrote for this book is informed by The Man (Woman) Machine, hereafter referred to as the Man-Machine for convenience and in deference to the Kraftwerk album of the same name. This is one-all draw in football terms, a win-win or 'cobotic' approach. This approach is already established in use within certain high-tech professions such as surgery, electronics, pharmaceuticals and opticians, so it is not a work of science fiction.

I spoke with Matt Bonam and Neil MacKillop at Astra Zeneca about their approach to working in an integrated way with machines. In particular, what advances in AI can offer us in terms of improving health across all three of Astra Zeneca's therapeutic areas: respiratory, oncology and cardiovascular. The dialogue was remarkable. Matt's unit aims to combine new digital technologies with products to help people and physicians better manage when and how medications are used in terms of their impact. This helps patients to optimise their adherence, their self-management and interaction with the physician. The development was triggered in 2012 when the team realised that digital technologies had become robust enough to revolutionise data collection and transmission. It became possible to collect data in real time and provide insights back in real time. This has enabled us to develop a much better approach to more personalised medicine: the right dose; right treatment; delivered at the right time.

> Patients are traditionally supported by seeing a physician at intervals and would be asked, "How have you been?" Their doctor's effectiveness is predicated on what the person can remember and what they are prepared to tell the doctor. What has changed is our ability to passively collect information about the patient, thus eliminating problems of memory or willingness to disclose information.

In the future, Matt and Neil pointed out that Astra Zeneca will have the ability to bring together the individual's data with anonymised information from the population they sit in. This will revolutionise what we are able to do for the patient's healthcare. This will allow the prediction of what will happen to them over the next few days. For example, for respiratory patients who exacerbate for COPD and asthma, the impact of that exacerbation could be life changing. The ability to look at data from an individual will save people's lives. In cardiac failure, Astra Zeneca aim to be able to predict a stroke or a heart attack 48 hours in the future, which offers the opportunity to take preventative action. "We will soon be able to more accurately predict the right dosage for the individual patient, taking into account their weight, health and metabolism with impacts on efficacy and reductions in side effects."

However, Twiss pointed out that technological revolution is always impeded by social evolution factors. I asked Matt to comment on the barriers to adoption and his answer was refreshing when compared with many people who attempt product push:

> We do not start with the technology, we start with the problem. If you are going to start with cool tech, unless you are a Steve Jobs, your technology is unlikely to diffuse into a crowded marketplace. Some of the technology used to enable better medication adherence

is one example. If we are asking someone to ingest a microchip every day and the patient must weigh this up in terms of benefit-risk. If for example you have had an organ transplant your social contract may well be different than someone with a less critical condition so it all depends on a number of factors.

We are navigating several hurdles with our approach. Privacy and security of data are crucial for patients, especially if they fear that the data will be used to penalise the individual, e.g. elective surgeries, insurance premiums. Data loss and impact of data loss must be weighed against the positive stories of lives saved/transformed by the technology. It is about having a contract on fair use of data and we take that very seriously. It is our job as leaders to make wise decisions that harmonise the opportunities that exist between man/woman and machine.

Brain Based Enterprises offers a view that the win-win posture is both desirable and achievable. Reaching this will not be a simple affair, nor is it likely to be a linear journey in all areas of our life and it is already apparent that these are not discrete choices in some areas of business and life. Barack Obama summed up the challenge well in his departure speech: "The next wave of economic dislocations won't come from overseas. It will come from the relentless pace of automation that makes a lot of good, middle-class jobs obsolete."

To engender harmonious collaborations and mergers between man, woman and machine will require us to answer some extremely difficult questions:

1. What shall we do with ourselves in a world where many jobs will have been turned over to machines? What will careers look like in such an age?
2. What then will the people who worked in our 'brawn-based industries' do to create a sense of contribution and value to society?
3. How shall education change in a world where what matters most is application of knowledge rather than acquisition and retention of information? What will we need to learn in order to live fulfilled lives?
4. What will our leisure time look like in such an age? How shall we fall in love?
5. How will we afford a life at leisure if we continue to exchange money for effort in terms of a working life?
6. What will we value? What will we no longer place importance in?
7. How shall we commune with our fellow man/woman? What will enjoyment look like?
8. What levels of privacy of our personal data shall we tolerate?
9. What place will there be for nostalgia?

Nostalgia ain't what it used to be

In considering a future society in which machines are omnipresent and integrated into everyday life, in some cases quite literally under our skin, it is very easy to be seduced into a dystopian future, where man and woman are enslaved by machines in a real-life version of *Attack of the Clones*. Indeed, while writing this book, King Filip of Belgium issued a warning that the digital revolution was contributing to a growing gap between the individual and government. Many of our seismic shifts in terms of unrest in the western world are not so much connected with Donald Trump and Brexit, but by deeper seated anxieties as people begin to see fundamental changes happening to their jobs, livelihoods and communities. President Trump's victory and the United Kingdom's surprising vote to leave the European Union were partly fuelled by a sense of paradise lost and a perception that our futures were controlled by others, alongside various promises to restore a sense of control to the people.

This came home to me when I was invited to attend a private viewing of a Bob Dylan painting and sculpture exhibition. What struck me was how Dylan had captured a lost industrial age, and 'nostalgic landscapes' such as coal mining, car factories, steel works, art deco cafés, heartbreak motels, Zephyrs, Zodiacs, signs of the Zodiac and so on. Yet, such retro-futures are unlikely to return given the inevitability of technologically driven change and the onward march of Moore's Law. In case you are not familiar with this, Intel co-founder Gordon Moore predicted in 1965 that the number of microchip transistors etched onto a microprocessor would double every two years. This also meant that computing power would double every two years. Moore's Law appears to be slowing yet his basic principle holds good. However, the Man-Machine paradox does not have to be an either/or affair, like *War of the Worlds*. In other words, nostalgia ain't what it used to be.

The crucial differentiator is how we respond to the machine age and how we manage to resolve the paradoxes of man, woman and machines. *Brain Based Enterprises* offers strategies and practices that will help you maximise the upside of the Fourth Industrial Revolution. That said, we all have to rethink exactly what we expect and how we intend to adapt in order to thrive in an age where AI drives disruptive technological growth with dramatic impacts on what we call civilisation. Rather than drowning in fake nostalgia let us begin by considering how we get through this thing called life.

What do you want from life?

> A foolproof plan and an airtight alibi,
> Real simulated Indian jewelry,
> A Gucci shoetree,
> A year's supply of antibiotics . . .
>
> 'What Do You Want from Life?' – The Tubes

Psychedelic punk poets The Tubes shone a satirical light on our hopes, dreams, foibles and fantasies with their dystopian rock anthem 'What Do You Want from Life?' You ought to check the song out to appreciate the full value of the rant at the end, which was decades ahead of its time. Yet their title is an incredibly good question for anyone trying to focus their energies and skills into what they do for a living and from life in general. I asked a beautiful woman the question. What she said took me by surprise:

> I want to feel confident in my own skin, improve my education and have the emotional intelligence to protect myself from self and other's criticism. Aside from that, I want to do a job that makes me feel valued, be paid well enough for it to enable me to give some of my time to things that matter. At the end of my life, I'd like people to be able to say that I left the planet in a better state than when I arrived in some ways. My footprints should be light on planet earth but purposeful.

I was expecting her to give me a list of consumer products! Well, actually I am only joking about such an obviously sexist and ageist assumption about my wife, yet this story rather points to our perverse views about happiness and how some of these are only skin deep. The question of what do you want from life is hard enough for many people to answer in the present moment, even harder if you attempt to answer it some time into the future. Perhaps it is a little easier to consider the question "What do we get from life?" In the western world we tend to get an education, some basic promises about health, a job with sufficient income to have some kind of life and so on. Some of us enjoy greater levels of wealth and therefore the potential to live a richer life while others must satisfy themselves with inner riches. Paradoxically the research on happiness shows some correlation between a rise in material wealth and an overall decrease in happiness. The CIPD report that a surprisingly high number of those earning more also say that money worries have affected their job performance. For instance:

- 30% of those earning £35 000–£44 999 report that financial anxieties have impacted on how they do their job.
- 20% of those earning £45 000–£59 999 and 14% of those enjoying an income of £60 000 or more all report their work performance suffering from financial worries.
- More than one in five (21%) senior managers and over one in four (27%) middle managers report that money fears affect their work, indicating that money worries affect all income groups.

In Dialogue III of this book we visit Gareth Jones at Chemistry, a 21st-century recruitment agency that has developed the tools to help people get better answers to the question "What do you want from life in 2030?" Is age a factor in all this?

The millennial fallacy

Biology is a constant, but careers are driven by psychology, sociology and anthropology.

There is a popular belief that millennials are somehow genetically different to Generation X/Y and that this somehow requires us to redesign work to meet their needs, wants, whims, foibles and fantasies. It would be quite remarkable if a species had fundamentally changed across a single generation and quite contrary to any ideas about evolution, bringing new meaning to *Planet of the Apes*. Talking with millennials I think we might have mistaken cause and effect and confused biology with psychology, sociology and anthropology here. Certainly socioeconomic factors surrounding work have changed, with greater uncertainties in career tenure, constant churn in jobs, a major recession and changes in the employment relationship and the 'psychological contract'. In some cases millennials conclude that loyalty to an enterprise is at best transient and not worth the trade. This, rather than 'genetic modification', might more adequately explain their desire for sabbaticals, job-hopping and what appears to be mere compliance to an enterprise over commitment.

Anthropology also plays its part in terms of how tribal behaviour affects expectations and behaviour at work; in other words millennial behaviours might simply be part of the latest 'corporate fashion'. In the gig economy, with low wages and 'start-stop' project-based work without commitment, pension contributions, holidays, sick pay, etc., some millennials are willing to trade other non-financial elements of the reward-recognition package. This might explain why some people claim that millennials crave constant instant approval via references and other recognition tokens such as awards, as these help such people manage their careers on LinkedIn etc. The need for approval might, therefore, be nothing to do with fundamental ego problems, just the social recognition that references say more than your CV in a connected business world. To suggest that these changes are down to fundamental biological factors is, therefore, to miss the impact of some other 'ologies'. In short, we have not changed genetically, but our circumstances have. Some millennials I speak with would love the idea of a job for life, if an enterprise could be found that nurtured their talents in the way that I experienced in my time spent at The Wellcome Foundation. Such places are much harder to find these days.

So, we do need to think about what people want from work and life and maybe these things are not so far different from those of other generations. In a recent survey 74% of staff surveyed said they wanted more freedom in their roles and 34% said their work was overly regulated. Paradoxically, computers and more structured processes at work, driven by algorithms, can restrict the freedoms that many people crave in doing their jobs.

One only has to experience phoning a bad call centre where management have structured the work and held on to discretionary power in such a way that frontline staff are unable to do anything other than repeat pre-scripted responses, causing frustration all round. This approach dehumanises and is evocative of the *Planet of the Apes* approach we discussed earlier.

Although the Man-Machine age might well offer a utopian future, CIPD CEO Peter Cheese pointed out that the bridging period could well be painful and difficult. An examination of any of the scenarios around the future of work, even the most positive, involves a large degree of redundancy of people who then need to have transferable skills. The big challenge will come in the next 20–30 years. We could end up with greater inequalities in the medium term without a properly managed approach and this will call on our best efforts in leading and managing people. This is not a factor of age, it is a factor of aptitude, willingness to learn and flex your knowledge, skills and experience into different career choices.

Cheese points out that we are already seeing the signs and drivers of what life will be like in 2030 for millennials:

- *Demography*: People living longer, working longer. We expect to have a more fungible existence driven by both need and opportunity and assisted by healthcare improvements.
- *The continuation of the rise of the gig economy facilitated by technology*: There has been a lot more evidence of people working for themselves, particularly older people, although it seems unclear as to how this will affect income and wealth for younger people who must at present still save for education, mortgages, pensions, etc.
- *A fragmentation of what we see as the homogeneous life of work toward more flexible career structures and flexible working*: Rather than flatter hierarchies coming from millennials as an expectation, this seems to be coming from enterprises as a response to the need for greater innovation velocity.
- Technology will enable us to work anywhere in the world through live translation and virtual reality at a very affordable cost, and this could transform knowledge work.

Our education systems will need to change radically to address these changes and we look at alternatives to the upload-download model that remains resilient but irrelevant in our current education system. Aside from this we will need to prepare people to be more adaptive to apply skills to different situations. Continuing Professional Development is not a nice-to-have in the Man-Machine age and we will all need a PSP or Personal Sanity Plan which balances head (IQ), heart (emotional intelligence; EQ) and soul (spiritual intelligence; SQ), rather than just focusing on professional skills and knowledge.

GROUND CONTROL

Learning to learn 2030

Find yourself a quiet space and equip it with artefacts that create a sense of relaxed attention for you. These might be objects, music, visual stimuli, tastes, smells, etc. Whatever it is will be entirely personal, but make sure it is a sacred space for you.

Wear a blindfold or put the lights down low for at least 20–30 minutes, ideally longer and remain still, just appreciating the moment as you muse upon life in 2030.

Reflect upon the things you would like to learn in your life without concern for how you might go about learning them. Trust your mind to remember those that matter most.

Review those things that are somehow now learnings that are now past their sell by date. Find ways to update or commit them to your store of unlearnings.

So, does this mean that we are pursuing the wrong things or do we need to reframe what we mean by happiness in the 21st century? Some of the taken-for-granted things of life are under review and it seems certain that our ideas about wealth, health and happiness are likely to be challenged in the Man-Machine age. We might, for example, have to become comfortable with the idea of not having a job for some parts of our life. We might have to find purpose in ways other than work. Perhaps we might have to get off money and material things as the hallmarks and opiates of personal progress and status in the world. Maslow's triangle could become inverted in such a world where self-actualisation is the main activity of life, with basic needs for food and shelter met for all.

In contemplating the myriad changes we might have to consider, the notion of "Money for Nothing" is one such idea. One of the pressing questions that we must answer is "How will we live long and prosper in a world where many of us do not have access to money through the thing we have called work?" Elon Musk proposes a universal basic income for all, a concept already being discussed and trialled in Switzerland, Finland, Canada, India and the Netherlands. A form of universal income has already been in operation in Alaska since 1982 where every person was given $1022 in 2016 as a basic income and the idea is not itself new, having been proposed by Thomas More via his book *Utopia* in 1516. However, this is not going to be easy to do in a connected world. For example, some countries' healthcare and education are paid for by private money, so this is a complex issue. It is in essence a 'VUCA or wicked problem'. We must understand and be able to navigate Volatility, Uncertainty, Complexity and Ambiguity if we are to thrive in the Man-Machine age. We need to be able to navigate the VUCA world to be effective as a Brain Based Leader.

CHAPTER 2

Wickedness, complexity and the Man-Machine age

Rittel and Webber coined the concept of 'wicked problems' in 1973. This foreshadowed the more popular notion of 'VUCA' issues and the IBM concept of Cynefin, which have come to the fore in recent times. The term VUCA stands for problems and opportunities that are Volatile, Uncertain, Complex and Ambiguous in nature. These do not lend themselves to simple solutions, indeed many VUCA issues are insoluble in so far as they can only be resolved rather than solved. We have been seduced with problem-solution thinking in a non-stop world and this is alluring for simple problems where there is no need to consider knock-on consequences of the solutions and where the consideration of options is unnecessary. For the simple things in life we tend to want our problems solved as quickly as possible and without fuss, for example when downloading a piece of music that somehow does not work on our chosen platform. As we add more complexity to our lives we will increasingly need to be able to resolve wickedness. Such problems do not lend themselves to problem-solution thinking. Here we explore strategies and tactics to deal with inherent wickedness.

Consider the problem of having an oversized carpet in your house as an oversimplified example of a wicked problem. It is certainly possible to move the rut around the room but almost impossible to eradicate the rut without re-laying the carpet, cutting the unwanted material off in the process. In the context of an enterprise, moving the rut around the room might mean shifting the problem from the HR division to Marketing to the IT division, etc. But the problem still remains unresolved in overall terms and each rearrangement creates other problems, some of which might be worse than the original problem. Re-laying the carpet in organisational terms is almost certainly not feasible, due to the need to maintain business continuity. It is essentially the equivalent of starting over in your enterprise and maybe reconfiguring the business from scratch. This is, perhaps, why we in the UK cannot 'fix' our NHS, our rail systems and other monolithic and complex enterprises that we rely on, as we cannot simply shut down and re-boot like a computer. VUCA problems are characterised by:

Volatility: VUCA problems do not stay in one place. They move and that makes them especially difficult to pin down, define, contain and stabilise. They are to the business world what Heisenberg's uncertainty principle is to physics. 'Solutions' for VUCA issues are also not solutions in the pure sense of the word, as they are often sub-optimal. Applying a poorly formed solution or a 'quick fix' may have negative consequences of equal or even greater long-term impact, yet busy managers like to control volatile problems and the need to juggle short-term expediency with long-term effectiveness is a constant tension. The long-term nature of VUCA issues sometimes means that resolution takes place while the issue is still 'moving' and the dynamic volatility of the issue therefore prevents full resolution. It would be tempting to think that doing nothing might be an expedient course of action, and timing is a crucial factor in the resolution of a VUCA problem. Yet, inaction is not in itself a good choice and this presents leaders with the dilemma of taking sometimes having to take sub-optimal action or doing nothing.

Consider the example of improving transport in London. It sounds like a well-specified goal at face value. Who would disagree with the goal? Let us suppose the Mayor of London decides to tackle one 'tamer' element of the wicked problem by installing cycle lanes? The cycle lanes do indeed improve the safety for cyclists but increase the danger for pedestrians jaywalking while on their phones. The lanes also slow traffic down considerably in a city characterised by a legacy road structure through road narrowing measures. Paradoxically, the congestion this creates sometimes causes cyclists to weave through traffic in areas where there are no cycle lanes and thus creates the potential for more accidents. I met the owner of a company who had done a lot of the work to build the cycle super-highways in London. He confidently told me that he thought he would likely be uninstalling the lanes within a few years once a new mayor was appointed and when people realised that attempts to discourage cars had failed, with intolerable amounts of congestion for motorists. Indeed, just as I write this, our MP for East Somerset Jacob Rees-Mogg, with a penchant for classic cars and classical language, has put forward the idea that motorists should not be penalised for wanting to drive in and out of cities, so it begins . . .

Unknown unknowns: One of the difficulties in cracking a VUCA issue is often that people do not know what needs to be known in order to make progress. Priorities are usually challenged. The debates that ensued following the UK's decision to leave the European Union were characterised by a tsunami of data but a desert of accurate information on which to make

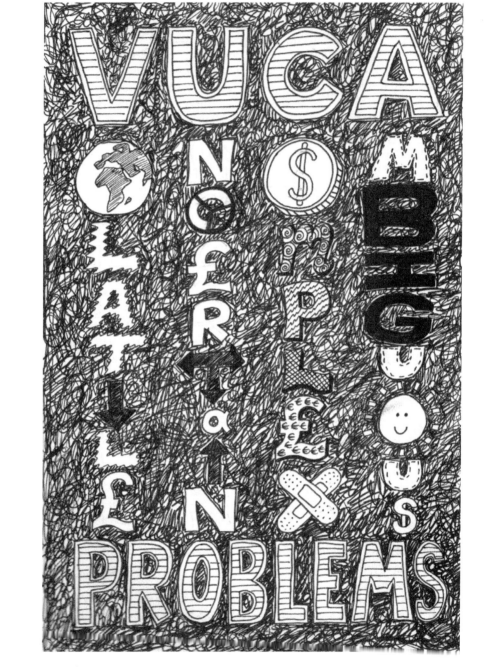

any coherent plans. This led to our prime minister's tautological 'plan', stating that "Brexit Means Brexit". Clearly the reductionism of an unknown unknown into a three-word sound bite makes it appealing at a superficial level. However, on closer inspection, the phrase was found to be content free. This led on to a multiplicity of almost weekly Brexit varieties, including Clean, Dirty, Red, White, Blue, Green, Hard, Soft, Variegated, Ventilated, Venerated Brexit et al., none of which adequately encapsulated the inherent unknowns. VUCA problems are characterised by uncertainty. One smart thing to do when tackling them is to research all the known unknowns. This has the tendency to tame the wickedness to some degree, leaving prime thought space for the major uncertainties. Columbus and Magellan's breakthrough discoveries thrived on uncertainty and it is the stuff of much entrepreneurship, as people like Sir Richard Branson, Sir Alan Sugar and others would testify. Yet even these 'adventure capitalists' build their adventures on solid foundations when you take a peek under the hood.

Responding to uncertainty is one of the biggest issues facing Pfizer Inc., the world-class healthcare company. Many employees in the pharmaceutical sector live in the world of order and control, reinforced by a necessarily tight regulatory system to ensure that the products are safe and effective. Yet the lifeblood of the pharmaceutical industry is innovation, which, by definition requires exploration of the 'unfamiliar'. The successful management of this paradox is one of the key issues that occupy top management attention:

> The thrust to innovate informs every aspect of business and life at Pfizer. We do everything we can to stimulate, organise, and direct creative development. That's how we control the innovation process and, as much as possible, keep it predictable. I say as much as possible, because there is always the capricious variable of chance. The unpredictable always plays its part, but we have tried to institutionalise opportunism.
>
> William C. Steere Jr, former Chairman
> and CEO, Pfizer Inc.

Turning away from macroeconomic issues toward personal development, in the gig economy, young people face higher levels of career uncertainty than they would have done in the Industrial Revolution. While the future of our careers is uncertain, it is possible to reduce the uncertainty levels by adopting the following postures:

- We need to update our skills to make ourselves employable in a disruptive world.
- We will need to manage our careers as a portfolio.
- We must learn to participate successfully in the gig economy.

If the half-life of technology and businesses is in sharp decline, one of the personal risks in managing your career in an uncertain world is that it is possible to 'reverse' yourself into career dead ends in the future. A disruptive environment and the possibility that you might need to have 3–5 phases of your career means that an agile approach to your own career portfolio management becomes an essential part of any smart leader's suite of strategies for an uncertain world. Leaning into the future is better than holding nostalgia for the past or remaining frozen in the present.

Complex connectedness: When dealing with a VUCA problem, it is impossible to disentangle the issue from its context. VUCA issues have multiple causations rather than single causes and in some cases it might be difficult to identify component causes. VUCA issues are interconnected and interdependent. This came home to me in sharp relief when acting as a mediator with a team of health professionals for the family of a dear friend who was dying from triple organ failure at the age of 30. While trying to hold the rage and grief of his family in the meeting I had to find a way to help them understand that his kidney failure was related to his liver failure and, in turn, the many other complications were related to the complex connectedness of the human body. This was not really like a car alternator breakdown or a computer software problem, where a new part or a plug-and-play solution would rectify the problem, as much as all would have liked to believe. VUCA problems live in a world of soft correlation rather than hard causation. People like to think of problems being caused by a single issue but this is rarely so in the case of complex connected problems. In our example of transport in London, cycle lanes might not cause pedestrian injuries but there might be some correlation between the issues. Traffic jams are only partly caused by traffic and so on, although the terminology might suggest otherwise. In the world of health, while it is well known that smoking increases the risks of cancer, giving up smoking might not stop someone from getting cancer, as there are many lifestyle factors that contribute to the disease, and so on.

Speaking to Carl Bate at Arthur D. Little revealed the difference between complex and complicated. Horst Siebert, the German economist, coined the phrase 'the cobra effect' to illustrate the effects of an incorrect understanding of the total view of a situation, and the misapplication of controls in an economy. The term stems from early 20th-century Delhi. The governors of the day were worried about the increasing number of venomous cobra snakes roaming the city and to solve the problem they offered a bounty for every dead cobra. Initially this was a successful strategy, with large numbers of snakes being killed. Over time, however, some enterprising citizens began to breed and slaughter cobras for the income and all of a sudden the governors were faced with too many cobra skins and too many bounty payments – the scheme was becoming unaffordable and was rescinded. But by then the cobra farmers had this large population of cobras to deal with. And what do you do if there's no market? You just release them. And this significantly, by a few orders of magnitude, worsened the cobra menace in Delhi.

Inherent ambiguity: Multiple stakeholders are often involved in the resolution of a wicked problem, many of whom will see the issue differently or will find it hard to actually even describe the issue in a clear way, and this makes for inherent ambiguity in the goals, scope and potential diagnosis and agreement about what the problem is. Looking at just a few of the stakeholders in our transport for London example:

- The Mayor of London might be concerned with seeking re-election and making the roads safer as a bare minimum. In extremis, some of his own concerns will be in conflict.
- Road transport lobby groups might be more interested with traffic flows.
- Commuters might be more concerned with getting to work quickly, and so on.
- Cyclists might be more interested in having free uninterrupted cycle lanes without people and/or traffic lights.

It is often hard to pick or converge opinions down to the issue that unifies all. Some people say that resolving a VUCA problem is like trying to nail jelly to the ceiling.

Consider this simple scenario built around an ambiguous new product. A colleague has invented a new way to clean your teeth. It is apparently a revolution, bears no resemblance to a toothbrush and, moreover, you can clean your teeth without the need for water. However, you are not allowed to see a prototype, nor have the opportunity to try it. What is your response to the device? You want to buy ten for the family now? Couldn't give a damn? Interested to find out more? Merely intrigued? Want to try it out before you decide?

Typical VUCA issues are world peace, universal happiness, a universal income and solving world poverty. In the case of world poverty it is clear that we have made huge progress in this area over the last 30 or so years, with the prospect that we could eradicate it within 20 years, although other factors might complicate eradication.

- In 1990, 43% of the citizens from developing countries lived in extreme poverty.
- By 2010 it was just half of the 1990 figure at 21%.

At the same time, our actions to eradicate poverty have also had other collateral effects such as migration, which have contributed to racist divisions in the western world via populist movements. None of these are reasons for stasis, of course, yet to be effective we must do the best thing we can at the time rather than anything or nothing. Yet, many times VUCA problems present themselves as burning platforms, in other words they are both urgent and important in time-management terms. This sometimes precludes their full resolution and promotes knee-jerk reactions.

The idea of a universal income is also utopian, yet the idea asks as many questions as it appears to solve and is therefore a VUCA opportunity. Musk, however, believes it could open up a new chapter in human life. Would some of us choose to receive a basic income in exchange for full employment, fewer hours worked and the opportunity to earn more by discretionary contribution to our collective net worth through the development of new knowledge? We explore this concept more in the epilogue with our visit to life in 2030:

> *Julie works 20 hours a week flexibly via a complex coordination of her client's needs, her family and herself. Julie elected to receive a basic income in exchange for full employment, less hours worked and the opportunity to earn more by discretionary contribution through an international grid of knowledge.*

According to Peter Cheese (CIPD CEO, 2017), "People will have time to do other things and more complex things, more interesting things. They will certainly have more leisure time".

David D'Souza at the CIPD asks some incisive strategic questions about Musk's vision and VUCA problems that need to be given attention by world leaders on all sides:

1. Financial markets, left to their own devices, are not good at accommodating a greater social purpose – do we need to take more of an interventionist stance to ensure greater societal benefit?
2. More leisure time requires more disposable income if we assume that money will remain as an exchange token for the thing we call work.
3. How will companies pushing automation make money if most citizens survive on a fixed, universal basic income?
4. What is the point of work? To get happiness? Make a difference? Recognition? Will the point of work change and how might it do so?
5. If whole chunks of your life are viewable on the Internet will we become more tolerating of mistakes at work?
6. How do you get a mortgage in the 'Gig Economy'?
7. People cry when their pets die. What will be the first piece of technology that you cry over the loss of? Do you remember your first download?

▬▬▬▬▬▬▬ **GROUND CONTROL** ▬▬▬▬▬▬▬

Rethinking society

It is the year 2030. Form a small working group and set aside a few hours to contemplate two or three of David D'Souza's questions.

Insist on running the event as a dialogue rather than a discussion. See our conversation on dialogue later in this book for a description of how these terms differ.

Resist as far as possible the tendency to close down dialogue, reach conclusions, decisions or actions such that the conversation ferments and spreads. Evaluate much later, say at one month after the dialogue.

Resolving wickedness

How then does one go about addressing a VUCA/wicked problem/opportunity? There is no single way to go about this but here are some suggestions for commencing:

1. Time to think is essential. Wicked problems must be understood well in order to have any chance of doing anything better than applying a sticking plaster to them.
2. At the same time, it is vital to suspend judgement about sub-optimal solutions that have been tried or suggested. A wicked problem is wicked because it has hitherto eluded all attempts to resolve the matter through 'plug-and-play' solutions or piecemeal approaches to problem solving.
3. Be prepared to apply systemic thinking to the topic. In particular, find ways to see the problem from multiple viewpoints and stakeholder perspectives in order to grapple with the whole-brain view of the problem.
4. Sometimes some clearance activity can help to 'tame' a wicked problem, by eradicating the 'knowable unknowns' through research. The more one can know about the known areas of a wicked problem the easier it is to focus on the uncertainties that actually count.
5. On some occasions, it is useful to invest a good amount of time converging to a point (the super-ordinate goal) to agree what the prime issue is. The issue, which, if addressed will have maximum impact on the sub-issues in the most helpful way. This requires skilled facilitation skills if dealing with groups, and expert coaching if dealing with individuals.
6. In other circumstances, it helps to begin to solve the problem through active experimentation/improvisation, discarding prototypes that do not work until a clear vision emerges from many attempts to 'hit the spot'. Much exploratory research and development operates on this basis although trial and error can be an expensive business. The classic examples of this are Edison's light bulb, which reputedly took 10 000 prototypes and Sir James

Dyson's vacuum cleaner, which involved 5127 prototypes. Dyson used the Edisonian/scientific approach to innovation, making just one change every time he developed a prototype.

7. In some cases a pincer action is needed. Perhaps clarifying questions of shared vision first and then finding ingenious solutions through experimentation. Re-clarifying the vision and then systematically removing the obstacles to reaching that vision.

8. Expert facilitation is needed to tackle VUCA problems and we look at this topic in Dialogue II.

9. Alongside facilitation, there is often a need for process management and tools and techniques. We explore divergent and convergent thinking later on in Dialogue I.

10. The values needed to tackle VUCA problems are those that cultivate a climate of creativity, i.e. curiosity, love, forgiveness and a sense of direction. We examine these within our review of 'Seven habits for the Man-Machine age' in Chapter 5.

To resolve a VUCA problem requires all of our intelligences: conventional IQ, EQ and SQ. How then do we create an enterprise that thinks individually and collectively in teams and as a whole system?

CHAPTER 3

The Brain Based Enterprise

I first conceived of the idea of a Brain Based Enterprise (BBE) in the shower while writing the book *Leading Innovation, Creativity and Enterprise*. To be completely correct I was in the shower thinking about the book rather than actually working on my laptop. Perhaps this will be possible in the future to capture those creative moments! Anyway a pithy definition helps begin our exploration of the BBE:

> A Brain Based Enterprise (BBE) is an enterprise that encourages people to bring their heads, hearts and souls to work.

You might well ask "why not just their brains?" Well, we need a wider palette of intelligences as mentioned: IQ, EQ and SQ as we shall discuss later. Arguably, however, our basic IQ will be less important than our EQ and SQ in a world in which much of the analytical work will be automated. We might, however, need much higher IQ skills to process the data and information, which machines will process on our behalf. A BBE is characterised by:

1. A happy marriage of people's passions, the enterprise's purpose and profitable outcomes, be they measured in financial values for a profit-seeking enterprise or social good for a non-profit-seeking one, be it a public or social enterprise.
2. An enterprise that maximises talent, in terms of leveraging people's abilities to use knowledge, skills, experience and wisdom. This is reflected in every way through the attraction process, the development of people to become continuous learners and the use of machines and AI to augment human endeavour for maximum effectiveness.
3. Teams that collaborate through sharing knowledge, insight and wisdom where it is often impossible to achieve the enterprise's ambitions by working alone due to the complexities of innovation and the need for skills not normally resident in one individual. A good example is the United Nations Weapons Inspectorate, where sadly, due to the

complexities of modern weapons, they need people who are experts in physics, computing, bioscience and other disciplines in order to have the relevant knowledge and skills to be effective.

4. An obsession with innovation as a modus operandi and a relentless thirst to never let today's successes become tomorrow's plateaux. Essentially to increase the churn rate between ideas and innovations, what we call the ROI (Return on Innovation) or what Arthur D. Little call 'Next Practice' over 'Best Practice'.

5. An open systems approach to the enterprise's boundaries. In some cases people will be collaborating with others who are not on the payroll and who are motivated by different things than that of the host enterprise. Brain Based Leaders must therefore be adept at motivating people who work for a mix of motives: staffers, freelance gig economy workers, volunteers, customers and possibly competitors.

6. Leaders who harness diverse talents and personalities and blend their skills in pursuit of the enterprise's aims while giving meaning to the thing we call work.

7. A culture that encourages productive synthesis of human- and machine-led endeavour and not a *War of the Worlds* approach to technology adoption and augmentation.

At an individual level, the atoms of a BBE are the people. Unless we get the atoms right we will not be successful at building molecules (teams) and macromolecules (enterprises). The field of study that we call Organisation Development begins from the ground up and we therefore begin by looking at individuals and intelligent contributions at a personal level before examining teams and the whole enterprise.

Brainy people

Our notions of what makes a brainy person will change in a world where we will not need rote memory in terms of recalling facts and data. However, all of us need a mental model of the area we are working on in order to be able to synthesise knowledge. So, recall and connectivity become more important than memory per se. My two sons are 'learnatics' with a great thirst for learning. As such they offer me a great stimulus to my own learning, as do all children. They constantly challenge my ideas and this helps me stay young. One day they pointed out that IQ has dropped by 13.35 points in the last 100 or so years and asked me "Will IQ be superseded by Q in the James Bond sense of the word?" I took this to mean something around the question is formal intelligence as measured by IQ tests the model form for the future? I would argue that as we mechanise there is an even greater need for those things that humans do so well if we are to coopете with machines. While we can probably design algorithms for humane qualities such as empathy, compromise, creativity, etc. nobody does it better than a human being.

Yet, their example points out that much of the essential knowledge required to function at work and in life is already codified on the Internet. This codification has taken place over the last few hundred years from the development of the first printing presses. Printing made it possible to write down instructions for things as simple as baking a cake to waging war. It has accelerated considerably with the advent of computing power and data storage. The noun 'Google' has become a verb and the question facing many people these days is 'To Google or not to Google?' The goal of learning becomes one of harnessing the plethora of data we collect and converting it to information, knowledge and wisdom. Yet, we are stuck in a rut of believing that education is about our abilities to retain facts, when most of the facts we need are available at our fingertips. In a world where we are drowning in data, how shall we learn to swim with information? We will need to make some significant shifts or upgrades in some familiar and some less familiar skills:

- To search for facts in a jungle of data. Asking more questions than seeking answers.
- To separate what really matters from what is shouting in our face. To pick out key information from gigabytes of data.
- To notice the difference between causation and correlation.
- To separate the important from the merely urgent.
- To look for connections between disparate pieces of information.
- To let go of the notion that we must know everything and replace it with the notion that we can know how to know everything we need to lead fulfilled lives.
- To take seriously the idea of continuous learning and a PSP (Personal Sanity Plan) covering IQ, EQ and SQ. Darwin's notion of survival of the fittest will take on a new importance in terms of mind, body and soul fitness.

If Continuous Personal Development (CPD) is vital for success, it helps to take a brief history lesson on the topic. Back in the day, I used to belong to the CIPD and took CPD very seriously, using a wide variety of methods. On reflection it seems that I was in a minority of about 10%. I recall that those of us who wanted to improve ourselves through learning even suffered subtle social disapproval from more casual members who thought that learning was for dummies. This will no longer do in the automation age. In short Bill Gates was right when he said, "Be nice to nerds. Chances are you will end up working for one."

Peter Cheese provided me with some insights on the issue of CPD. Alongside the declining half-life of products, services and enterprises themselves, the upskill/reskill cycle will be much more frequent and this will require those enterprises to develop people not just for their current occupation but also to prepare them for the next one. He sees three levels of skills needed for the future:

Employability skills: These include literacy, numeracy skills and the notion of resilience in order to manage a career, which might span several changes of focus. The ability to market yourself will also be very important in a world where we work globally. We discuss the issue of personal and collective branding later on in this book.

Core skills: Examples will include digital skills, risk, basic financial understanding for starting businesses, learning to learn – how do you develop someone's capacity to learn? We discuss this under the heading of learnacy later on in Dialogue I.

Emotional intelligence: For example critical thinking skills, empathy and the ability to relate to people. Again, we pick this theme up under our review of seven intelligences for the future.

> I can Google any subject under the sun and I get tens of thousands of references, but then I must apply critical thinking to the information. This also throws up the question of what do I actually believe in a post-truth world?
>
> Peter Cheese

> Perhaps the one skill that humans have also been good at will become the most essential of all – that of "sceptical questioning" or "critical thinking". It often baffles me when I see people re-tweet or post clearly nonsensical information or "news" to others in the social media world. These individuals never seem to stop and think to themselves – "can this actually be true?"
>
> The old cliché of a lie being able to "travel half-way round the world before the truth has got out of bed" has never been more apt. So in a professional world where a lot of data is going to be presented pre-organised, visualised and perhaps even qualitatively assessed by machines, the ability to stop and calmly think could be the most powerful skill of all. And that is not necessarily an easy one to learn.
>
> Simon Warren, MD, CaseWare

How then will we augment our humanity with AI? I went in search of some clues . . .

Artificially intelligent?

We are entering a world where machine learning is a reality. In this respect Google is an Artificial Intelligence company. Google Translate used to operate on a principle called phrase-based translation, which offered me great amusement from time to time as people attempted to translate my articles from Russian into English using Google Translate.

TABLE 3.1

What the writer intended	What Google Translate thought it said
We invited Peter Cook to present on his book "Best Practice Creativity". The organiser called to say that Cook was unable to obtain a Russian visa. So, I read his book. His photograph looked like a rock star. The 50-year-old owner of Human Dynamics blends music and business in his seminars and audience members participate. His work may seem frivolous but his clients see great benefits in his creativity. Even the CEO of Kent County Council once appeared as Elvis to break down the distance between him and the staff. Cook believes that business should be fun as well as purposeful.	To past in autumn to me they by mail sent Peter Cook's book "[Kreativ] it brings money" they invited to its presentation. The lost organiser rang after a certain time and he reported the cancellation of measure – Cook could not obtain Russian visa. Honestly saying, precisely, in this fact it me it drew – to read to the end its turbid book so I was not able. After looking at Cook's photograph. I saw face of chute. The fifty year owner of [komsaltingovoy] firm walks with the guitar on the companies and wriggles before the managers. Then I revealed that this strange approach brings fruits – somebody of the clients of Peter Cook see in his tomfoolery benefit. For example, Cook learned the head of the town council of county Kent to appear to his subordinates in the means of Elvis Presley. "To the secrecy of firm" Cook attempted to prove that the real manager must be [pankom].

While writing this book, Google Translate was replaced by the Google Neural Machine Translation system (GNMT). It achieved much better translations by inventing its own language. The important transformation here was that the software actually learned to make the translation process more efficient. I have still not yet been tempted to pass my article back through the software for fear of some new transformations of meaning. My colleague, data genius and author Jason Bell also tried an experiment to see if AI could write a book. He said:

> It turns out that it's not that bad but very rough around the edges. TensorFlow is better at some things than others. This is one of the positives. However, the training took all night on a modest laptop. Text generation takes a few seconds, so an 11,000 word novella in less than two minutes is do-able. Does it make any sense or have flow? Not really.

Astra Zeneca's example earlier on shows us one view of what is possible from technology and AI. Yet it is well known that human beings do not always act in accordance with their own best interests in questions of personal development and health. Turning our attention to financial services, the following example shows us what is starting to be possible in a world of augmented intelligence. In this visit I went to meet Simon Warren at CaseWare to find out how AI is, and will continue, affecting business (www.caseware.co.uk). CaseWare is devoted to helping accountants do a better job by innovating in the space of accounting software used by accountants and auditors throughout the world, for auditing, financial reporting, management reporting and taxation. The business has been developing cloud-based applications for about four years and one of the primary missions behind this project is to design software for a 'data-driven audit'. This means adopting automation, machine learning and AI wherever possible to eliminate the areas of inefficiency and risk throughout the audit process.

In the accounting sphere it is still early days for machine learning, but there are probably two distinct areas where artificial intelligence can make significant differences to the general auditor or accountant. Firstly, in the area of data transfer/exchange between systems and secondly in making sense of unstructured data, finding patterns and drawing conclusions from that information.

Data exchange can be a very simple and logical process but it is tricky to apply the solution without an agreed global "taxonomy" that labels similar things with the same name. Despite moves to use a common dictionary people place things in different areas and "label" them differently. Machine learning could solve these issues by being able to "learn" from the behaviour of users. CaseWare is doing this with its core cloud platform, under the name of "Automapping".

Secondly, AI can be used to make sense of the very scruffy world of social media data, professional articles, half-baked journalistic opinion, etc. This is important, because one fundamental aspect of any audit is the "Understanding the business" phase of planning. This is not just about understanding what the business actually does (or how it does it) but also what else is going on in the same industry, and perhaps what are others saying about the business or sector. If AI was to really be able to make sense of this noise (and ignore the load of "false positives") then we could solve another key audit challenge – the identification of risk. Audit risk is a concept that the general public misunderstand, believing it to be about the risk of mistakes, risk of a business getting things wrong, etc. This is the risk that the auditor fails to spot a significant mistake that could undermine their conclusion that accounts present a "true and fair" view of the business' performance. Failure to get this right can, and has, resulted in serious lawsuits.

So risk is close to an auditor's heart, and only AI can possibly hunt through all of the information available to a modern reader and attempt to identify potential risks. Obviously this was something that accountants relied on years of experience to be able to do at a senior level.

But, and here's the kicker. What if a firm of young ambitious accountants was to deploy all the technology available to them to shortcut and automate their work? They could undercut fees dramatically and actually spend more time advising their clients rather than simply meeting regulatory requirements. That is the potential disruption that AI could bring to the professional world.

Simon Warren, CaseWare

Embedded in Simon's final reflection is the decision as to whether given enterprises will adopt the Man-Machine strategy or any of the alternatives, including *Planet of the Apes*. While it seems obvious that it would make sense to adopt technology, I recall that lawyers refused to use a fax machine or e-mail for many years, so maybe this is not such a no-brainer. If we are to hand much of this work over to machines, what then counts for intelligence?

CHAPTER 4

Intelligences for a machine-led world

While the last few decades have provided us with massive leaps in our understanding of the human brain, I suspect we will say we knew nothing in 2030 as our knowledge increases exponentially. Our desire to simplify the brain has led us up a few garden paths over the years. For example, the handy 'shorthand' of the left and right brain developed by Roger Sperry has been discredited, although it remains a useful shorthand for identifying the different functions that we must perform as human beings and the idea that there is some specialisation in the different parts of the brain. Much has also been made of the brain as a computer and it is an alluring simplification, yet our brains are much more complex and flexible than any computer currently available. Philip Ball of the Royal Society of Chemistry says it succinctly: "It's simplistic but largely unavoidable to portray the brain as a vast bureaucracy of specialised departments, some in constant communication and others barely aware of their mutual existence."

So, what do we know? Our brains are mostly occupied by the cerebral cortex, divided in each hemisphere into the frontal, temporal, parietal and occipital lobes. They are able to cope with a great deal of information. On occasion, when our senses are working overtime, we become overwhelmed and become less effective. This contradicts the oft-quoted notion that we are good at multi-tasking and there is much research across the sexes that now disproves this illusion. The implications are that we need to break information into manageable chunks and be focused on our main needs rather than wandering aimlessly through the data jungle. Highly effective leaders are great bite size information processors and cognitive librarians, finding ways to hold information in internal compartments and algorithms of the mind.

Our brains continue to develop through our lives but they thrive on stimulation. This contradicts the notion that we cannot learn into our old age, although some people experience isolation as they get older and this points to an important social remedy for staying young through socialisation. Neuroplasticity means that our brains can grow new neurones and adapt to new situations throughout our lives. Importantly our ability to acquire, retain and use information is not thought to be IQ dependent, rather it is a function of our emotional state or what could be called our level of engagement with learning. Simply stated, we learn best when we want to learn best. Stress and anxiety are obstacles to learning new things. We thrive on novelty, which releases dopamine, the so-called happy drug. This perhaps explains how we give disproportionately high levels of attention to well-designed advertisements.

Learning is also a social process, which explains the importance of bringing adults together in some common cause and also a common geographical space. Some studies show that the oft-quoted idea from Neuro-Linguistic Programming (NLP) that we have a primary learning channel via what people call VAKOG (Visual, Auditory, Kinaesthetic, Olfactory and Gustatory) senses is false. In other words, we are not visual learners, feelers, etc. That said, the best teachers clearly reach more of their students by ensuring their stories and teachings are rich in the five main senses. A quick scan of great works of literature also demonstrates that we love sensory-rich imagery.

Intelligence on intelligence

> Humans no longer need to upload and download information.
>
> Our 'hard drives' will need to be reformatted . . .
>
> Intelligence is not as smart as it used to be.

The more intelligent we become the more it seems we become confused about what intelligence is. Klaus Schwab, author of *The Fourth Industrial Revolution*, talks of four forms of intelligence:

1. **Contextual** (The mind – how we apply knowledge).
2. **Emotional** (The heart – self awareness, self-regulation, motivation, empathy and social skills).
3. **Inspired** (The soul – moving from me to we-centredness and questioning purpose).
4. **Physical** (The body – health and wellbeing).

There is nothing terribly new in this classification. People have wondered how we become intelligent since the world began. I have used the Kolb learning cycle to great effect over the years as a design strategy for helping to improve the intelligence of individuals, teams and enterprises. Broadly speaking Kolb considers four modes of learning, ranging from direct experimentation, concept formation, reflection and using pragmatism. Yet, the critics say that Kolb cannot be proved in science to have any basis of validity as a theory. However, I would suggest that this is an unfair test. The Kolb learning cycle is not a law of physics. It is a practical construct and not all things that cannot be proved by scientific methods are invalid. Kolb has a lot of face validity with 'what works' on an everyday level. Others, however, also see learning and intelligence differently. Howard Gardner seems not to be sure if there are nine or ten forms of intelligence, having wavered on the question of spiritual intelligence, perhaps in order to be taken more seriously by hard-bitten business people who dislike 'tree hugging' strategies for business. Regardless of the validation of Gardner's model, it also has great face validity and utility. It is regularly used by teachers to engage their students, along with the ideas about VAKOG from the field of NLP. These also have practical value in terms of reaching all the senses and therefore stimulate our brains to learn. Gardner's intelligences are therefore interesting, and they are worthy of exploration here.

Musical, rhythmic and harmonic intelligence: People with good musical intelligence can often sing, play instruments and compose music. They might have sensitivity to rhythm although this is not guaranteed. I know many great guitar players that have little sensitivity to rhythm (have you ever known a musician who cannot dance?), although great bass players are almost universally gifted with good sensitivity to rhythm.

> If I were not a physicist, I would probably be a musician. I often think in music. I live my daydreams in music. I see my life in terms of music.
>
> Einstein

Visual-spatial intelligence: Visual-spatial people demonstrate good hand-to-eye coordination and have the ability to visualise things in three dimensions. Classically many artists and designers possess visual-spatial intelligence. Madeleina Kay who provided the illustrations for this book has this and many other related intelligences in good supply.

> I think I understand something about space. I think the job of a sculptor is spatial as much as it is to do with form.
>
> Anish Kapoor

Verbal-linguistic intelligence: Verbal-linguistic types are typically good at reading, writing, telling stories and memorising facts. When combined with musical intelligence, such people can make good songwriters.

> To succeed, you will soon learn, as I did, the importance of a solid foundation in the basics of education – literacy, both verbal and numerical, and communication skills.
>
> Alan Greenspan

Logical-mathematical intelligence: Logical-mathematical people are good at performing abstractions, reasoning, numbers and critical thinking.

Accountants and financial specialists are classical professions that need people with such skills, although machines now do much of the logical work. This requires them to become much more interpreters of the data and facts to inform better decisions.

J.S. Bach was one of the greatest composers of all time. His main achievement was the synthesis and development of late Baroque with the tunefulness and popular appeal of his material. He drew upon the harmonic and formal frameworks of German, French, Italian and English music, while building his own identity. Bach used a mathematical precision in his music. In other words, Bach was an 'all round learner' using both musical and logical intelligences in his work.

Bodily-kinaesthetic intelligence: Bodily-kinaesthetic people are good at handling themselves and objects skilfully. They might also have good timing, goal orientation associated with physical tasks, along with the ability to focus their energy. It is what Schwab calls physical intelligence.

Interpersonal intelligence: People with good interpersonal intelligence are sensitive to others' moods, feelings, temperaments, motivations, and often good at working in teams. Essentially part of what Schwab calls emotional intelligence. This is essentially a skill of reading the world around you.

Intrapersonal intelligence: People with good intrapersonal intelligence have a deep understanding of the self; what one's strengths or weaknesses are, what makes one unique, being able to predict one's own reactions or emotions. This is essentially a skill of having mastery of your inner world and perhaps equates to what Peter Senge called Personal Mastery in *The Fifth Discipline*.

Naturalistic intelligence: Gardner said that if he were to rewrite *Frames of Mind*, he would probably add the intelligence of the naturalist. This seems to be the recognition of a systemic thinking intelligence, of how things connect as part of a system. It seems that there is a desperate need for systemic thinking, given the joined-up nature of the world's problems. It is also a rare skill from my own experience, with many people only able to see issues from their own heads.

Existential intelligence: Gardner did not commit to a spiritual intelligence, but suggested that an 'existential' intelligence might be a useful construct. These last two elements relate to what Schwab calls inspired, what I call soul or what Jennifer Sertl calls Spiritual Intelligence (SQ). We explore this further when we examine communications and influence.

Gardner said in 2016 that he is considering adding a teaching-pedagogical intelligence 'which allows us to be able to teach successfully to other people'. I sense a tendency to keep adding elements to it rather than keeping it simple.

In this context, I prefer just three umbrella elements that essentially embrace Gardner's 9/10 intelligences and Schwab's model – The Head (IQ), Heart (EQ) and Soul (SQ). Schwab's physical intelligence can be seen as an application of knowledge to one's own wellbeing. Traditionally we have selected people for their IQ and sometimes sacked them for their EQ (or lack of it). Formal intelligence rather than EQ and SQ is indeed much easier to test for under time constraints, yet increasingly what we know is not what we can do. In the future, low-level IQ might be less important than EQ and SQ as data processing power and analytical thinking pass from our memories to a memory stick, leaving us to up our game in other areas. We are likely to need higher order IQ elements such as creativity and improved decision-making skills. We explore these next after a brief divergence into the world of ignorance, foolishness and un-intelligence.

MATHEMATICAL CREATIVITY

Rethinking intelligence

Form a diverse team to discuss the following questions:

- What intelligences do we need to add for the machine age?
- What intelligences do we need to dump or delegate to machines?
- How could we multiply our intelligences to make us mentally fit for the machine age?
- How could we divide our intelligences by collaborating better so that all 'of us are smarter than one of us'?

Ignorance is bliss: un-intelligence

> Real knowledge is to know the extent of one's ignorance.
>
> Confucius

> The fool doth think he is wise, but the wise man knows himself to be a fool.
>
> William Shakespeare

> He knows everything but he lacks inexperience.
>
> Howard Gardner

I was asked to volunteer to attend a brainstorming session at Nokia a while back. I should add that it did not produce the Nokia 3310! Asked to search for novel ideas on a particular topic I was simultaneously astonished and dismayed as many participants in the session reached for their phones to ask Google for the answers, thus validating my Shakespearian software sonnet "To Google or not to Google – that is the question". It is a pity Nokia did not look online to foresee their takeover by Microsoft! Yet, much innovation arises from the unknown and the unknowable! In a data world of 'knowns', how do we welcome the unknown into our lives in order to create SCA (Sustainable Coopetive Advantage)? Should we protect such a precious human quality or consign it to the dustbin of the Fourth Industrial Revolution? Our brainstorming example highlights the question of what will the notion of expertise mean in a world where much data processing will be turned over to machines? What does it take to be an expert in a world full of intelligence? What role does naivety play?

1. Meta level expertise becomes the ability to solve problems that have never been faced before rather than subject-specific expertise. For this we must be T-shaped. In other words this is about having the ability to talk across disciplines while retaining one specialist skill as the root of your platform of expertise.
2. The ability to cross-pollinate expertise remains an essential humane skill. This of course produces both ingenious strategies and mistakes, yet our progress depends on unexpected leaps of the imagination. Sure, computers can do the mass-permutations much more efficiently but only humans can spot the trend. In conversation with Sony Music CEO Doug Morris, he pinpointed the subtle human skills that distinguish great from good A&R people in the music industry as one of 'seeing round corners'. This is still an essential human skill.
3. The ability to not know is an intensely valuable resource. The Dunning-Kruger effect suggests to us that we pretend to know more than we actually do. A corollary of that is that it is genuinely intelligent to not know the answers to the really important questions, even if it is socially unattractive in a busy world where people expect answers and full stops. Ignorance really is bliss if it leads to greater levels of enquiry in corporate life.

Where then does the psychological and physical space for ignorance and human creativity reside in a programmed world? Should we actively protect it rather like we have to protect the environment or, in the words of Jeff Goldblum when challenged about chaos in the film *Jurassic Park*, "Will nature find a way"? If not knowing is a core skill of coping with VUCA problems, what can we be more certain about in terms of the habits that will help us ride the waves of the unknown and unknowable in the Man-Machine age?

CHAPTER 5

Seven habits for the Man-Machine age

In a world where many things can and will be automated or handed over to machines, we have a unique opportunity to maximise those things that make us uniquely human. Through a combination of research, practical empiricism, experience and future gazing I thought it helpful to set these out as a framework for leaders and future orientated people wishing to prepare themselves to operate in the Man-Machine age. The seven habits are, in no implied order of importance:

1. The head, heart and soul of leadership
2. Communications and influence
3. Creativity and creative thinking
4. Precision decisions
5. Innovation excellence
6. Learning and plasticity
7. Branding for a complex world

1 The head, heart and soul of leadership

Whereas the manager's primary function is to optimise the work of an enterprise, making it as efficient as possible, the leader's job is to induce change in an enterprise to increase its effectiveness. The distinction is perhaps an artificial one, as both management and leadership are needed for an intelligent and vibrant enterprise. In other words, most managers need to be leaders and vice versa. We explore questions of team leadership in Dialogue II of this book but we start with the question of self-leadership and the thoughts of Jennifer Sertl, author of *Strategy, Leadership and the Soul* and network colleague from the US. Jennifer dares to use the other S word . . . not strategy, but soul in a business book. We have been playing with ideas of ethics, sustainability and spirituality in leadership for several decades and perhaps the S word has finally come of age. To paraphrase:

What the world needs now is beyond leadership; what is required is Transleadership. So many books are written on leadership and strategy. Here are some terms I'd like to anchor:

Strategy: We are convinced that in order to lead your company in the business environment of the 21st century, it is essential for you to master the ability to invent your company's future, particularly in the current rapidly changing strategic landscapes of your business. Therefore, the old ways of designing a strategy need to change. You will need to *constantly* rethink your strategy, not just once every few years.

Leadership: Leadership styles and challenges have dramatically changed and will continue to change from the old world models. In order to handle successfully the age's enormous complexity and to improve your ability in the role of a leader, you will need to become highly skilled at sensing relevance in all areas of life and business, and to create synergistic relationships between all parties.

Soul: To accomplish the alignment between strategy and leadership, we contend that your values and inner beliefs should be in harmony with that of your organisation and vice versa. Only in this way, we believe you can maximise your organisation's power and efficiency and create a working environment that allows you and your people to find satisfaction and fulfilment in your work and your lives.

At a personal level or what Jennifer calls the soul, leadership comes down to the balance of passion, purpose and profit. It is impossible to achieve this for your enterprise unless you have balance in your own life. What then can we do about balance and wellbeing? We have access to more data about their health, wealth and happiness than any previous generation. But does more data give us a greater sense of wellbeing? Data is estimated to be rising by 40% per year, and is expected to reach 45 ZB by 2020. For a balanced life (swimming with information, knowledge and wisdom rather than drowning in data), we need to feed all aspects of our being, in other words our minds, bodies and souls. Here is my best advice for achieving balance in a busy world, based on sound research in the area and a healthy dose of experience in 'what works'.

Time to think

Wellbeing is all about good time management. Yes, you can work flat out for 'eight days a week', but one of the trade-offs of working in the Brain Based Economy is to develop the habit of working when there is demand and taking time out when there is not. The trick is to actually do this rather than working through, which can lead to a life of slavery. After nearly

25 years of working for (and against) myself in this respect, I recommend these time-management strategies:

What matters most?

One of the most important things I ever learned was the so-called urgent and important grid. I think it has been forgotten in an age of digital over-stimulation. The grid helps you allocate time to the most important things that matter to you over the long term. It also identifies those items that require sustained effort (eating elephants) over the long term and those tasks that you need to learn to delegate or turn into a short routine.

Good prioritisation is especially important in a world where your day can easily be interrupted by so many distractions from social media, fitbits and so on. Some people I meet are driven by urgency and not importance in the overall scheme of things. While this is natural, as our brains crave the novelty and excitement created by urgency, it is not healthy as we then allocate too much time to these things, at the expense of those things that are on our main pathway to success.

I have a daily routine to clear the urgent but not important items by dealing with them in one succinct move. This is difficult in a globally connected world if you are to be responsive, but it is even more necessary if your time is not to be frittered away around other people's disorganisation. The mantra used to be 'only ever touch a piece of paper once' and it is transferable to the Internet age. Do it once, do it quickly, don't do it again. We will meet our future family Johnny, Julie, Esmerelda, Thomas and James again in the epilogue, but here is a small snippet from their life in 2030, which outlines how we might be able to reach a more effective use of our time with the assistance of AI and machines.

Julie's personal digital assistant Rover made the breakfast and collected, collated and prioritised her overnight e-mails. Rover even took two video calls during the night to gather rainfall and other data and convert this into information needed for an agricultural project Julie is working on. Mindfulness and physical exercise precede brainwork and the data from her morning routine is automatically fed into Julie's PSP. All of Julie's home appliances are enabled for her to speak to Rover anywhere in her house while he gets on with the housework. She talks to Rover via the fridge this morning, which gives her exercise class and meditation session.

Rover then conducts a business briefing and runs through the day's meetings and calls that Julie must make. This leaves Julie to do what she does best. This level of structure and organisation allows Julie to be more agile and responsive to the various disruptions of business life in 2030.

Don't climb every mountain

Leadership is as much about what you say no to, as well as yes. Staying focused but also remaining open to opportunities is not just a clever play on words. Manic focus prevents you from developing your business and it might block off new ideas. Be firm but kind when saying no to others to maintain relationships. Sir Richard Branson is excellent in this regard, receiving many proposals but always being clear to say firmly but politely if he is not interested. It is easy to say yes to something but much harder to say no without offence. This is a skill of great leaders.

Get the balance right

Consider this seemingly frivolous example. Spending time playing with your children is important but it is not urgent in pure time-management terms, is it? Surely you could play with them later? But you have 190 e-mails in your inbox . . . Take this strategy to extremes and your family might forget who you are! This might sound ridiculous but I do know some parents that manage to get these two priorities in the wrong order and our story in the epilogue is testimony to the advantages that can accrue when we get this right. Protect family time above all else. The strategy of 'eating elephants' is a good one to learn, whereby you nibble away at your biggest tasks systematically. Use this strategy for important but not urgent items. I only managed to write this book because I am ruthless about using the 'elephant eating' principle, marking out reasonably sized chunks of the day and writing overnight when I can get several hours of uninterrupted time accompanied by music and an occasional glass of wine. Frank Zappa adds some existentialist pearls of wisdom on time management for dramatic contrast: "A composer's job involves the decoration of fragments of time. Without music, time is just a bunch of boring production deadlines or dates by which bills must be paid."

GROUND CONTROL

Balancing head, heart and soul

Travelling is a great activity to rebalance. Take a slow train journey where you deliberately decide to do nothing but relax. No texting, social media, nil, nada, nothing. Make a deliberate point of getting a window seat so that you can enjoy the view, untrammelled by other matters. Let your mind wander, perhaps considering how people live in the different places you travel to. Write down any thoughts that occur to you. Some time after your journey, re-read your list and see what secrets it holds for you in terms of your professional or private life.

What Matters Most?

URGENT

DIARY

URGENT BUT NOT IMPORTANT

DELEGATE OR TURN INTO A SHORT ROUTINE

URGENT

IMPORTANT

ALLOCATE YOUR BEST TIME TO THIS

NOT URGENT NOT IMPORTANT

BIN

EAT THE ELEPHANT

NOT URGENT

NOT IMPORTANT ⟶ IMPORTANT

Free your mind

It is estimated that the average person receives more information per day in 1999 than they received in a lifetime in 1900 and this is a huge processing burden. Eminent neuroscientist and musician Dr Daniel Levitin suggests that to be more creative and effective we should allow 10 to 15 minutes to daydream every few hours. Levitin also suggests that a 15-minute nap is an effective strategy for wellness. Any longer than this tricks your body into thinking it is about to go to sleep, which has less positive effects on wellbeing.

Work hard, play hard

It is important to find a mode of exercise that you actually enjoy rather than trying to impose a fitness regime on yourself that you hate. I personally prefer swimming and cycling, but it is really about finding your sweet spot. Movement matters especially if your work cycle is sedentary. A brisk 15-minute walk toward the end of the day can make your final two hours of work much more productive. Although it might seem to break the laws of thermodynamics, if you expend energy you gain energy.

Enjoy what you do

All work and no play really does make us dull. In my case I love to play music and have cheekily integrated this into my work, as part of the ultimate time-management strategy where work = play. If you do not have the option of turning your hobby into work, make sure you make time for leisure pursuits. Some examples of these strategies in action are shown in our epilogue.

Go with the flow

Great musicians often reach what Mihaly Csikszentmihalyi calls the state of 'flow', where they are completely absorbed with the task at hand, where nothing else seems to matter and effort is effortless. They are often also acutely aware of what is going on around them. In other words, they have both internal and external mastery. In contrast, bad musicians live only inside their own heads. The music artist Prince was a good example of what Csikszentmihalyi meant by 'flow', able to focus on his own performance effortlessly while remaining in touch with the band, the lighting technicians and, most importantly, his audiences. I interviewed virtuoso jazz and classical guitarist John Etheridge as part of some research into the strategies of masters. Etheridge performed with Stéphane Grappelli, Nigel Kennedy and John Williams among many others. Etheridge recognised the state of flow through his own playing and through his work with other masters and this relates to our discussion on SQ. We pick the theme of flow up in Dialogue III.

Finding your own sacred time and space for mindfulness is an important part of any entrepreneur's PSP (Personal Sanity Plan)

MATHEMATICAL CREATIVITY

Rethinking work/life balance

- What could I add to better balance my work and life?
- What could I remove to better balance my work and life?
- How could I multiply to accelerate the time I have to spend on the things that increase my sense of purpose?
- How could I better divide my time to radically reduce my off-purpose moments?

Commit to learning

As well as all the above, to maintain wellness in your business, devote time toward continuous learning in an age where the 'half-life' of knowledge is in freefall. Learning can take many forms and work itself is often more valuable than a training course. Wellness really does boil down to a happy balance between work, learning and play. Get the balance right and prosper.

Life in the fast lane

The whole question of life in the fast lane fell into sharp relief for me recently when I had a breast cancer scare. Fortunately this proved to be a false alarm, but it gave me the perfect opportunity to consider what mattered most and what could wait. We need a two-pronged approach to a connected world to give us perspective as well as responsiveness. I went in search of examples of fast information and slower wisdom.

BBEs help us to access more information at times of our choosing, allowing us to live in more spontaneous 'last-minute' ways. Just think of the last time you booked cinema tickets, air travel, a brief encounter and so on. However, it is not enough to just have *more* information. We need *better* information to inform better decisions.

Yet there are occasions when making last-minute decisions restricts the options available to us or forces us into making sub-optimal choices. While the information and technology revolution enables us to be more spontaneous, some good things in life arise from careful planning.

Slow down to go faster

Neuroscientists estimate that our experiences of 'being fully present' are fleeting moments that last just three to four seconds on average. There is increasing evidence to suggest that we are increasingly suffering from 'DADD' (Data Attention Deficit Disorder), for example it is estimated that office workers in the USA check their e-mails up to 30 times an hour. What then can we do to improve our ability to contemplate for longer periods of time when it matters, in terms of decision-making, business strategy and practice? Some things in life benefit from incubation and the use of what Professor Guy Claxton calls our 'tortoise minds', rather than our 'hare brains'. The idea of mindfulness is not new, but the term has helped to articulate the need for reflective practice in a busy business world, assisted by books such as *Time to Think* by Nancy Kline which points out that thinking for ourselves is still a radical act.

I went to meet entrepreneur Mark Sillitoe at the Anniversary Olympic Games in the Queen Elizabeth Park, where Usain Bolt won the 100 metres at his usual break neck speed. Mark invested in our Olympic legacy by starting a business to maintain the fleet of widebeam barges built specially for the Olympic Games using clean technologies in a sustainable ecosystem. A cruise on the river gave me a rare moment for mindful contemplation in the heart of the city. Of course, one does not need to take a river cruise to achieve a state of mindfulness and there are many time-honoured ways to give space to life in order to think carefully about things that matter. In my own case I have written large chunks of this book on trains, having taken the three-hour trip to London instead of the 42-minute high-speed option. This has given me some seven hours of uninterrupted time per day without access to the Internet to give focus and depth to my thinking and doing. If we are to live in a constantly connected world, all of us need the occasional pit stop for reflection and growth. Finding your own sacred time and space for mindfulness is an important part of any leader's PSP.

Broadcaster and futurist Ben Hammersley bears witness to the need for mindfulness in our approaches to personal leadership. He also shines the light on some of the more trendy ideas about technology and fads of virtual working. We will remain human even if assisted by machines and our need to commune in geographical spaces is a 'fad' that has lasted since we began living in caves.

> The death of the open-plan office is a myth, for various reasons. Firstly, we learn more and more every day about the psychological optimisation of different types of work. The need for quiet, for rest, for correct stimulation, for a sense of meaning and for other specifically human qualities – by which we are consciously or not influenced. I believe, for example, that the open-plan office is a finance-director's dream retrofitted with bullshit justifications

around it being good for creativity. It's patently, and scientifically provably not so, the realisation of such will take another 20 years to shake through the business world. The same for company-wide chat systems, or hot-desking, or even a good deal of social media: an enormous amount of today's cutting edge business social practices will become laughable over the next 20 years.

Not only the tortoise but also the hare

In an "I want it all, I want it now" society, we must make wise decisions to balance our long- and short-term goals. This means that on occasions we must behave like the tortoise, at other times like the hare. I am reminded of this important maxim from Hyman Schachtel, which applies to an accelerated culture: "Happiness is not having what you want, but wanting what you have."

Sleeping appears to enhance the connection between nerve cells in the brain. A scientific study from the Harvard Business School and the University of Rochester revealed that the brain consolidates learned memories while sleeping at night. It becomes increasingly clear that there is a positive correlation between good nutrition and brain development. For example, it is thought that fatty acids present in seafood and fish can improve memory function by about 15%. Exercise also has a profound impact on our ability to learn.

You cannot lead others unless you are personally balanced across head, heart and soul. Great leadership of others starts with a little self-care so that you can be of service to others. However you go about it, commit to your PSP today to be your best:

1. Give yourself time to think.
2. Determine what matters most and give that your best efforts.
3. Do not climb every business mountain: say no when it counts.
4. Get the balance right between urgency and importance.
5. Free your mind by allowing yourself some low power consumption time every day.
6. Find ways to exercise that you enjoy so that it is something you can practise on an everyday basis.
7. Enjoy what you do by fusing what earns your living with what turns you on.
8. Learn how to enter the state of flow or effortless mastery.
9. Commit to continuous learning to increase your value in a Brain Based Economy.
10. Manage life in the fast lane by planning carefully so that you can be agile and respond to last-minute demands.
11. Slow your thinking down from time to time to execute faster.
12. Sleep well to work, learn and play.

GROUND CONTROL

Your Personal Sanity Plan

What grounds you, so that you feel in a state of flow? It might be a hobby, an interest, your work, a physical activity, stillness and so on. Use Gardner's intelligences to prompt your thinking as a checklist.

Make space for this by building it into your daily routine as part of your PSP.

2 Communications and influence

We live in an increasingly fragmented and busy world, with many competing activities and stimuli for our attention, time and money. Compared with 50 years ago, we have multiplied the number of ways we can communicate and this provides certain freedoms to live spontaneously. Yet, more communication devices and faster communications do not always make for better communications. In some cases, more and faster communications actually impede clarity. I observed this in stark relief when I organised a campaign to stop the UK's Brexit using intelligent pop music to combat populism on steroids. The EU referendum was won by naked populism, extremely clever but ambiguous communications and a large cash injection on the part of the Leave campaign. It was also affected seriously by what took place on Facebook, Twitter et al. In comparison, the Remain campaign was well-intended but fragmented and unprofessional, perhaps resembling the BBC comedy programme *Dad's Army*. In trying to maximise the impact of volunteers within various Remain campaign groups I encountered huge amounts of goodwill but some ineffective communications strategies. These took immense efforts to rectify, partly because of the degree of passion embedded in members of the movement. In particular, last-minute communications often meant that opportunities could not be seized due to the relevant people not all being in the same place at the same time and so on. This provided object lessons in managing communications within immature teams trying to use social media as a business communication tool, when it is not.

Success in communications can be reduced to four easy to say things, although they are often are hard to put into practice:

The message

Successful communicators use very clear, potent messages to engage and coalesce people around a goal or a project. For example, business people often set SMART goals for their projects, Specific, Measurable Action orientated, Realistic, Time dependent. Fuzzy messages drive fuzzy actions and fuzzy outcomes. In short, fail to plan, plan to fail.

Source Channel Receiver

HAVE A POTENT MESSAGE

CHOOSE THE RIGHT MESSENGER

CHOOSE THE RIGHT CHANNEL

ENSURE RECEIVER IS AWAKE, ALERT & RECEPTIVE

Applying this to our EU referendum example, it becomes clear why people believed the message that we could spend £350 million per week on our NHS instead of the EU by "taking back control". Although the message proved to be false and was retracted the day after the vote had been cast, this did not matter to people who wanted to believe the message. Irrespective of your views on the matter, it was undeniably a clear and potent message in terms of our model. It was carefully calculated to create 'order control certainty' in the minds of voters, in other words 'not VUCA'. The notion of 'taking back control' has since proved to be a nominalisation in linguistic terms, i.e. the process of turning a word from a verb into a noun, as it became clear that people realised that they do not exactly know what they were taking back control of, when, where, and so on.

In business situations where things are unclear the successful leader creates clarity for those they lead, even if that clarity is the first step on a longer journey. This is because we are mostly conditioned to enjoy certainty over uncertainty. That said, audacious business strategies are sometimes fuzzy at the first formulation and the job of leaders is to make fuzziness compellingly clear for those that they lead. If that is not feasible, the next best alternative is to get them to 'live with looseness', without leading them up a garden path with lies. Research on communications has wide implications for leaders:

1. First, let us consider the issue of one-sided versus two-sided messages. One-sided messages work best when the receivers already agree with the argument, or when they are unlikely to hear counter-arguments. This might explain why people read newspapers that already accord with their views and clearly worked with our example of the £350 million for the NHS. This rather demonstrates that we are essentially in echo chambers for much of the time where we are only ever confronted with views that we are already consonant with.

   Two-sided messages tend to be more effective when the receivers initially disagree with the argument, where they are well educated, or when they are likely to hear counter-arguments. Arguing on both sides of the issue tends to be more persuasive in our communications with intelligent people. The ramifications of this innocent sounding sound bite are massive in terms of thinking about your choice of persuasive communications, as many of us do not like to appear to argue away from our preference, yet it can be very effective.

2. When communicating to persuade it is generally better to draw a conclusion in the message rather than letting others attempt to infer it themselves. The risks of not drawing a conclusion include that a different one might be drawn or that no conclusion will be drawn from the passive supply of information. We will return to this theme when discussing directive facilitation style in Dialogue II.

3. Repetition of a message can increase persuasiveness if used cleverly. However over-repetition can wear out a message as well. Repeating ideas rather than exact messages might be the best solution to avoid message fatigue.

4.   Rather than presenting features, it is better to provide benefits, as some people do not translate features into benefits. A good way of forcing yourself to do this is to ask yourself the question 'What does this mean for the person I am talking with?' This requires the use of what we call the 2nd position in NLP.

The messenger

Successful communicators use a messenger or messengers that will be heard. I have tried many experiments where I have taken the visuals and audio away from the person delivering them and found considerable differences in the receptivity of messages, especially when the messenger is controversial.

For example, I tested a speech given by ex Prime Minister Tony Blair, talking about the need to end our Brexit process. When I simply showed the text of his speech to a group of people who did not know who had said it, their agreement with the messages was generally good. However, when I tested Blair's words matched with video and audio of him speaking on the same people, the receptivity of his message was severely impaired or fundamentally disagreed with, with people offering visceral reactions such as "warmonger", "liar" and so on.

I did a similar test with Sir Bob Geldof's famous standoff in a fishing boat on the River Thames with our UKIP leader Nigel Farage over his support of fishermen. I was surprised to note that even people who totally agreed with Geldof's message rejected it once they knew who had said it, based on reactions such as "elitist", "rich idiot" and various other visceral expletives. The successful influencer chooses the right person or persons to deliver the message. This is not always themselves.

If you are an inventor or a leader whose job it is to bring novel ideas to your enterprise it is particularly important to balance your innate passion for your idea with the need to persuade others of its value. Selling an idea often requires us to be less passionate than we are as the 'owners' of that idea. Remember the point about two-sided arguments being more persuasive than one-sided ones in many circumstances where the messenger has something to gain from the outcome. If you find it impossible to be dispassionate and balanced about your obsession, find someone who can represent your interests in an appropriate way to your customers or stakeholders.

In general, a messenger is perceived to be more influential when the receiver perceives them to be high rather than low in credibility. This explains why leaders need to operate from a strong platform of expertise to be successful. We explore the issue of power, expertise and authority further in Dialogue II.

Honesty and trustworthiness are also vitally important to be an effective communicator. Therefore, the messenger's influence is weakened when the audience perceives they have something to gain from the communication. Bad salespeople have turned this into the phrase "I'm not trying to sell you something . . .", which often means exactly the opposite!

People are more easily persuaded by individuals they perceive to be similar to themselves. Yet the paradox for leaders is that often they are trying to change people, and this implies that they are engines of difference or even polar opposites of the people they try to influence. Sure, it is possible to gain more favour by using insights from NLP on gaining rapport, but the authentic road forward is to find ways to legitimise and deal with cognitive dissonance. We explore this topic further in Dialogue III.

All of this information on communications and influence can be used with congruence and flair as well as as an instrument of manipulation. Successful leaders know the difference and influence with integrity.

The channel

Successful communicators choose the best channel(s) or media for the job at hand, not just the most convenient one(s). When we communicate we often have a range of goals in mind, from informing, to persuading, confronting, facilitating etc. Impersonal channels can be counter-productive when giving 'hard to hear' messages and this explains why people often fall out on social media channels when trying to deliver complex and emotional messages if they are any more difficult than "I love you". The relative poverty of social media as a channel for communicating nuanced messages is counter-balanced by people's shortage of time to do anything more effective and we are now in the age where deaths are announced on Facebook rather than in person, sometimes for reasons of efficiency but also with some downsides in terms of humanity.

The multiplicity of communication channels has also increased enormously in the last 20 years from text to instant messaging across multiple platforms, video conferencing and so on, yet our fundamental skills of communicating have not changed. Sometimes the most efficient channels are not the most effective. Personal channels such as 1:1 dialogue are expensive in terms of time but they may be very effective. Impersonal channels are much more efficient but can be quite ineffective. The successful communicator reaches for the best tool for the job rather than the one most readily available.

Two other insights from the field of NLP are worthy of note here:

1. The linguistic aspects of a message are vital in terms of how effective a message is. Professor Albert Mehrabian conducted some research on personal communications in 1970 and concluded that the syntax (words), tone of voice and body language account for 7%, 38% and 55%, respectively, of personal communication. The figures are perhaps less important than the overall point, that the words chosen are but a small part of the overall communication. That said, all we have in many modern communication media (text, e-mail, messenger) is the syntax or

words. This explains why there can be so much confusion when trying to explain complex things on these media.

2.   We regularly delete, distort and generalise messages through our own filters. This prompts NLP specialists to point out that "the map is not the territory". Quite literally, a map of Italy is not quite the same as the experience of visiting the country or eating a fine meal in Rome. What then is the relevance of deletion, distortion and generalisation in terms of giving clear, potent and accurate messages to people?

First, people are fond of **deleting** context-sensitive information when sending brief instant messages or texts. Simple messages do not tend to suffer from this strategy; for example, "I'll meet you at the Kings Cross St Pancras Café Nero at 6.30 pm" is specific and clear. However, some people try to use the same channel to discuss matters of strategy, complexity and so on with some amusing and disastrous consequences. For example, this is a real-life request for assistance received by a LinkedIn message from someone I did not really know.

> "Peter, I want culture change."

Of course, the obvious response if you believe it is a serious request is to state that you can help and ask for some background to the need . . . whether it is the person or the company that needs/wants culture change, what the culture is and why it needs changing and so on. But when no real answers come back, it becomes obvious that you have started too far ahead in the communications cycle.

Deletion of information is also quite common in my experience, when people take for granted information that you do not have access to, without which the message makes no sense at all, for example, "He's a failure". A failure at what? And so on. Here is another professional request for help from a colleague. People do say that I am quite intuitive, but I am not a mind reader . . .

> "Do you mind if I get a bit political? My coaching thing requires me to confront the big scary stuff. Wingman coming with. Terrified but will be worth it. Felt a bit broken in the mix, but think that may be par for the course. Part of the process".

I remain mystified as to who or what Wingman is or was, although I did look the term up on Wikipedia but it still made no sense!

Distortion of information occurs when there is an inferred cause and effect relationship, for example: "He never brings me flowers so he doesn't love me". There are, of course, lots of reasons why flowers may not appear.

Generalisation is an interesting area. This is the tendency of people to assume that what happens to them is true of all people. Words such as 'all', 'everyone', 'never', 'always' contain the hallmarks of a generalisation. In the context of mass communications, generalised messages are attractive as their potential 'market' is much bigger than specific messages. However, they can be too general to engage people in productive action and they can lead to fuzzy outcomes, no outcome at all or the wrong outcome.

The receiver

Successful communicators ensure that those they are communicating with, i.e. the receiver(s), are awake, alert and receptive. Sometimes this is the most important work you can do, to prepare people to hear what you have to say. Timing can be a crucial determinant of success. Hard to hear ideas might need some 'warm-up' to get the receiver in the mood to receive. Sometimes a skilled communicator will use several staged attempts to build up interest and desire to hear what is to be said.

Timing and location are also crucial if you are to reach your intended receiver and have the desired outcome. It is what I call the 'Martini' effect after the retro advertisement – **not** any time, any place, anywhere. More like the right time, the right place, etc. Ideas always have their day and the successful communicator chooses the right time and the right place to launch their ideas and strategies. It is arguable that Clive Sinclair's C5 environmental scooter might have been more successful if it had been launched at a time when environmental consciousness was at a greater level. People often seize on the only opportunity they believe they have to communicate, for a host of reasons, e.g. limited access, convenience and so on. Sometimes it is better to mark out a time when the receivers are ready and willing to listen. This is a fine judgement and marks out the sheep from the goats in terms of communications excellence.

During my work with the UK Remain movement over 12 months I noticed a number of masters of their art in terms of communications' excellence, but also rather more classic communication errors. These mainly arose not out of a lack of ability but more out of people's busy-ness and in some cases a lack of a business-like approach to busy-ness. However, these offer great insights into how not to do things as a set of reversed out lessons on how to succeed:

1. Diffuse **messages** led to a dissipation of energy, inter-group conflict and the eventual departure of people from the many fragmented Remain movement sub-groups. It became apparent that the global goal of stopping Brexit masked a huge series of discontinuous sub-goals such as save the NHS, micro political goals, a dislike of global capitalism, hatred of individual politicians on all sides, a wish to bloody the nose of politics in general, a hankering for England's green and pleasant

land, farming subsidies, fishing rights and so on. When mixed with the primary goal of stopping Brexit, they became complex and unwieldy through lack of focus and increased 'wickedness'. Eventually, this led to fracture points and the split of the movement into sub-units which then competed with each other. I noted that people would rather leave the movement than deal with the conflict that would be needed to achieve a more coherent and cohesive approach. In pure Organisation Development (OD) terms the movement needed interventions at pretty much every level of the 'OD Matrix'. However, the movement lacked sufficient trust to take advice from experts, due to its geographical dispersion and the fact that most of the people knew little or nothing about each other's talents.

2. A lack of any focal points or leaders of the movement meant that there were too many **messengers** of variable quality. This was a serious hold back factor in gaining interest and input from businesses, who saw no focal points within the movement. As a result they were unwilling to back the movement either visibly or via private sponsorship. The exception to the rule here was Gina Miller, the woman who took our Government to the Supreme Court and who won her case to preserve our democracy. I connected Gina to Sir Richard Branson and secured her some support for her campaign. In direct contrast to other Remain movement groups, she was clear with her message and expectations and this produced results.

3. Use of messaging approaches and social media platforms in attempts to galvanise the movement was a good example of using the most convenient **channels** rather than the most effective ones. The misunderstanding and lack of trust arising from this combination of virtual teams and the wrong communication channels was in some cases toxic. A classic manifestation of this was an inability of the Remain movement to trend on Twitter. This was because they could not gain agreement on a single hashtag to use in a Facebook group discussion. As a result of this seemingly trivial issue the movement was unable to get national press coverage for their work and in so doing reach further with their message. Even simple things become difficult if the wrong communications methods are used. As Tom Peters points out in *The Little Big Things* the small things impact on the big things if they are not done properly.

4. The **receivers** were not awake, alert or receptive for the most part. Parliamentary paralysis occurred in the two major parties (Conservative and Labour) around the phrase 'the will of the people' thus the movement's messages were not received or acted upon in Westminster. For some time the third party (Liberal Democrats) also tacitly supported this position. Because there was no political will to support the movement, popular support gradually dwindled. In effect the Remain movement was 'shouting at the wind'.

TABLE 5.1

Level of change	Depth of change		
	Behaviour (what is happening?)	Structure (what system is needed?)	Context (what is the setting?)
Enterprise	Poor morale, corrosive rather than creative tension, conspiracy theories, poor market focus. **Options**: Survey feedback; benchmarking.	Wrong goals; wrong or misunderstood strategy; wrong structure for purpose; lack of external measurement systems. **Options**: Change structure.	Wrong place; wrong market; wrong people; wrong technology; wrong time. **Options**: Change strategy, location, layout; change culture; liquidate the business.
Inter-group	Poor cooperation, unhealthy conflict, unresolved feelings. **Options**: Inter-group confrontation, role clarification and negotiation.	Silo based approaches to projects, interactions difficult. **Options**: Redefine responsibilities, change reporting relationships, boundary crossers.	Different sub-unit values, lifestyle, physical distance. **Options**: Reduce mental and physical distance, job swaps, improve social interaction.
Group	Poor relationships, climate, commitment, poor leadership style. **Options**: Process consultation, team development.	Poor task and role definitions, leader's role overloaded. **Options**: Redesign work or jobs, autonomous team working.	Poor group composition, environment, resources, personality clashes. **Options**: Change technology, layout, group composition.
Individual	Poor fit of individual with goals, poor response to change, no learning opportunities. **Options**: Coaching and career counselling, job design, career development strategies.	Poor job definition, tasks too easy or too difficult. **Options**: Job redesign, management by objectives.	Poor selection, promotion and training, mismatch between rewards and objectives. **Options**: Change 'raw materials', improve training, align incentives with performance.

The multiplicity of messages, messengers and channels contrived to make it produce a very low signal:noise ratio. That said, the movement did the best it could, given its fragmentation and lack of strategy. It is very probable that it could have achieved so much more with some strategy, leadership and great collaboration methods.

In simplifying the communications model it is wise to realise that there are several types of receivers in any communication interaction. It is useful to distinguish between:

> **Gatekeepers**: The gatekeepers control the entry and exit points to the people who hold opinions and make decisions about your message. These people range from receptionists to security personnel and PAs. They do not usually hold highly paid positions in the enterprise but they can determine access to decision-makers and influencers. Ignore them at your peril and do not bypass them for speed. Karma works in mysterious ways . . .

> **Influencers**: Such people have wide networks and have the power to diffuse your message much further. In the medical world these are often called key opinion formers. Decision-makers typically listen to their views in order to make their final decision and they are likely to require expert contributions from you.

> **Decision-makers**: The people who make decisions and commit resources to your project or enterprise. Ultimately they decide whether your message will gather traction. They might not necessarily be experts in your field of interest and you should recognise this in your communications with them.

People waste a great deal of time asking the wrong questions of the wrong stakeholders. It is no use asking a gatekeeper to sign a cheque, nor is it always useful to ask a decision-maker for their opinion of the technical merits of an innovative new product idea. It could even backfire on your strategy by putting them in a place of discomfort. I have observed this happening even with some of the most senior people in enterprises who frankly should know better, so it is well worth thinking through.

If you are wishing to communicate to influence and know your receivers, it is also worth considering some general personality traits that can help or hinder your cause.

- People who have low self-esteem tend to be more persuadable than those with high self-esteem.
- Authoritarian personalities who are concerned about power and status are more influenced by messages from authority figures whereas non-authoritarian types are more susceptible to messages from anonymous sources.

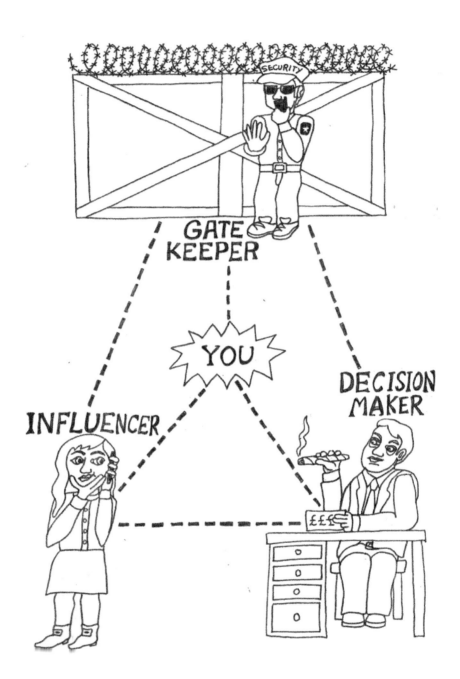

- Those high in anxiety are hard to persuade. If you face an anxious person in a difficult communications encounter, your first job is to remove their anxiety.
- People who are high in rich imagery, fantasies and dreams tend to be more empathetic toward others and are more persuadable. In plain language this explains why sales people often like being sold to!
- People of high general intelligence are more influenced by messages based on impressive logical arguments and are less likely to be influenced by messages with false, illogical or irrelevant arguments. They may be especially sensitive to short messages that appear to be unsubstantiated in our 140-character world of Twitter soundbites. There are important implications for short versus long messages here.

Of course, generalisations can be generally unhelpful. It is always wise to work with the specific realities of each situation, perhaps holding this knowledge as a set of heuristics or rules of thumb rather than absolute truths.

When thinking about the people on the receiving end of our communications, it is also worth adapting some ideas from the field of marketing if you are communicating to influence or persuade. Everett Rogers' diffusion curve identifies five discrete groups of people as receivers, who exhibit different responses to new things. Although this model was focused mostly on new product diffusion into the marketplace, it is just as relevant when considering questions of communication more generally. The five categories are:

Innovators: Circa 2.5% of a typical population – somewhat uncharitably referred to as 'nerds', these people will tend to be the first people to embrace something new. However, they might not be good advocates of your message as they do not always have access to good networks.

Early adopters: Circa 13.5% of a typical population – often more gregarious and admired by their peers. In other words, this group have friends who listen to them and form their opinions based on their views. Sometimes people refer to these people as tastemakers.

Late adopters: Circa 34% of a typical population – will look for signs of approval by the early adopters. Essentially passive in terms of opinions at the outset and therefore requiring a great deal of energy to get them to commit.

Late majority: Circa 34% of a typical population – might come on board when they perceive it is as safe to do so or when the risk has dropped to an acceptable level.

Laggards: Circa 16% of a typical population – will typically resist change until there is no alternative but to give in.

At least 68% of the population are what I would call the 'indifferent majority'. People waste millions trying to get these people to adopt a new product or concept before they have brought on board the people who they respect and listen to. It is really worth giving this some thought when considering an important communication, as you sometimes only have one chance to get it right, or wrong.

Conventional wisdom on adoption of new products and concepts suggests that you target the innovators first, i.e. those who are already positively predisposed to the message and build momentum from the easy targets. Unconventional wisdom also points out that the people at the other end of the curve have negative energy toward your message, but at least they are not indifferent. Inside a company, they might well be influential cynics. To ignore them is perilous. What this group have are often real concerns, for example safety, cost, etc. If these concerns are properly addressed, the laggards can become your best advocates. Furthermore the late majority are influenced by the laggards to some degree. Thus it becomes possible to 'squeeze' the 'indifferent majority' from both sides.

The key to all successful communications is careful preparation. This allows you to take advantage of life's occasional surprises. For this you need creativity and creative thinking, which we address next.

3 Creativity and creative thinking

> Necessity is the mother of invention, it is true – but its father is creativity, and knowledge is the midwife.
>
> Jonathan Schattke (M.S. Nuclear Engineering &
> Mathematics, Missouri University of
> Science & Technology)

To master creativity and what I call good creative thinking we must master the two thinking styles: divergent and convergent thinking. Divergent thinking is what we traditionally think of as creativity. It opens up options, is characterised by a lack of constraint, the notion that many ideas are healthy and that judgement is suspended in the interest of generating novelty, which, when combined and developed produces ideas with innovation potential. Divergent thinking is typified by popular creativity techniques such as Classical Brainstorming, Six Thinking Hats, TRIZ, Superheroes, Synectics and Mind Mapping. However, brainstorming is frequently done badly and this gives creativity a bad name. I watched in sadness as a group of young people attempted to organise a 'hackathon'. As soon as an idea was generated a tech person would repeat that the idea was already covered in his lengthy report on the subject. I sensed that he was possibly frustrated that the leader had not taken the trouble to read it, but the impact of this unmoderated contribution was ultimately destructive to the purpose. Eventually contributions dwindled to a full stop. Everyone looked puzzled as they had obviously never seen a creative thinking session organised and facilitated properly and had no basis of comparison, nor any idea what to do about it.

Convergent thinking closes down options to a point, e.g. the systematic evaluation of a range of options down to a final decision. It is given much less attention than divergent thinking but is far more important if we are to gain access to innovations that confer SCA. It is estimated that only 4% of new product ideas reach the marketplace. Imagine the impact on your enterprise if you were able to double that ratio? And multiply it by five? So much time is devoted to creativity in enterprises when rather more time should be devoted to idea development and the conversion of raw ideas into market-ready innovations to improve the success rate of new product and service development. The trouble is that divergent thinking is generally the fun part of business and convergence seen as the boring/analytical/hard work part. It should not be seen this way. Without convergence there can be no ROI (Return on Innovation). Successful companies ensure that converging is done carefully to ensure that requisite novelty is not lost but ideas are developed such that they are 'oven-proof' for the harsh world of the open market. Instead of filtering novel ideas through the normal business criteria, it is important that they are evaluated more carefully, using criteria such as relative novelty, appropriateness for the future and feasibility using existing resources or ones that can be appropriated. If an idea is to be rejected or recycled, successful convergence kills the idea but not the originator of the idea and this is a hallmark of Brain Based Leadership.

On the subject of divergence, there are plenty of good books on tools and methodologies that support creativity. Our recurring theme of 'Mathematical Creativity' in this book is one such routine that is easy to use as an augmentation of Classical Brainstorming. There is value and purpose in having some shared rules of the road when participating with others in team-based creativity sessions. I am not going to spend a great deal of time on what I call 'better brainstorming' techniques here. Instead I am more interested in the psychological and physical habits that produce creative ideas naturally, as these tend to be more portable for individuals and encourage what I call 'natural born creativity'. These were exemplified in the 'altered states' that were the basis of Brian Eno's 'Oblique Strategies', Roger Van Ouch's 'Creative Whack Pack' and various other psychedelic experiments in the 1970s. It is, however, neither essential nor helpful to add artificial stimulants in order to think differently. In most cases it needs to happen naturally in business, so here I offer you eight R's of highly creative people which you can try on as simple natural extensions of your own skills in this area.

R1 Randomise

There are many examples of great ideas being inspired by 'random stimuli' such as the discovery of Velcro which was inspired by taking a walk in a field. Creativity tools such as SCAMPER, Excursions, Catalogue, The Blindfold technique, etc. build on our unique ability to generate great ideas from random stimuli. Essentially we are talking about being 'outside' the space where your thinking currently lies and using a random provocation to simulate this state of mind. The randomise strategy works on the principle of what Arthur Koestler termed 'bisociation', which distorts a problem or opportunity from its original frame of reference.

Try this exercise. Take an issue of interest or concern in your life and spend some time defining it carefully. For example:

> "I'd like to be able to balance a busy life with sacred time for friends, family and leisure".

Go outside for a walk and collect ten items from nature. If, for example, you collected a leaf, ask what the leaf has to do with the issue in question. Doubtless you will generate a wealth of ideas from this stimulus, perhaps the idea of seasonality, or how the leaf stores energy for what matters most for its health and so on. In any case, the important move is to apply these provocations to the issue at hand. The approach works just as well when randomly browsing a magazine or catalogue. It was a selection of lifestyle magazines rather than an intense search through hundreds of medical papers that produced the breakthrough idea to extend product patent life for pharmaceutical giant Pfizer during a 24-hour summit meeting we held some years back.

R2 Reframe

Comedians often use the creative tool of exaggeration in order to make the familiar seem strange and/or funny. Reframing also changes the point of view or perspective to change our perception of a situation. By the same token, many great business ideas are the results of creative extensions, frame shifting or distortions of current reality. The idea of cats' eyes came from the creative extension of imagining how much easier it would be to see at night if cats lit the way on dark streets with their reflective eyes. Rather than then requiring thousands of cats to lie in wait on motorways at night, which would involve cats sitting in specially created wells in the road and being more obedient than is feasible or even desirable for the feline form, the inventor set about embodying the reflective quality from cats' eyes into a robust design that could be embedded into tarmac. This is much easier on the cats, who prefer to pursue their own interests, and much lower mainte-nance for the humans in terms of herding them.

R3 Retreat

The discipline known as NLP has received a variable press, based on the misuse of NLP for what could best be described as 'power selling' and the evangelical approach of some NLP practitioners. This of course is not the fault of NLP but due to some of its overly cheery cheerleaders and pushy proselytisers. That said, some very practical, durable and ethical principles exist inside the genre when used with head, heart and soul. One such principle is that of the idea of being dissociated, what NLP calls second and third position and what I am calling *retreat* to fit in with our 8 R's! The following is an attempt to debunk the NLP jargon.

Many of us spend a lot of our daily lives living inside our own bodies so to speak, in other words viewing the world from our own perspective. This is what NLP calls 1st position, being fully associated or fully present. It is often helpful to adopt 2nd position (viewing the world from another person's skin) and 3rd position (completely dissociated, rather like seeing the world from an alien viewpoint). To sum up:

- Your own viewpoint or 1st position, fully associated. This is you seeing things as they are from your own perspective. Often this is a visceral or gut-based outlook on things. Put crudely, you, inside your own trousers or skirt, so to speak.
- Another person's viewpoint or 2nd position, partly dissociated. This would be someone with an interest in the topic, but who sees it differently from you. Perhaps a customer, stakeholder, critical friend, etc. Some skills of projection are useful to put yourself into someone else's mind.
- Another planet's viewpoint or 3rd position, fully dissociated. Someone with no interest in the topic who can bring a fresh eye to the table. Detachment and focus are essential prerequisites for business and personal development in my long experience.

Creativity techniques that rely on the *retreat* or dissociation strategy include Superheroes, Disney Creativity Strategy, Six Thinking Hats, X-Factor Creativity and some approaches based on meditation and imagery manipulation, etc. Retreating might sound as if you are not facing your problems, yet putting distance between problems can put you in the perfect thought space to see issues for what they are rather than what they seem to be. This is very different to avoidance.

You can also use these 'perceptual positions' in sequence as an individual. In teams, it is possible to assign sub-groups with the different positions and facilitate a 'synthesis' of the ideas from the three perspectives in order to come up with ideas that are both novel, appropriate and feasible. In my work as a strategy consultant I have used perceptual positions in 'series' or in 'parallel', depending on the client need, the depth of enquiry and the time available.

Take multiple viewpoints on your innovation and ensure your strategy for gaining acceptance includes these – what I call the Janus effect.

R4 Restrict

Constraints are a great spur to creativity and there are many examples of innovations that have been prompted through the navigation of a constraint or restriction, such as Sir James Dyson's invention of the dual cyclone vacuum cleaner, inspired by his Hoover that would not suck due to the dustbag being full. Rather than complaining, he set about rethinking the constraint of the bag, starting from the viewpoint of getting rid of the constraint. The theory of constraints has applications across a wide range of industries and pursuits, for example the arts. I spoke with a theatre director who pointed out that great actors, faced with an unintended obstacle on a stage, use the obstacle, rather than seeing it as a constraint. Using restriction through navigating constraints is part of the skill set of the master improviser. Try imposing restrictions on your thinking, even artificial ones as thought experiments, in order to release your creativity.

R5 Reverse

The act of reversal is tremendously powerful in helping us focus on what we do want/need in a situation. Reversal is not about focusing on what we do not want, rather we must come up with a complete reframe of the problem or opportunity. By generating a perverse and extreme reversal we usually alter our state, which puts us in a position to see the issue with new eyes. Reversal reveals areas of the issue that have often been left unexplored. For example, imagine your enterprise were seeking to improve customer perception of their product or service, a perverse reversal would be:

> "How can we make our products so dangerous/undesirable/ faulty and so on, such that we put ourselves out of business for good?"

Generating options on such a provocation and then inspecting the options for their embedded goodness often generates ideas that are hard to think of using traditional brainstorming approaches. Reverse yourself into great ideas.

R6 Relax

Tension is important for creativity, but too much tension puts us into a state of paralysis in terms of generative thinking. As we have discussed, stress and anxiety flip us over into unresourceful states for learning and creativity. Putting someone into a crisis situation and then asking them to do anything other than come up with the default fight or flight response is unlikely to deliver results for all but the most resilient and well-trained individuals. The state of 'relaxed attention' or 'flow' is a much more helpful state for releasing creativity. Some business people are prone to thinking that such states are the realm of soothsayers and healers, yet it is possible to be balanced, centred and resourceful in a suit and without the need to lie down on a yoga mat. We discuss what Mihaly Csikszentmihalyi called 'flow' in Dialogue III, taking our examples of effortless mastery from the class A musicians.

R7 Release

When trying to think creatively one easy state changer is that of using catharsis to unburden yourself in some way. Catharsis is quite simply the act of getting something off your chest and there are a variety of ways of doing this ranging from quiet reflection through to primal screaming! Humour is a great doorway into catharsis. British Airways once had a corporate jester within senior management to help break some of the seriousness that pervades an engineering culture and the 'boredroom'. The jester was not Sir Richard Branson, although I gather he performed this role for free when he broke BA's monopoly, much to my friend Dr Andrew Sentance's upset when Richard took BA's board on over their state monopoly over landing slots for their planes. Almost any change in emotions may be just as good to alter your state of mind. We explore catharsis as a facilitation style in Dialogue II.

R8 Romance

Much business life is analytical and unromantic in nature. For much of life this makes perfect sense as business decisions should follow a certain kind of logic to sustain the enterprise and its wider stakeholders. However, force of habit often forces us to express business problems in an unemotional way when it is unhelpful to do so. Try re-expressing a problem in a romantic way to create a shift in thinking. For example, instead of saying "How can we double sales performance?" say "How can we encourage our customers to become life long lovers?" The extensions that this generates often outperform options generated by random search techniques on their own. As with all strategies for creativity, these tend to improve the efficiency (speed) and effectiveness (degree of useful departure from current reality), rather than just thinking aloud.

GROUND CONTROL

Applying the 8 R's

Take an issue of interest or concern. It might be something personal to you or an issue of importance to your immediate team. Alternatively, offer some consultancy support to a voluntary enterprise that you know.

After some initial clarification of the issue and its structure, apply some of the 8 R's to the topic, allowing a freeform dialogue to ensue.

At some stage, aim to summarise your insights and, if possible, at some later stage, review the options to make a selection of the most novel, acceptable and feasible ones for further development.

A culture of creativity

What then can we say that is sensible about the generation of a climate and culture that supports creativity and how techniques can enhance this? The groundbreaking MBA programme 'Creativity, Innovation and Change' was instructive in changing my entire fortunes as a business leader. Unlike most MBA programmes, it was taught experientially rather than being an assembly of business models. This meant that the learning was retained permanently and deeply and not as a bundle of knowledge stored in a recess of my mind. It is worth repeating some of the lessons I learned here, lest they suffer from suffocation in the Internet age. Leaders can inculcate cultures that support creativity by paying attention and living the behaviours behind these principles:

Curiosity: In the words of Professor Charles Handy, curiosity made the cat. It also made Albert Einstein, Steve Jobs, Anita Roddick, Richard Branson and J.K. Rowling. Curiosity is the systematic habit of asking frighteningly good questions, testing boundaries around wicked problems and opportunities. It is sometimes about exploring the big picture and the detail or what I call 'seeing the wood AND the trees'. Artists, scientists and engineers often have this quality in great supply, some business people less so. It is a habit that can be practised and learned if you are open to the idea of not having instant answers to your questions.

Love: As I write this, it becomes obvious from the Harvey Weinstein affair that some leaders have taken the word love too literally, using their enterprises as a kind of executive casting couch. In its true meaning here the word love is meant to signify collaboration and developing your enterprise as a family. It requires genuinely participative approaches to organisation improvement. Love is a word used by companies such as Innocent Drinks and Metro Bank to describe their culture. If love is too emotive a word to use in your enterprise, try care instead.

Forgiveness: if you are to have a culture of creativity, there will be mistakes. If mistakes are punished, your enterprise's creativity will die and, with it, your IP (Innovation Potential). Forgiveness is required at all stages of a project or enterprise: beginnings, middles and ends. In other words, false starts to projects and enterprises, mistakes along the way and unexpected outcomes and results. As a leader you are judged on your responses to what happens. 3M are famous for demonstrating this at the outset of their enterprise, having acquired three mountains for mining purposes and found them to be of no use for their intended purpose. Another example of forgiveness occurred when Virgin Atlantic decided to do a promotion based on the Austin Powers movie *The Spy Who Shagged Me* with billboards featuring 'Virgin Shaglantic'. It was judged that Virgin's corporate immune system would have almost certainly said no to this, so the person responsible adopted Richard Branson's mantra "Screw it, let's do it" and forgiveness was asked instead of permission.

A sense of direction: Without developing a sense of direction, leaders cannot hope to develop a creative enterprise that consistently delivers innovation. Of course, this can happen through participation or direction. Leaders must decide which approach is best in a given situation. The ability to find a sense of direction is the differentiator for artists who are successful. Many artists are really good at curiosity, forgiveness and love. Without a sense of direction their creativity might not reach a market if that is their desire. In the music world this separates those artists who make a commercial success of their careers from those that remain in their bedrooms or attics.

In terms of creating a climate and culture that fosters creativity, leaders would do well to live these four values on an everyday basis. This is quite easy to do in good times. It is much harder but even more important to do in hard times when exploration and ingenuity are often sacrificed for expediency and short-termism. While this is not a book about tools and techniques for creativity and creative thinking, a few words on the topic are worthwhile, since they occupy a lot of time in any enterprise's life as the 'shared recipes that bind people together'. Techniques are simply the written down or codified knowledge of 'what works' in the field. Alongside techniques and tools for creativity, we do need a systematic process to improve the efficiency and effectiveness of your creative thinking and we look at this first.

Systematic creativity

There are many different proprietary processes for systematic divergent and convergent thinking and I favour the most simple three-stage iterative structure. This focuses on defining the problem/opportunity first before looking

A SYSTEMATIC A-Z PROCESS

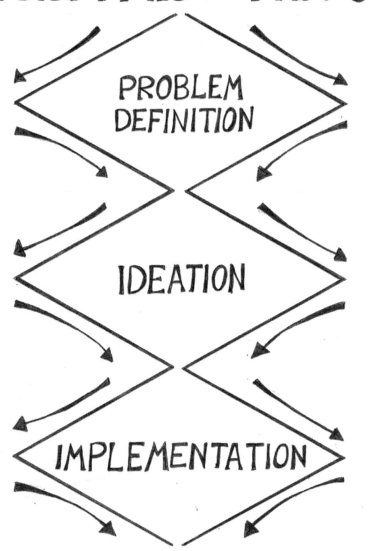

PROBLEM DEFINITION

IDEATION

IMPLEMENTATION

at creative options and skilfully evaluating and choosing best-fit resolutions and, finally, identifying a pathway to implement the chosen resolution. This is, in effect, a series of staged sequences of divergent and convergent thinking.

Starting with the question of problem/opportunity identification, skilled business consultants often say that there are several versions of a problem amenable to creative thinking. The problem/opportunity as *presented* and, after some dialogue, the problem/opportunity that comes to be *understood* and shared by those responsible for resolving it. It is vital that you work on the real problem or opportunity if there is to be long-term value in your work as a leader. This normally requires some initial diagnostic work except in the simplest of situations. The signs that tell you there is need for problem/opportunity identification are when people say things like "We haven't got a clue what to do", "We've no idea where we are going", "We've no idea how to get there", and so on. Techniques and tools to clarify a complex problem tend to help us to:

- understand the big picture and the small details;
- separate what matters from the background;
- separate what is important from what is urgent;
- identify real versus imaginary constraints and choices;
- know what success might look like;
- identify the most elegant ways into the topic, i.e. those that are both the most effective and efficient routes to start working on the topic.

It is easy to be too unfocused and nebulous. Tightening the topic area to the point where the 'aha' moment happens is time well spent as it saves lots of time later on in the process. The sorts of techniques that help include asking the question "Why?" repetitively. 'Bug Listing' offers a cathartic way to get the problem off your chest by legitimising dissent and can help us to understand the background and the needs the solution must address. More intuitive ways to help understand the underlying issues can be developed using tools such as 'extended metaphor' and also help to examine the problem from many different viewpoints using Janusian thinking. On occasion it helps to use structured, goal-focused tools such as the POSERS checklist from NLP and on other occasions mapping techniques such as rich pictures and multiple cause-effect diagrams are essential to map the underlying complexity and help see the wood and the trees.

Once people have converged on an agreed problem definition, it is usual to move on to option finding. A well-constructed idea-generation session improves the efficiency of ideas, i.e. how many novel ideas are generated in the time available. It also improves the effectiveness of idea generation, i.e. the degree of useful departure from current thinking. Not all brainstorming sessions require radical ideas, so there is no implied suggestion that wackiness is a feature of effectiveness in idea generation. Effectiveness can better be measured by the degree to which the ideas are novel, appropriate and feasible, otherwise known as the NAF criteria. You know when you need to use a bit of mental escapology when people say things like: "Current approaches don't get us far enough", or "We need to renew our strategy and tactics". Techniques for option finding enable you to:

- generate a range of incremental, radical or unthinkable ideas;
- create some useful tension or shared vision for change among stake-holders;
- develop existing ideas so that they produce continuing returns on your investment.

Of course, the most familiar technique for creative thinking is Classical Brainstorming. The technique is widely used and abused and tends to advantage extroverts who gain energy from the externalisation of their ideas. Brainwriting is a useful variant that helps to unlock the ideas from introverts who perhaps prefer the inner world of expression. Other useful techniques for divergent thinking include 'Wishing' and 'Reversal', which can help you reach unthinkable ideas very quickly. Sometimes the need is to bring the ideas back to the practical reality we are faced with, and techniques such as force fitting help with that. Other techniques build on some people's natural abilities and preferences for putting themselves in an NLP 2nd or 3rd position such as the 'Disney Creativity Strategy', 'Superheroes' and 'Six Thinking Hats'. These particularly suit people who are good at adopting roles outside of themselves and this brings a new meaning to NLP: "Now Let's Pretend".

It is said that we are only capable of holding 7 +/– 2 items in our conscious mind at a given time. What happens when we have 150 ideas from a brainstorming session then? The dumb move is to discount the 150 and go back to the idea you first thought of. The smart money is to use a thought organiser that allows you to see the wood and the trees, plus connections between ideas, from which you can formulate a strategy and so on. You know when it is time to organise and group ideas when people ask questions like "We have idea overload – I'm going to lunch", "I can't see the wood from the trees", "There's so much c . . . p here that I think we should adopt the idea I thought of in the first place", and so on. Thought organisers enable you to:

- understand connections and causations between issues;
- separate the important issues from 'noise';
- identify entry points, paths of least resistance and obstacles to progress.

If people are having difficulty seeing if ideas 'fit' with the problem as defined, Ishikawa (Fishbone) analysis helps the team to see the links. If the bulk of the ideas for solutions have a series of themes to them, Mind Mapping can group them efficiently. Rich Pictures force us into helping the ideas to coalesce. To render complexity easier to understand, multiple cause and effect diagrams pull together allied ideas. Having 150 ideas can cause an overload problem in itself.

It is one thing doing a superb brainstorming and thought organising session, quite another to converge with care. Careless decision-making can invalidate even the best innovative thinking through the use of 'business as usual' criteria to evaluate novel ideas, which by their very nature are untried and untested. That is not to say that innovative ideas should not be pressure tested – indeed, they must if your company's risk profile is to be met. They must, however, be treated differently from existing business propositions, otherwise most if not all will be screened out by the process, with the result that people judge brainstorming to be a waste of time as 'you end up with the same answer as when you started'.

You know when it is time to take a careful approach to making wise decisions when people say things like "I think my idea is the best", "Why bother brainstorming, I think we all know the answer?", "We haven't a clue what to do", and so on. Techniques for this stage help to:

- organise ideas and note duplicates;
- appraise them down to a manageable number without losing the novelty;
- combine the front-runners into an approach that hangs together;
- agree an outright winner if only one blockbuster idea is needed.

A range of techniques can be employed here from simple voting approaches to grids and matrices to carefully preserve the novelty of the ideas while realistically assessing their potential to be capable of realisation using resources you already have or can acquire. We focus in greater depth on decision-making shortly.

Once you have carefully selected an option the next step is to identify an implementation pathway for your decision so that it becomes part of business as usual. The devil is in the detail and execution requires meticulous planning and navigation of the obstacles to implementation. You know when it is time to implement your idea when people say things like "The idea is simple, but nobody accepts it", "The idea is complex and will not be understood", "The idea upsets the status quo and the egos of certain individuals and groups in the company", "The idea is risky and we are not in the risk business", and so on. Techniques for this stage help to:

- package the idea in ways that increase its perceived and real value;
- present the idea so that it can be understood and adopted by others;
- create a clear pathway for execution;
- analyse helpers and hinderers and devise a strategy to address the power dynamics;
- eliminate or reduce the risk of the solution.

A number of tools are available to help, ranging from simple checklists such as the 4W's and H through to Force Field analysis, which can help you understand and manage the power dynamics behind implementation. There is also a suite of project management type techniques such as Critical Path Analysis and decision trees.

In summary, BBEs have a culture and climate that supports creativity and the conversion of bright ideas into sustainable and profitable innovations. They generally install the underlying thinking skills and beliefs into the DNA of the business via careful selection of naturally creative people supported by the 'habits' we have discussed. If there is need to 'make creativity go faster' or to have some shared rules of the road, then having some shared processes and techniques and tools will generally make the conversion of creativity into innovation more efficient and effective. Yet the installation of tools, techniques and processes into a poor climate and culture will generally be less effective.

> **Culture first, processes, tools and tricks later.**

4 Precision decisions

> Good judgement comes from experience. Experience comes from bad judgement.
>
> Tom Watson – IBM

I often cycle when working and travelling in London. It is the perfect place to observe the random and complex adaptive behaviour of human beings. I note with some amusement and occasional trepidation that these days I often nearly run over pedestrians walking across roads while addicted to mobile devices, as they seem only to respond to the audio stimuli from cars. Some say that our brains are like computers, yet current computer systems are far less complex than our brains and the analogy is at best a partial one and more likely a very poor approximation. This will change rapidly in the Man-Machine age.

Yet our random behaviour as humans in public spaces will be a major impediment to the implementation of driverless cars and other automations if they are to travel at a reasonable speed. That said, we can also expect that our decision-making will improve in a Brain Based world where rationality takes precedent over ego and human emotion. Embedded in my previous casual remark, though, is a whole hornet's nest of organisational vipers in the VUCA world of business. We regularly make poor decisions as human beings, in spite of compelling evidence that we should choose otherwise. People continue to smoke cigarettes in spite of the body of evidence that suggests this can kill. A high percentage of people continue to eat and drink in an unhealthy way after a heart attack, in spite of clear advice from their doctor that this is a warning of the need for a lifestyle change. Consider these examples of irrational decision-making, which range from the sublime and amusing to the ridiculous and vaguely insane.

A local council banned conker trees for fear that a conker may insert itself into a child's head while playing in the park. (Editor's note for our international cousins – a 'conker' is the name for the prickly seeds from Horse Chestnut trees). Clearly 'conker attack' has a low probability of occurrence and constitutes a low impact in terms of serious harm! Yet our well-meaning public service managers saw fit to issue an outright ban to the prickly monsters.

An overenthusiastic member of staff (stationmaster Dave) at my local train station told me that chaining my bicycle outside the station on some railings in the street was "a health and safety risk". Upon further enquiry as to the risk he was unable to identify one, although I was expecting him to come up with terrorism as a catch all excuse, which would have been hard to push back as the opium of the people. When pressed for his reason he said that he had identified a risk that it might "ladder ladies tights or stockings". This was once again highly improbable, considering that the bicycle was parked in an area of zero impact, save for the laddered lady's lost vanity in an area of low tights' or stockings' density. Despite writing to the CEO of SouthEastern I could not get any adequate answer for the perceived 'threats to fishnets'.

When working in corporate life I have noticed that some IT departments consider that Skype is insecure and block its use in companies. Although it is true that voice over IP (VoIP) communications are insecure, apparently Skype is the networking medium of choice for terrorist cells. Somewhat perversely I am minded to say that this would appear to be a pretty good endorsement of its security!! (Far more of the risk is executives losing their phones and laptops on trains, or even more so, moving between companies and taking their entire 'hard drive', i.e. their brains, with them.) Skype might have some security concerns but the whole thing seems out of proportion with the actual risk and the alternative leaky strategies to contain knowledge and commercial intelligence.

Yet, nobody seems to think that it was risky for Michigan Republican Senator Christina Bond to carry a gun in her underwear. Senator Bond, or 007 as she came to be known, apparently shot herself in a bizarre tragedy, yet why were we surprised that she shot herself? Moreover why was it reported as an accident in the US media rather than an accident waiting to happen? When we look at risk rationally, we can see that it is possible to confuse the risk of 'conker attack' with falling over on a raised paving stone, flying Aeroflot in the 1980s or accidentally shooting yourself from your underwear.

Risk=Probability×Impact

HIGH

PROBABILITY

PAVING SLAB TRIP HAZARD | BRA SHOOTING MISHAP

CONKER ATTACK | FLYING AEROFLOT

LOW

LOW   IMPACT   HIGH

It is more dangerous to cross the road than 'conker attack', flying and most of the things we assume are risky. Smart thinkers consider the probability of a risk occurring and its impact rather than assuming that all of life is a risk. We appear to have become obsessed with risk rather than risk management. This is one area where machines might help us make better decisions, almost like having Mr Spock from *Star Trek* on the team to balance out our reactions from our 'crocodile brain', which regulates our fight or flight response, is prone to recency bias and so on.

You might well want to say to me, "Peter, the risks of conker attack and bra holsters are frivolous examples", yet, the failure of Pfizer's inhalable insulin product Exubera is a much more serious affair. Exubera was a breakthrough medicine, offering patients a needle-free life for their insulin. The inhalation device that was devised for the product was almost the size of a small fire extinguisher and became the product's 'Achilles heel'. Why, therefore, was this obvious product defect not spotted, especially given the scrutiny that every microscopic aspect of a new pharmaceutical product receives? The CEO at the time knew that Pfizer did not have much in the way of an R&D pipeline and declared that Exubera would be launched whatever happened and invited anyone who said to the contrary to apply for a new job. Quite unsurprisingly, nobody did. It is a supreme example of a decision that was handled poorly by humans to the enterprise's ultimate cost of $2.8 billion due to a defect that was obvious to all but the CEO. It is arguable that this decision would have been better handed over to a machine who would have told the CEO dispassionately that he was about to make a major mistake. Then the only obstacle would have been the CEO's ability to listen, take note of the information and do something about it.

Human beings suffer from a number of biases that cause them to make irrational decisions and we can look forward to some improvements in our decision-making processes in the Man-Machine age if only we have the courage and wisdom to listen to what the advances in data management will offer us. The benefits of a balanced approach to decision-making that makes the best uses of what logic can offer us plus the human touch are many, including:

- much better strategic decisions by enterprises that are informed by information but not slaves to data;
- improved designs that grab customers and impact the ultimate user experience;
- reduced failure rates of innovative products/services;
- improved diffusion rates into society – riding the adoption curve quicker, which is especially important in a world of shorter product lifecycles; and
- much better customer engagement and attachment to your brand.

The blood/brain barrier

The science fiction TV series *Star Trek* envisioned a world in which the logical functions of decision-making (Mr Spock) were separated from the emotional side (Captain Kirk) and which often used a mediator (Dr McCoy) who attempted to bring head and heart into balance. However, Kirk often won the battle for hearts over minds. This mirrors what happens in business and society when our heads are over-ruled by our hearts. It is almost always a mistake when head, heart and soul are separated in decision-making, be it a personal decision such as buying a house or a car, or a vital business decision such as whether to enter a new market.

It is estimated that adults make around 35 000 decisions every day and many of our decisions are unconscious and, in a sense, artificially intelligent, such as getting up, protecting ourselves from danger on the roads and so on. But what happens when we know what to do but then act in ways that are directly in opposition to our decision? Neuroscience is helping us to understand the balance between our collective synapses and our corporate corpuscles, yet understanding why decisions do not always get executed is merely part of our ability to change those decisions. Can we reach a point where our decisions are much more balanced between head, heart and soul?

Daniel Kahneman's book, *Thinking Fast and Slow* outlined two different modes of decision-making. He called automatic, unconscious thinking 'system 1' and a more deliberate and measured approach 'system 2'. System 1 drives quick reactions, such as avoiding an accident, whereas system 2 helps us solve complex problems. There is nothing inherently new in this. The Jewish Kabala separates *hokma* (wisdom) and *binah* (intelligence). *Hokma* is seen as being linked to 'right brain' thinking with *binah* more connected with 'left brain' analytical thinking. Professor Guy Claxton discusses something similar in his book *Hare Brain, Tortoise Mind*. It would clearly be inappropriate to organise a focus group to decide whether to dodge a speeding bullet. Equally, it is probably a bad idea to organise a snap opinion poll to decide on the UK's social, economic and political future. Yet our hare brains can also be used (inappropriately) to process complex problems where instant decisions might be sub-optimal. Politicians sometimes use such devices to persuade us to accept simple answers to complex problems using attractive slogans that perhaps have no real substance on deeper inspection, but which appear to offer a solution. Examples in recent times include "Lock Her Up" (Hilary Clinton), "Build a Wall" (Mexico), "MAGA" and "Take Back Control". The ideal length for such slogans seems to be three words and ideally something that has rhythm and resonant simplicity.

Machines offer us dispassionate insights into decisions we can make as leaders, but only if we care to listen and act upon the knowledge. We have the possibility of severely limiting the failure rate of innovative products and services but the onus falls upon us to act in accordance with that logic. Humans have not had a great track record at listening to advice that does not accord with our own paradigm up till now. We might well be ready to make a great leap forward if we are prepared to listen to the insights that machines can provide to facilitate wise decisions, yet human processes such as denial and the Dunning-Kruger effect must be addressed if we are to get better in this area. To achieve this we need better information and better receptivity to information.

Informing good decisions

We are bedevilled by biases as human beings while they also make us charming, funny, silly and occasionally vulnerable. People believe things to be true in spite of compelling evidence to suggest otherwise. Examples abound, such as when an EE Sales representative told me with great authority that there are terrorist incidents *every day* on the streets of Britain. After some exploration of his assumptions it turned out that his friend had been at the Arianna Grande concert in Manchester when there was a tragic terrorist attack. Although his friend had not been injured, the incident had been generalised as an everyday occurrence in his mind. He had, in effect, been himself a victim of what psychologists call availability, recency and confirmation bias. The plain fact of the matter is that there were many more deaths from terrorist attacks in the 1970s and the 1980s, and in terms of their impact, we should really be more concerned that there are five road deaths every day on Britain's roads, some five times more than the very worst years of terrorist attacks in 1972 and 1988. Air pollution is now a significant killer, contributing to 40 000 premature deaths per year in the UK. Yet, we appear to rate events that appear in the media more highly than the everyday facts of life and death.

I hypothesise that people's experience becomes their data in a world in which they are rained on by data from the Internet, that the newspapers contain a distorted kind of truth and that they are overwhelmed by 'facts'. Our 'bounded rationality' is indeed bounded as we are unable to source all the data to make informed decisions, nor is it rational, due to our ability to prioritise more recent and more dramatic events over ones with greater impact. The currency of truth is devalued in such a world and we are all poorer for it.

Embedded in the need for making better decisions is, therefore, the need for much better approaches to our management of information. Frank Zappa takes a characteristically existentialist view on information management: "Information is not knowledge, knowledge is not wisdom, wisdom is not truth, truth is not beauty, beauty is not love, love is not music. Music is the best."

Our relentless hunger for data makes the need for better information management even more pressing and we must reform the data–wisdom paradox as this story illustrates.

I called James at the customer relations' department of Student Finance England who manages student loans for young people in the UK. They were pestering my son and myself to provide 'proof' that he was not currently working. He was not. I called to explain that there was no need for me, nor him, to fill in the time-consuming forms they provide, as they already have a foolproof system in place to take his loan back as taxation at source from his wages. Thus they would know when he started work and their request for data was not needed. James replied "We have to have the data". When I asked why, he simply repeated "For storage". When I pointed out that data has no purpose if it is merely to be stored and not used, James insisted that "Everyone else does it". He was unable to refer me to someone who could not repeat this broken record. I called again and heard similar answers, including one young woman, who had been a student herself but was only able to tell me, "Your son will be charged interest if he did not comply". This story illustrates an inflexible system, people who are unable to listen and respond and, moreover, a complete misunderstanding of the relationship between data and wisdom. This was clearly frustrating for all concerned and to no ultimate value to either party. We need to reform the system for a new age and there is clearly much to do and a big hill to climb in some enterprises.

We traditionally think of the hierarchy from data to wisdom where:

- Data are unstructured facts – growing at an exponential rate.
- Information is structured data.
- Knowledge is the use of information to pursue goals, i.e. applied to a need.
- Wisdom is the application of good judgement using knowledge.

In the information age, three important tectonic plates are acting on this hierarchy.

1. We are drowning in data, thus the shape of the data–wisdom triangle is flattening out, although human data processing power remains the same. As knowledge quantity goes up, if human processing power stays the same, knowledge quality must decline.
2. As a consequence we either have less time to convert data to wisdom or must choose to live with what Herbert and Simon called 'bounded rationality'. This is where we choose to operate with less than perfect information. We might, at best, be operating with naivety or ignorance in some situations.
3. What counts for wisdom is changing rapidly, as the half-life of what are considered stable business concepts in society declines. Taken-for-granted notions of first-mover advantage, competitive strategy, strategic alignment and so on are all under challenge and we explore these later.

Wisdom is the application of good judgement using knowledge

WISDOM

USE of INFORMATION to PURSUE GOALS

KNOWLEDGE

INFORMATION: STRUCTURED FACTS

DATA: UNSTRUCTURED FACTS

We have also seen rapid shifts in what is defined as wisdom with the advent of post-truth politics where taken-for-granted truths are dispelled one day and then transformed the next, with no explanation or apology when previous 'truths' are reflected back to the perpetrators. This is clearly a perverted use of knowledge and devalues the currency of trust, which is vital for all business to continue. Nonetheless, the availability of distributed knowledge is overall a massive advantage to individuals and society, but it requires us to adjust our strategies for scrutinising and using knowledge in a frenetic world. Here are five principles for dealing with data overload and information poverty:

1. Be sceptical but not cynical about facts in a busy business world over-loaded with data.
2. Triangulate information and data by cross-checking data to look for congruence and inconsistencies.
3. Err on the side of trusting people if they demonstrate that they are worthy of that trust, rather than starting out needing the proof.
4. If there is insufficient information or data to pursue a course of action, create a test that enables you to gather early confirmatory or discon-firming data.
5. Ultimately, if you do not have sufficient data to make a good decision, you always have the option to delay, ask for better information or say no.

GROUND CONTROL

Balancing mind body and soul

Think of an important decision you have taken or one you plan to take.

Consider the balance of information on which the decision is to be based. What does logic say to you? What does your heart say? And your higher purpose or soul?

Take one element of the information away? Does it alter the decision? What does that tell you?

5 Innovation excellence

If creativity is the input to the inventive process, then innovation is the output. Business leaders are mostly interested in innovation over creativity, yet there is not universal understanding or acceptance that you cannot have one without the other. There is also considerable confusion in the world of business as to the interchangeability of these two terms. This leads to the belief that a brainstorming session or a hackathon is all that is needed for innovation. Yet this is often only the beginning of the process. These things often generate the raw ideas that must then be developed into viable and sustainable innovations. Given the statistics we mentioned earlier about the extremely poor conversion rate of ideas : innovations, there is a massive opportunity to be grasped by BBEs. With just a small incremental improvement in the conversion rate the success of an enterprise can be transformed.

Innovation operates at three levels. It can be *strategic*. This includes brand building and development, building the enterprise's unique position, restructuring the company to maintain an edge. Examples include Tesla Inc. and IBM, which grew from selling computers to enterprise solutions. The UK Automobile Association repositioned itself as the '4th emergency service'. This added 2.5 million customers (nearly 20%) to their business and the idea for this came from a ground floor staff member. This demonstrates that strategy can be distributed to the customer interface in service-led enterprises if leaders have good listening posts for great ideas. In IKEA's case, their brand is built on customer experience and they have used intelligence to help their customers make better choices of furniture for their homes through their Catalogue app. This helps customers envision furniture items placed in their own homes. Virgin are masters of innovation within branding and have conducted some notable businesses out of branding alone, including Virgin Atlantic and a considerable number of glorious failures including Virgin Brides.

> I think because there aren't many virgin brides, it never took off.
>
> Sir Richard Branson

Innovation is most often understood as a *product* or *service*. This requires the exploitation of novel ideas to deliver something of value to the marketplace, or the reconfiguration of an existing product or service so that it is more in tune with market demand. Examples of product and service innovation include fire (400000 BC), the wheel (3400 BC), the printing press (1440), the steam engine (1712), semiconductors (1896), the transistor (1947), the Fender Stratocaster (1954) (OK, that one is a personal choice and perhaps not groundbreaking!), the World Wide Web (1990). Much R&D attempts to improve the ROI (Return on Iteration) ratio toward the development of successful new products and services. Whereas there has been an emphasis on pushing new products and services into existence in the 20th century, the statistics of new product introduction are often poor. These days, the Internet allows for strategies that encourage customer engagement and pull strategies on the basis that participation can breed commitment.

However, much innovation is about internal *process* improvement, in other words finding new ways to do old things. Examples include shortening

the distance or number of steps between the enterprise and its customers. In a busy world, shorter and smarter processes have the potential to give your enterprise SCA. Amazon are a good example with their 'one click and you're done' promise. There is much process innovation work to be done in public services, who have tended to transplant bureaucratic manual systems into computer-based ones, which often makes the service delivery more cumbersome for the end user but with less recourse to be able to get service delivery due to the lack of an ability to speak to a flexible and responsive human being. Top of my hit list for improved process re-engineering is Her Majesty's Courts & Tribunals Service (HMCTS) who have managed to finesse the ultimate in mind-numbing Kafkaesque customer service and some parts of our NHS, which, despite the undoubted skill and commitment of professional staff, is sometimes frustrated by antiquated and unnecessarily complex administration and management.

Improving innovation probability

The relationship between creativity and innovation is probabilistic. The best we can have is the idea that we can make it more probable to convert ideas into sustainable innovations. What then must enterprises pay attention to in order to increase the likelihood of successful innovations?

Idea development Great companies are great at rapid idea development, pushing the MVP (Minimum Viable Product) through successive iterations as rapidly as possible to make the idea ready for the market. It is rare for an idea to be fully formed at first inception, yet continuous iteration may make it unwieldy and the successful innovator ensures that idea development refines the idea such that it improves its fitness for purpose without losing its edge. In short we must iterate to innovate and the faster we can get that process working the greater the likelihood that we will find something of interest to our customers and markets. The essential condition is a fusion of style and substance that produces desire and functionality. This is the embodiment of the oft-quoted phrase, "I try to fail as fast as I can".

Yet failure without learning is of no practical use. Entrepreneurs and innovators must understand that failure contains all the seeds of success built into the experience if only they are prepared to stop, listen and learn. All too often, a failed project is buried in the organisation's deep memory, sometimes so deep that organisational amnesia breaks out. All the golden secrets to success are entombed along with the project. Few people ever look back in a fast paced enterprise to their ultimate peril. Some of my success as a creativity consultant over nearly 25 years has come down to leading executives into dark corners to examine ideas that have been forgotten or ignored for a host of reasons. At a personal level there are powerful forces within us that contrive to stop us admitting that we made errors. This requires exceptional emotional intelligence to confess to ourselves that we made a bad decision, let alone to others we work with and whose confidence we share.

Idea elegance   Quite simply, if your idea has not got a great name or a beautifully simple concept attached to it, you will find it harder to diffuse the innovation into the market. With this in mind, great innovators are unafraid to study art, music and other 'non-business' disciplines to understand concepts such as beauty, resonance, simplicity and so on. The wheel is an example of an idea that is elegant in that it has been adapted many times while still preserving the essence of form and function. The wheel quite literally makes the world go round. Giving your product or business a great name matters a great deal in a world of declining attention spans . . . I will just say that again . . . Giving your product or business a great name matters a great deal in a world of declining attention spans. Say it short, say it powerfully and say it in ways that your customer will understand.

Market readiness   Innovators are fascinated with what I call market intimacy. This is not the same as being led by market research. Business mythology says that enterprises like Apple and Fender refused to be led by market research, yet perhaps the truth is closer to the idea that they refused to be led *blindly* by market research. It is simply not intelligent to ignore the wealth of data that exists on just about every little thing we do. Yet data cannot tell us much about things that have never been done before. As with most things the smart leader blends data with wisdom in their search for novelty that someone wants or needs in sufficient quantity that it offers a sustainable profit or purpose.

The Fender Stratocaster guitar is one such example of a product that has managed to retain a premium price in a market of fierce competition purely through a combination of great design linked to a brand name that continues to defeat 'me-too' competitors. Leo Fender designed the Fender Stratocaster without reference or deference to market research strategies or techniques. He challenged the prevailing paradigm by designing a guitar that was made from two separate pieces of wood (the neck and body), when they were previously made from one piece of wood by luthiers. He attached the neck to the guitar using four wood screws, challenging the almost sacred viewpoint at that time, that guitar making was a craft. Fender's guitar was essentially the Model T Ford of the guitar world, transforming guitar making into an industrial process rather than a cottage industry. Fender also introduced a number of innovations. He crucially understood that great design combines form and function, that market research cannot always tell you about new product innovation and that product design is insufficient to ensure your innovation diffuses into the market. Fender was also great at marketing his products and especially understood the power of endorsements in gaining diffusion for his products. This is a point we shall return to when we examine MyMVision, an innovative app development to connect musicians to their global value chain.

I still note that the mistake is made to push, push, push when the statistics on the diffusion of what I call 'better mousetraps' is fairly unpromising. I believe that the problem here is that inventors and entrepreneurs quite literally fall in love with their ideas. They then assume that everyone else is just as romantically attracted. We need to put distance between ourselves and our ideas in order to see them as others do. Once we are in this place we have the possibility of discovering ways of generating market pull rather than product push. We now have the ability to engage customers at the design stage and this is one way to increase the probability of product adoption.

Evolution vs. revolution There is safety in evolutionary innovation as the next product or service usually builds on the safe foundations of an existing market need and an established customer base, but there may be no sustainable advantage or differentiation long term. Revolutionary innovation is, of course, high stakes and potentially high cost, yet it might be one of the few things that gives you a sustainable edge in a business world where business development is a bit like copying and pasting into a word processor. Guy Watson, CEO of Riverford Farms takes up the vexed question of evolution versus revolution in our next insight from an innovative enterprise coming up shortly.

Streetwise innovation tactics Small companies want to behave in ways that make them seem bigger. Large companies want to behave in ways that make them seem smaller. The winning move is to find ways to accrue genuine advantages that come from size while minimising the liabilities. There is much emphasis on the big 'S' of structure, i.e. large-scale organisational structures that fundamentally reorganise the way work is done. However, there is much value that can be created by using small 's' structural changes to gain from everyday changes that create a small company ethos in a large enterprise. A few examples will help you think through some of your own that will work in your company.

████████ **GROUND CONTROL** ████████

Streetwise innovation tactics

Try some of these daily habits out to improve your innovation excellence:

- Shut down computers and 'gadgets' at a certain time on a regular basis to indulge in unstructured dialogue.
- If you have a 'blamestorming' culture, agree that blame is to be rotated on a purely arbitrary basis. Elect a 'scapegoat of the month' to absorb blame, much in the same way that carbon is used to absorb spare neutrons in a nuclear reactor.
- Bring back political incorrectness – never mind the aha moment; double entendre and humour (the ha ha moment) are some of the places where people discover new ideas. Do not marginalise others in the process. It is possible to be provocative without being personally offensive.
- Reintroduce tea ladies/men and the tea break as a place where representatives of the 'whole enterprise' can bounce ideas around. The tea break is the original think tank and ought to be reinstated as the knowledge-management hub of 21st-century companies. Aside from the health consequences, the smoking room was an environment in which ideas flowed, although I personally never smoked.
- Remove all explicit and implicit structural impediments to conversation, e.g. time, space, personality, role, titles. It's good to talk.

What is your team's ROI?

> Not everything that counts can be counted and not everything that can be counted counts.
>
> Albert Einstein

Most business leaders are familiar with the concept of ROI or Return on Investment. In a world where rapid prototyping and incremental development is more important than one-time product development, what matters more is the extent to which you can make radical improvements on each product iteration. This leads to the updated notion of ROI or Return on Iteration. This leads us into the wicked problem of measurement and control of innovation. Measurement plays an important part in getting people to recognise success in most walks of life. Yet too many measures can be crippling in many walks of life. They are especially so at the front end of innovation due to the fragility of embryonic ideas. However, some measures for innovation may be of value:

- How frequently is the business plan revised to take account of external circumstances?
- How many 'sacred cows' are destroyed per year? In other words out-of-date business models, ideas that have repeatedly failed to reach a

threshold level of performance? At the very least these should be looked at for serious redevelopment.

- How many of your products or services were developed in the last two years and the last year? In a world of product churn, it is wise to be aware of the half-life of your products and take steps to improve them before they pass over the mid-way point of their S-curve.
- How many suggestions do you receive per employee? This is both a measure of employee engagement and the sign of a healthy innovation input pipeline.
- Percentage of suggestions implemented. This is both a measure of employee commitment and the sign of a healthy innovation output pipeline.
- R&D efficiency ratio: percentage of R&D projects converted to successful innovations.
- Percentage change in time taken from concept to launch. We discuss the potential for first-mover disadvantage in Dialogue III of this book.
- Time to recoup R&D investment.
- Number of processes successfully re-engineered.

A 'hardy perennial' approach that helps us stay focused in the field of performance measurement is the *balanced scorecard*, championed by Kaplan and Norton in 1992. This focuses attention on the need to balance hard and soft results with short and longer-term strategy. As such it is an advance on having thousands of disconnected and unmeaningful measures that typify average players in the field.

The strengths of the scorecard are in its simplicity and the fact that it brings together hard and soft measures. As such it is vital that such an approach does not develop into an unwieldy set of purely numerical measures, as this loses the point of its creation. Aliaxis, who produce innovative building products, adapted the format into three critical indicators that can be easily understood by everybody and were a step improvement as they reduce the complexity of the model by 25%. In a busy world, we need simple processes to help us understand complex things. Any form of reductionist thinking that does not 'dumb down' the complexity but somehow 'dumbs it up' by improving access to a business idea and reducing the number of things to occupy our RAM as human beings is an OK development by me. Aliaxis have dumbed up Kaplan and Norton's model thus:

BUS: How is the business doing?

CUS: How are we meeting customer needs?

US: How are we doing internally?

The BUS, CUS, US language is an easily tradable 'shorthand' that can be used to increase focus on where improvements are needed. BUS or

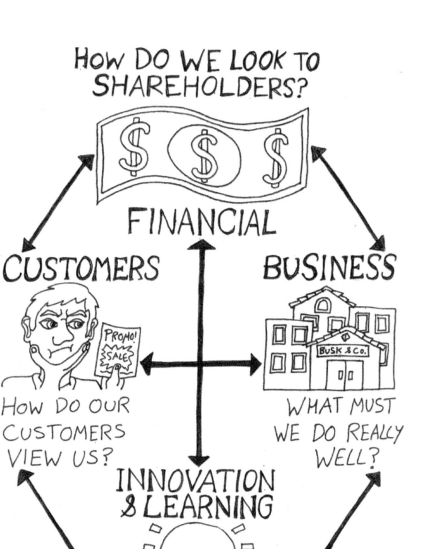

HOW DO WE LOOK TO SHAREHOLDERS?

FINANCIAL

CUSTOMERS

BUSINESS

BUSK & CO.

HOW DO OUR CUSTOMERS VIEW US?

WHAT MUST WE DO REALLY WELL?

INNOVATION & LEARNING

HOW CAN WE CONSTANTLY IMPROVE AND ADD VALUE?

business/financial measures include closeness to budgeted profit. CUS or external customer measures reflect achievement against required levels of order completeness and timeliness of delivery. These measures are, in turn, interpreted in terms relevant to local teams. This is a good example of a simple system in use to 'tame' a wicked problem.

The anatomy of an innovator

Innovation is not just the realm of technology firms. It is as old as our wheel. This example shows just how it permeates every aspect of our lives as we visit Riverford Farms, an organic farm owned and managed by Guy Watson. Guy specialises in a sustainable and ethical approach to business and this permeates his whole life and ethos in a model approach that others would do well to live up to. He alludes to the need to match revolutionary innovation with the evolutionary kind, to know when to innovate and when to consolidate and to the restless mindset of the innovator.

> We were double winners at the Soil Association Best of Organic Market awards this month; best and most innovative organic farmer. The urge to innovate stems from our restless dissatisfaction with the way things are, a determination to find a better way and constant pushing of the boundaries. It got man out of the cave, brought us the Industrial Revolution, the Green Revolution and the Internet but arguably also the Enclosures Act, climate change, deforestation, gun powder and industrialised farming. Clearly it can be a force for both good and bad; as yet we are incapable of distinguishing the useful from the destructive before lunging forward into the chaos that ensues when we let the marketplace decide. The innovations that are scaled up are invariably the profitable ones (usually to a small minority), not necessarily balanced, beneficial to all or thought through in their consequences for humankind and the planet.
>
> I am an irrepressible innovator and sometimes loathe the restless dissatisfaction that comes with it. I know it makes life hard for my staff and those around me and have determined to take time to celebrate achievements before dashing on. On this occasion, celebration involved a lot of organic vodka, imbibed on a warm London night with some self-satisfaction.
>
> To be a good, maybe even the best, organic farmer requires much more balance, and some wisdom. Innovation has its place but, unless preceded by a lot of observation, patience and a bit of humility we would be charging around creating clever solutions to the wrong problems. Last week we were clearing up the yard and I noticed a number of my early inventions disappearing into the

skip (I couldn't help retrieving the long-abandoned, barely used, lie-down weeder; a genius idea that my staff hated). Mercifully, over most of my 30 years of organic growing my impetuous nature has been balanced by our more considered farm team, particularly John, our cautious farms manager of 25 years. I appreciate his patience and consideration but will never emulate it; I will be an innovator to the grave. To succeed and persist another 30 years we need both approaches, and the wisdom to recognise when each is appropriate; when to risk my revolutionary leaps and when to progress in John's cautious steps.

Guy Watson, Riverford Farms, www.riverford.co.uk

6 Learning and plasticity

Educating the mind without educating the heart is no education at all.

Aristotle

Like most things connected with the future, the jury is out on just what humans will need to tilt the balance toward the intelligences that are needed for a machine-enabled world. I would, however, argue for a rebalancing of the importance of each type for a sustainable world in which we profit from machines and robots, etc. In the industrial age, it was important for us to carry our IQ around with us. Our education systems were guided toward this goal through 'uploading and downloading' information onto examination papers, through our attempts to impress each other with our retention of facts and the ability to organise and reformulate facts to suit particular needs. Retention of facts may no longer be needed apart from entertainment purposes at dinner parties and quiz shows. What matters more is our ability to apply information and knowledge.

As a child, it was important to carry many facts around in one's brain. In hindsight, this was a sensible strategy as a two-year-old's brain is approximately 80% of adult size, so we have plenty of capacity. In any case it is estimated that we only use approximately 3% of our entire brain capacity in our lives, unlike most computers. The development of what could loosely be called 'Learning to Learn Technologies' were crude, so I had to use a DIY approach, developing my own approaches to install the required knowledge to pass exams and so on. Some of my methods were not efficient in today's terms even though they were naively quite effective. These included the repetition of French vocabulary in my head before going to bed and then recalling it on awakening, essentially a rote learning method, repeating the phrases in my head many times until I had linked them to their meanings. In other cases I manufactured surprisingly effective ways of assembling knowledge and wisdom onto small cards containing images, words and other triggers such as mnemonics, which I would 'photograph'

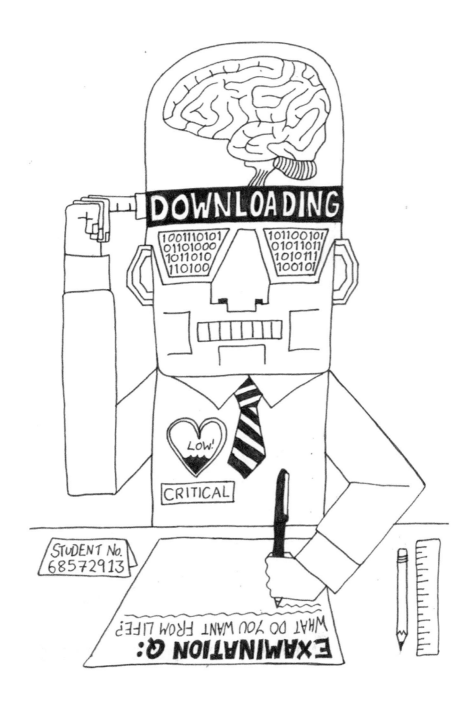

in my mind's eye. All this pre-dated the advent of "Key Facts" cards and then Mind Maps™ by Tony Buzan and a suite of visual memory method-ologies such as rich picturing and cognitive mapping. I learned many other methods of acquiring, retaining and organising information later on, but, to be frank, the amount of information now available has outpaced my ability to learn so I must modify my strategy for learning. Given that there has been an exponential growth in the amount of data we are exposed to on a daily basis, we have two choices on how to handle it as individuals. We can either drown in data or swim with information. Some of us are clearly switching off as a strategy, since the average attention span has declined from 12 seconds in 2000 to 8.25 in 2015. That is nearly one second less than the attention span of a goldfish, although, in fairness, the goldfish's environment has not altered that much in the same time. We must become much better at solving the question of how to improve the signal:noise ratio in terms of finding and using the information we need to succeed.

We know that children learn best when teaching engages with their own natural exuberance, energy and curiosity. Yet much educational pedagogy still expects children to sit still, as passive recipients of knowledge, disen-gaged with learning. The 'upload-download' model, whereby teachers input knowledge in order for children to write it back down on an exam paper is also broken in an age where application of knowledge is more important than knowledge acquisition. Also, much of our work life requires collabora-tion so why do we rely on feeding the individual child in school? Education has a lot of learning to do about learning in the Man-Machine age. It is something I spent some time discussing with Professor Ken Robinson some years back when he had just written his groundbreaking book on educa-tion called *All Our Futures*. The essence of this book was that creativity in education was a core skill across all subjects and that it could and should not be confined to the art department. His findings were widely ignored by the government of the day who had commissioned the project. Perhaps they will listen now. I also spoke with Greg Smith of Arthur D. Little more recently on how education must change in order to prepare people for a world in which the intimacy between people and machines is increased? In a nutshell, he said that the measure of success must move from the things you know to the questions you can ask. Acquiring knowledge through facts must be replaced by acquiring knowledge through lines of enquiry. So a futurist school manifesto will balance lessons in IQ (head), EQ (heart) and SQ (soul). We are likely to be focused on meta-knowledge (how we use knowledge) rather than just concentrating on the acquisition and retention of knowledge per se. It might well include lessons on:

- asking better questions of oneself and others;
- searching data, information and knowledge for unique wisdom;
- synthesising quantitative data and qualitative insights;
- systemic thinking – seeing connections between the arts, the sciences and the humanities;

- interacting with one's emotions and relating to others' feelings and emotions;
- finding one's soul/spiritual intelligence; and
- making best use of machines.

Although there is little hard evidence to support the existence of spiritual intelligence, Howard Gardner alluded to its existence when he augmented his theory of multiple intelligences in 1999 with what he called 'existential intelligence'. Just because we cannot quantify something it does not mean that it does not exist. Society does seem to have become afraid to believe in anything these days unless there is quantitative research-based evidence behind the concept, perhaps because of the proliferation of information sources, often contradictory information and the advent of the term 'fake news' which has devalued the currency of the truth. Yet, many of us are prepared to buy health foods, read tarot cards and pray, none of which are supported by hard evidence. Are we simply too hard on things that are by their very nature empirical in nature amid a data-led world?

GROUND CONTROL

Splitting synapses

Examine a taken-for-granted belief that you hold, such as it is good to live within your means, or that it is good to keep your workplace tidy.

Examine the basis of that belief. Is it common sense or is it supported by evidence?

What are the alternative viewpoints? Are there ways of safely testing the alternatives?

What then works in the field of multiplying your personal intelligence? Let us lift some more durable needles out from the haystack in this area from the last 50 years of activity for busy people. Never mind last week's fads. We are looking at what works in this area, from classic methods that have stood the test of time to advances in this area that will last more than a week.

Never mind the neuroscience

Humour can be dissected, as a frog can, but the thing dies in the process and the innards are discouraging to any but the pure scientific mind.

E.B. White

Perhaps the ultimate test of the convergence between man and machine will come when a computer can do a stand-up comedy routine without assistance.

Rather than telling just a pre-prepared joke, can the computer 'warm the audience up', sense the context in which the joke would need to be adapted and so on? Once the computer had made the audience laugh, could it act upon emotional intelligence to build on the situation and vary the script until they could take no more?

Neuroscience offers us massive opportunities to discover how we might be more intelligent individually and collectively. Unfortunately the word 'neuro' has also become some kind of catchphrase to be added on to virtually any product or service to revitalise it, rather like the word nano-technology has been added to hairspray to befuddle us. Before we look at what advances in neuroscience can offer us, let us take a brief diversionary muse into some early failures in my quest to fuse man and machine in perfect harmony.

Having wrestled with machines for much of my life as a musician, I spent a lot of my early life trying to get machines to do things that humans do easily. My Man-Machine experiments came to a head in 1978 when we augmented our drummer Simon on stage at a concert in the town hall with a spin drier loaded with a brick to create an industrial backdrop to our music. We did not do this as an act of cruelty to Simon but one of kindness, as he was incredibly shy and did not want to be seen on stage. Instead he played 'in synch' with the spin drier behind the stage curtain, although that experiment did not work well due to the dominance of the spin drier and its arrhythmic qualities. Most of my experiments with drum machines and early computers were not as satisfying as the interactions I have had with live percussionists and drummers, due to their ability to learn, unlearn and relearn. The process of creating new neural pathways in our brains is called neuroplasticity. This is our brain's way of becoming more effective and efficient. As we age some of our neural pathways grow stronger and others diminish. But we are still able to learn all through our lives if we are motivated to do so. In this respect humans differ from machines, most of which do not currently learn, unlearn or relearn. Our abilities to learn, unlearn and relearn are some of the most precious capabilities that differentiate us from machines at this time. We would do well to enhance these capabilities as we enter the age of machine intelligence. How then is the brain organised for thinking?

Keiron Sparrowhawk leads My Cognition, a company devoted to cognitive fitness and our ability to enhance it. Major advances in neuroscience over the past 30 years have built on two centuries of psychological and cognitive research, to give us a better understanding of five domains that form the main part of our cognitive function. These are: executive function; working memory; episodic memory; attention; and processing speed.

> **Executive function**: The executive function allows us to plan, organise and be creative. It also controls how we fully utilise our cognition across all five cognitive domains. Things you can do to enhance your executive function

include keeping or taking back some planning responsibility and preventing these skills from diminishing, and encouraging constructive criticism from your team to testing your convictions and keeping you focused.

Working memory: This is the 'workspace' of our minds. Ultimately, it is our ability to make decisions and solve problems. To boost working memory take time to explain concepts, ideas and work processes to others. As well as benefitting your work colleagues, the process of teaching helps you to consolidate information and archive it, while making way for more long-term memory. Sleep is critical to learning and memory. To avoid sleep deprivation, 95% of adults need between seven-and-a-half to nine hours sleep a night, so 'getting by' on a few hours' sleep is a false economy, because your working memory will suffer. Get into a regular sleep schedule and try not to break your routine.

Processing speed: Processing speed is the ability to act with speed and accuracy. Boost your processing speed by re-energising meetings. Cut the length of them down by 10%. If that works, try cutting them down again by another 10%. Speed meetings force attendees to be more concise and focused, but given that the average employee spends 62 hours in meetings a month, a 10% saving will give you six hours of your life back every month. Maintain an active and diverse social life. Humans are inherently social animals and, fortunately, from the simplest of conversations to the liveliest of debates, the dynamics of social interactions flex our cognitive skills and boost our mood. Take time every day to indulge your social nature and engage with those around you.

Episodic memory: Episodic memory is the ability to recall events, people and places in context to a relevant situation. It is what helps us learn from experiences and impart wisdom to others. Enhance this domain using imagery. For example, recall a list of individual items in sequence by conjuring up a striking image of all the items together. This technique is up to three times more effective than trying to learn by repetition. Positive relationships also help protect against memory loss. Nurture personal relationships, do not take people for granted, and ensure that you do not let others take you for granted either. Make a habit of telling the one you love that you love them – every day.

Attention: This is the ability to concentrate and focus. It enables us to selectively focus on a task, even when being distracted. Attention can be given a powerful and immediate injection through regular exercise. A healthy level of cardiovascular fitness is clinically proven to increase the attentional function of the brain. Therefore, walking, cycling or running to work, hitting the gym, or even making sure that you always take the stairs all make vital contributions to keeping you sharper and more energised for longer. Aside from exercise, we also improve our attention by paying attention. The best leaders are intuitive listeners; they spend more time listening and learning than they do talking. Try talking less and listening more to your colleagues, family and friends. It will boost your attention, improve your communication, and help you to better read situations and understand what is sometimes, crucially, not being said or heard.

Our plasticity differentiates us from machines that are, of course, currently brilliant at logic. The point at which machines can match our ability to think creatively is a long way off and creativity will be a core skill that helps us work in harmony with machines. The following stories illustrate the different ways that people learn.

The chemistry of learning

It was a chilly day in February 1971 and I was 12 years old. I was tucked up in the house as usual in the living room with my chemistry set. My mum was doing her own chemistry experiments by burning my fish finger sandwiches in the kitchen in her usual way. In front of me, an array of test tubes and flasks, a methylated spirit burner, a tripod and a crucible. The air hung with acrid smoke as I attempted various chemistry experiments with my Lotts' chemistry set, suitably augmented with various items I had bought in bulk from the chemist's shop without parental supervision, question or challenge: ammonia, hydrochloric acid, flowers of sulphur, copper sulphate, potassium nitrate, hydrogen peroxide. Some of the experiments were quite dangerous! I was in effect a learning junkie and also read avidly around the subject of chemistry. As a result I became top of the class in the subject and suffered the usual Anglo-Saxon bullying that accompanied educational success in an English grammar school environment. I later on realised that I was more of an exception rather than the norm in my nerdishness and thirst for learning, yet I still feel I would be ready for a world in which the only source of personal competitive advantage is the ability to learn fast and to be inquisitive. As an aside, just imagine what would happen if a 10 year old went to the local chemist's shop to procure such items at such tender years in the current age?

This story is a good example of what Kolb would call active experimentation in order to learn. In my experience, just trying stuff is insufficient to guarantee learning. We have all done experiments but failed to learn from them. To learn well, we need to also have ambition, goals, interest, capability, a means of learning and willpower. So often in my life as a university tutor, I have noticed that there is no shortage of capability among the people I have dealt with but often the desire to learn, which is connected with interest and willpower, is missing. The old adage "You can lead a horse to water, but you cannot make it drink" springs to mind. Clearly we need to ignite the

willpower of our children in learning if we are to succeed as faster learners. This includes allowing them to experiment and, occasionally, to fail.

In other cases, learning can be a social process. Reading aloud or listening to stories is one of the most 'cerebrally' engaging experiences a child can have. Watching TV for 15 000 hours only generates about 30 minutes of brain activity. However, reading aloud fires up children's brains because they have to use their imagination. This activity stimulates the electricity in the brain, promoting brain development by strengthening brain pathways. Do we read books anymore, however? Perhaps I am preaching to the converted as you are clearly reading this one!

7 Branding for a complex world

In a world where the signal:noise ratio is in sharp decline due to communications overload, an effective brand can help you and your enterprise stand out from the crowd. Supermarket brands are a kind of shorthand for your enterprise's products and services. Your brand is a manifestation of the bundle of promises you intend to deliver. In a cluttered and complex world branding is a way of helping people find your enterprise, its products and services. How then does the gentle art and discipline of branding work in an age when many brands are virtual and transient? How are enterprises evolving their approach to branding to address the challenges of the Fourth Industrial Revolution where intelligence, information and imagination are the hallmarks of success? To brand your enterprise you must engage all the senses to reach people's heads, hearts and souls. To begin, here are six of the best rules every brand builder should remember and some examples of enterprises that are using these rules to help them stand out from the crowd:

1. Not everyone can or should become a brand.
2. Ensure your brand connects passion and purpose.
3. Do not build your brand on sand.
4. Social media is only part of the branding story.
5. Endorsements are an important part of any brand.
6. PR is more reliable and effective than branding if done well.

Stand on the shoulders of giants

ColaLife is a not-for-profit enterprise inspired by the thought that Coca-Cola seems to get everywhere in developing countries, yet simple life-saving medicines do not. They asked the question why and started to work on a number of fronts to cheekily brand themselves with the 'cola' tag as a disruptor by delivering small changes that make big, self-sustaining improvements. Not everyone can become a brand and while ColaLife do not have the resources to become a brand themselves, like a Fortune 500 enterprise, they have cleverly stood on the shoulders of giants in ways that give them presence while complementing Coca-Cola's drive toward improved ethical credentials, working with companies such as Glaxo SmithKline (GSK) and Johnson & Johnson to save lives in Africa.

Their work is in the field of Oral Rehydration Salts (ORS) and zinc for childhood diarrhoea. More than a decade since this treatment became the global standard, 99% of diarrhoea cases are still not treated with ORS with zinc and diarrhoea is still the world's second biggest killer of young children. This told co-founders Simon and Jane Berry that current efforts to improve access are not sufficient and are working too slowly. Simon and Jane are living embodiments of a company that connects passion and purpose. Here Simon speaks of how they came to have the idea and the transformations that have happened to realise their dream of "making death from diarrhoea history".

> One of the things Coca-Cola taught us: you have to deliver on expectation – every time. Quality and trust are everything – even and especially for poor people with few resources to risk.
>
> Jane Berry

ColaLife uses the power of horizontal online strategy, having more than 10 000 online supporters, and interest from many global stakeholders. These help to give a tiny enterprise the power to source expertise – and even information sharing – among unlikely partners such as UNICEF, J&J, GSK, Coca-Cola, SABMiller and health agencies across the world.

The power of connection

MyMVision connects musicians around the world with live music venues, music schools, recording studios, rehearsal rooms and the entire value chain via an IOS and Android app. MyM facilitates the professional careers of artists, helping them at every step of their journey, from the cradle to the stage and beyond. Launched in 2017 by Internet of Artists, a London-based company boasting a fully Italian creative team, MyM has masterminded social media and collaborations with giants, building their brand on solid foundations, with already more than 100 000 active profiles in over 15 countries. Founder Riccardo Torriani identified several of our branding rules as being pivotal to the development of their BBE:

> Brand building through social media is only part of our story. We have developed several strategic collaborations with partners to give us scale and reach. Nobody wants to be the first person to try an innovation and our musicians can partner with world-class musicians across the planet. We have also benefitted from endorsements from professionals who have worked with Prince through to Ozzy Osbourne.

Moments of truth matter

Your brand can be built or destroyed in seconds through social media. Some enterprises choose not to have social media presence because of this. It does not matter as people will talk about you anyway. As Jeff Bezos says: "Your brand is what people say about you when you are not in the room."

Brands matter, especially when a problem arises in your enterprise. Your response to circumstances when your enterprise is challenged is what marketers call a 'moment of truth' as it reveals your brand values in an unvarnished way. I was deeply impressed by the behaviour of Line 6 CEO Marcus Ryle in this respect. Line 6 are a high-tech electronics firm that make guitar processors among a range of other musical equipment. I had a mechanical problem with a guitar effects unit, the flagship Line 6 POD 500X, which is used by the likes of Bill Nelson, Elbow, Avril Lavigne and session musicians who work with Eric Clapton, Pink and Van Morrison. The problem occurred shortly after the unit was out of warranty but I considered the fault not to be down to fair wear and tear. I could make no progress with Yamaha's call centre, who handle Line 6's routine affairs on their behalf and decided to persist by inviting the CEO to connect with me on LinkedIn, having explained why I wanted to speak to him briefly. I could not be more impressed with the turnaround that Marcus performed after he made some detailed enquiries of me. Moreover, I was totally impressed because he handled the issue personally, when I am sure he had better things to do. If more enterprises were able to act in this way, their reputations would soar and their repeat business with it.

Brand on the run

Nub Records is an independent record company that collaborates with Warner Bros to achieve global reach and punch above their weight in the music business. The owner, Mark Christopher Lee, first set Nub up as an independent label for his own band:

> We were getting played a lot on BBC Radio 1 and were offered a lot of what I thought were dodgy deals by record labels. So I decided to start a label myself. We were one of the first digital only labels back in 2005 and we now have a deal with Sony.

Mark started sending music to the legendary VP of Warner Music – Seymour Stein who famously signed Madonna as well as The Ramones – Seymour loved what Nub were doing and their DIY Punk ethos. Since that time Nub has entered the *Guinness Book of Records* with their series of 100 × 30 albums. The concept is 100 songs all 30 seconds long, as a protest against lack of royalties from music-streaming services such as Spotify – 100 × 30 unintentionally broke the world record for the maximum number of songs on a 74-minute digital CD. It also fits perfectly inside our emerging world of DADD where the average length of video watched online is 2.7 minutes. The award sees them featured alongside Justin Bieber in the *Guinness Book of Records*, which Mark found hilarious. Nub Records are living proof that David can conquer Goliath with a clever strategy. Nub Records are a good example of a brand that has used the power of networks, endorsements and PR to build a brand from a small base without huge budgets and access to branding agencies.

The lessons from these branding stories may be summed up:

1. If you cannot or do not want to develop a brand, find ways to connect with others who can or already do have a brand that you can work with for mutual advantage.
2. Your brand connects your soul and purpose to your daily work. Ensure you are in synch.
3. Work with giants to scale your brand to grow faster and reach further.
4. Use the full range of marketing communications to develop your brand: traditional media, social media, endorsements and PR, etc.
5. Use branding to improve the signal:noise ratio of your enterprise in a complex world.

Synthesis

We must face up to the Man-Machine paradox rather than avoid the inevitable. The winning move for the Fourth Industrial Revolution is for humans to operate in synergy with machines, information and intelligence.

If we choose to operate in the Man-Machine quadrant this offers us the choice of gaining self-actualisation through the genuine release of the drudgery of working life, although we will need to pay the price in terms of becoming lifelong learners. Replacing drudgery with self-actualisation is not a bad trade-off although we might have to make other trade-offs in the process.

We live in a VUCA world. To survive and thrive, we must master complexity thinking and learn to improvise as part of a deliberate strategy rather than slavishly following rigid plans. We continue to develop the theme of strategic improvisation in Dialogue III.

BBEs are ones in which we fully engage the heads, hearts and souls of the people we employ or collaborate with. Enterprises that operate with high IQ, EQ and SQ are positioned perfectly to perform better in a disruptive business world.

Brain Based Leaders are also exceptional at balancing head (IQ), heart (EQ) and soul (SQ). It is no longer true that the most conventionally intelligent leaders will make the best ones in a world where information is freely distributed. However, there will always be a role for smart practitioners who can convert the tsunami of data into valuable information knowledge and wisdom.

In a world of communications overload, the Brain Based Leader masters the art and discipline of persuasive and potent communications, providing they lead with resonant simplicity and truthful communications in a busy, complex and confusing world. Instead of 'dumbing down' communications, Brain Based Leaders 'dumb up' their communications by being brief, rich in content, potent and respectful to their recipients.

Brain Based leaders create cultures where creativity and creative thinking are part of business as unusual. At the same time, they encourage others to make wise decisions, based on a balance of head, heart and soul without undue bias from the human condition. In doing so they set their people up to maximise the conversion of good ideas into innovation excellence for maximum ROI.

A BBE is a living organism rather than a two-dimensional organogram. Learning and plasticity are embedded into the enterprise's DNA. We will explore enterprise plasticity further in Dialogue III.

DIALOGUE TWO

Brainy teams
(collective intelligence)

CHAPTER 6

Leading brainy teams

> I am not afraid of an army of lions led by a sheep.
> I am afraid of an army of sheep led by a lion.
>
> Alexander the Great

We began by comparing four postures for the emerging relationship with man/woman and machines. We now move on to consider intelligent teams. Will we face the *War of the Worlds* scenario? This would be a full-on competitive approach with unhealthy competition between team members and a ghetto protectionist mentality toward the use of machines to enhance human potential for the good of the individuals, teams and society. Or will we opt for the Man-Machine approach? We would see teams working in an integrated way with machines, using machines for what they do best and human skills when they are of greatest advantage. Teams network their EQ, human skills, creativities and idiosyncrasies and augment themselves with machines and AI to make the best use of their time on planet Earth. The choice is in our hands and this relies crucially on leading brainy teams, which is where we begin.

My early experience was in leading and managing R&D teams in new pharmaceutical product development. Together we innovated in bringing human insulin safely to diabetes sufferers and the first HIV/AIDS treatment to the world. I considered myself very privileged at having been entrusted to do this work. The urgency and importance of the task was brought home to me as my best friend from school had contracted HIV and, of course, we had no idea as to what the future would hold for sufferers from this disease at the time. The project involved working with a bunch of pharmacists, chemists and regulatory people to deliver the AZT/Zidovudine/Retrovir drug safely to the patient in record time against a background of a highly regulated pharmaceutical environment. This was essentially a challenge of leading teams of brainy people to do things quickly, when our normal modus operandi would have been to work deliberately but perhaps more slowly. Paradoxically, intelligent teams need someone to help them keep focused on goals, harness human capabilities, make relationships work between opposites and so on. Good leadership and management are needed even more for brainy teams than ones that face simple tasks and where simple obedience and adherence to procedure is the order of the day. In particular scientists are good at unvarnished conversations that sometimes pay little heed to the emotional lives of their fellow team members. This, when combined with the undoubted passions and commitment inherent within the not-for-profit environment of The Wellcome Foundation made the need for skilful team leadership of prime importance.

Management is all about optimising a system, in other words, efficiency, whereas leadership is about changing the system, in other words, effectiveness. Of course, both management, leadership, effectiveness and efficiency are needed in most situations but the balance of these ingredients varies. Some people's jobs comprise more management than leadership and most people's jobs require some elements of self-leadership, especially in an age where work may happen across enterprises, much of it with people who do not share the same physical space or deep relationships. So management and leadership will need to change in the Man-Machine age from ideas of control and command toward those of community and commitment.

Leadership is both what I call a digital and analogue activity. It is digital, because wise leaders use facts and data rather than just hunch and lunch (intuition, gut feeling) to inform decisions and behaviour. It is analogue because human beings are hugely individual in their motivations and also occasionally illogical in their decisions and behaviour. This requires leaders to adjust, flex and finesse their strategies to the people they lead, sometimes on a completely personalised basis. We know well from our discussion about bra holsters and conkers in Dialogue I that data and logic do not always inform human behaviour and any leader operating only with the bounded rationality inside their head is likely to be ineffective at reaching the emotional core of those they lead. Perhaps this explains the old adage, "You don't have to be mad to work here, but it helps".

Views of leadership have changed over the ages, from ideas about war propounded by Sun Tzu and Machiavelli's treatment via *The Prince* which focused on questions of influence and manipulation, through to the beginnings of a psychological approach around 100 years ago. It could be said that leadership thinking has mirrored the age in which the ideas were put forward. At the height of the industrial age, Frederick Taylor put forward the idea of scientific management, which focused on the organisation of work in the best way to gain output from workers. Henry Ford was a great advocate of Taylorism and believed that his factories could be organised along the lines of scientific management and detailed work study. Fordism tended to ignore the influence of the human being but was clearly a grand design for the industrial age when leaders could operate through command and control and, to some extent, the employees could be treated as units of production. As an aside, we may be re-entering that era through the current obsession with gig economy working, Uber jobs, zero-hour contracts and the like.

Later on in the 20th century, Fordism and Taylorism were superseded by sociocultural ideas about leadership and notions that the leader was the most important variable and could flex and bend their style to fit the situation. This eventually produced theories and models of Situational Leadership and the desirable notion of being a 9 : 9 leader, meaning a leader who is outstanding at balancing concern for the task (9) with concern for the people (9). After all, who would want to be a 5 : 7 leader or worse? Desirable though it might seem that we can be all things to all people, more recently the issue of authenticity has begun to take hold as a major idea in modern leadership thinking. This is perhaps because of the perceived decline in trust levels in modern business and a recognition that the leadership talents involved in modern enterprises do not always reside in one single individual. In the last 20 or so years, the task of leadership has also shifted focus toward the management of complexity, uncertainty and the unknowable through the seminal work of Ralph Stacey and Dave Snowden's Cynefin framework, which offered five domains to help business leaders decide on the best approach to make sense of their own behaviour and that of others: simple, complicated, complex, chaotic and disorder. There is overlap with our exploration of VUCA issues here and leaders need to prepare to manage these habitats in business.

Leaders can derive power and authority from a number of places:

1. Your formal *position* (CEO, Head of Informatics, enterprise-given title etc.). Position power gives you the platform to give out orders but does not necessarily provide you with influence. Increasingly many of us have no position power as portfolio workers.
2. The *resources* you can command or marshal toward a goal (time, money, people). Resource power enables you to throw money and people at problems, but does not necessary command respect itself.
3. Your professional *expertise*. For example, if you are a pharmacist, engineer, social worker and so on, this might buy you respect in your professional field.
4. Your *social capital* through networks. It is not so much what you know but who you know and access to these people that counts here. This is your ability to get things done through others. In my case I was able to broker an introduction for Gina Miller to Sir Richard Branson. This was to help her win her case at the Supreme Court and challenge the legal basis of our government's attempt to turn back 400 years of sovereignty. This is a tangible example of the importance of networks.
5. The *information* you hold (not data, but truly your ability to use information to advantage). Clearly in an information-based economy, this is a key element of your personal platform as a leader, which is why the mastery of knowledge management for precision decision is a key issue for Brain Based Leaders.
6. Your *personal power*. Another way to think about this is the word charisma. It also equates to what we termed spiritual intelligence (SQ) in Dialogue I. We will discuss charisma in greater depth in a moment.

Each of these elements of power can be used in a positive way (give) or in terms of withholding (take) in more Machiavellian styles of leadership, such as negotiation, co-option, explicit or implicit or coercion. Whereas it was once true that leaders could rely on those things that an enterprise could *give* them (principally position power and resource power) to maintain authority, the basis of leadership is being challenged around the world. Portfolio working and gig economy jobs often leave us without any enterprise-given sources of power. In any case leaders are no longer respected for position or resource power alone, as people challenge the norms of authority. We see this in everyday life where there is reduced deference to powerful people, celebrities and/or people with titles, such as monarchs, presidents and politicians. Leaders in a Brain Based Economy must command respect through authority earned rather than given. So, power gained from your professional expertise, networks, information and charisma are the main building blocks of your platform of authority as a leader, with information mastery as the rising star in the Brain Based Economy. This is a very different way of leading. A word or two on the vexed question of charisma is also worth spending time on.

Although there is probably little proof in evidential terms that charisma, personal power or SQ is a 'thing', most of us know when we have been in a room with someone who possesses it. Having met Sir Richard Branson, Roberta Flack, Nadine Hack, Bob Geldof, Gina Miller, Professor Charles Handy et al., it is quite clear that these people have whatever 'it' is, even if you do not like or agree with anything they say. It is quite telling to watch Branson speaking to people in a packed room. To the person he is speaking with it seems as if they are the only person in the room. I am told by network colleagues that Tony Blair, Barack Obama, Nelson Mandela, Michelle Obama, Prince, Lady Diana Spencer, Lady Gaga, Steve Jobs, Madonna and Anita Roddick also possess this quality.

Charisma, personal power or SQ is the quality that causes people to walk over hot coals to deliver for you. Of course, this has a positive and potentially negative quality in terms of getting people to do their best and brainwashing them to consider doing their worst. We need the former.

It takes two: dialogue

> It takes two to know one.
>
> Gregory Bateson

What will the art of conversation mean in a connected world? Will chatbots who bite replace ladies who latte? Will we cease to use language to communicate and replace it with direct thought transmission? What will the workplace look like from the point of view of the physical and psychological environment? Will we still geolocate to cross-pollinate? How will we make technology work to our advantage? How will we avoid a dystopian future where we lose our grip on humanity and our human potential? Here we will look at the changing notions of conversation, dialogue, debate and discussion across time zones, geographies and species.

We have already tried some simple communication experiments working with machines. From using two tin cans and a piece of string to communicate, we are used to signing into our phone with our face, iris or fingerprint. I used to let my Toyota Hybrid park itself before insurance companies intervened to place artificial legal obstacles in the way of AI. Domino's Pizza use virtual assistants to handle orders. We have also seen some fairly disastrous attempts in trying to do human things using inhuman approaches, such as sacking people by text or messenger as The Accident Group found out – it was no accident, however, just a reputational car crash! As we automate, leaders would do well to double their education in humanity and the humanities. What then can we learn from psychology, sociology and anthropology about the value of analogue conversation in a digital world?

The word dialogue is derived from the Greek word διάλογος meaning conversation through speech. We are much more used to the words debate or discussion in modern business. I was once told that discussion comes from the root form of the words percussion and concussion, 'to beat around' or 'break things up' and this is an abiding experience for some meetings we have attended in corporate life. Whether or not the derivation is true is, perhaps, unimportant; it is certainly true that many meetings are effectively mass debates. These often result in what I call 'psychic concussion', a mind-numbing experience for all and one that devalues the purpose and experience of work for individuals, teams and the enterprise. There are important differences in the meaning of dialogue. Teams need to focus on dialogue rather than debate and discussion to reach better conversation levels in BBEs.

Physicist David Bohm wrote extensively on dialogue or 'skilful conversation' as a means of accessing much deeper thought patterns than is usual in social intercourse. I have been privileged to attend several dialogue sessions at creativity retreats at The Centre for Management Creativity and the experience is well worth having. Some of the principles behind dialogue have been at the heart of some of the more 'difficult conversations' on the world stage, such as Nelson Mandela's transition to power, the Good Friday agreement in Northern Ireland and Sir Richard Branson's 'Elders' group, which seeks to develop thought leadership on wicked problems that face the world and influence world leaders to make wise choices on such matters.

The 'rules for dialogue' are both deceptively simple and also potentially terrifying for leaders and managers.

- A dialogue often has no objective or agenda.
- Judgemental behaviour is set aside.
- Decisions are not made.

. . . and so on.

In this sense we still have some way to go with Siri, Alexa and other chatbots, as they can only give you 'answers'. Many of our current online devices are guided toward what can be described as 'relational thinking'; for example, Amazon always suggests items you might like based on your purchasing history. While this might be good for sales, it is rather less useful for strategic thinking, novelty and innovation, which are really about marking out your enterprise's offering in a unique and compellingly different way. As with all things, we need meetings for those things where there is need for short-term decisions and actions. We also need dialogue and extended conversation to help us resolve wicked problems, see the future and position ourselves opportunistically to take appropriate advantage of it.

> We must have an empty space where we are not obliged to anything, nor to come to any conclusions, nor to say anything or not say anything.
>
> David Bohm

The emphasis in dialogue is to see things anew and find new meanings. In that sense it shares one of the 'rules for creativity' in brainstorming, that of building on conversation rather than attempting to make judgements, close down expansive thinking or converge to a point. Think of a table tennis match for 40 people where the goal is to keep the ball in the air for as long as possible and not score points against your opponents. Of course, such behaviour is in conflict with the human tendency to compete to win. This is why dialogue sessions and wicked problem resolution require professional facilitation and management. The principles of dialogue also apply to Dialectic Conversation, except that in this form, there is some deliberate attempt to set up a creative tension/conflict of ideas using the ancient Greek tradition of 'thesis' and 'antithesis'. However Dialectic Conversation differs from debate in so far as there is a deliberate attempt to use opposing viewpoints in order to create something new via the process of 'synthesis'. A modern version of Dialectic Conversation is what I call 'Non-Linear Conversation' (NLC).

NCLs work on the principle of setting up a 'thesis', contrasting this with an 'antithesis' or something completely irrelevant and then attempting to 'synthesise' the two together to a higher ground rather than a compromise or lower order level. NLCs are non-logical in the sense that they ask people to ensure that the next idea is not linked to the previous one and they encourage random interventions. They therefore tend to break the cycle of analysis and logic. Because such conversations require the acceptance of cognitive dissonance as a basic rite of passage, it is essential that they are accompanied by the use of dialogue as a methodology of conversation. A 'micro-lite' version of NLCs is the technique known as the wildest idea method, where people are asked to come up with the most unusual idea for a period in an innovative thinking session. The NLC approach is more useful if 'stronger medicine' is needed.

We need to seriously up our game in the area of nuanced conversation in a complex world. We are also some way off being able to have a counselling

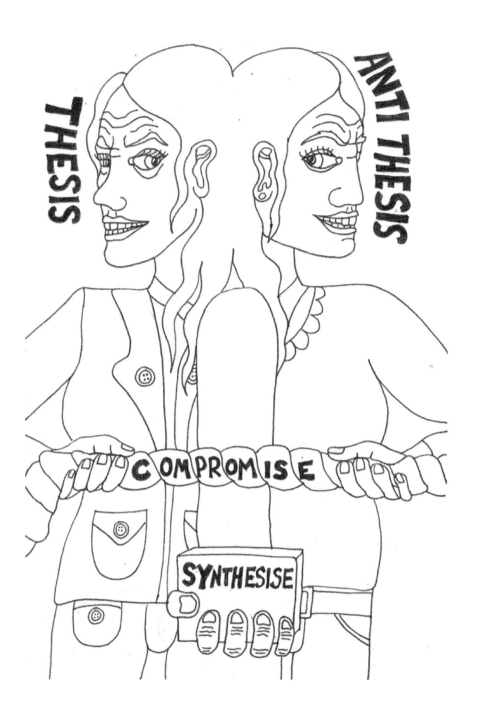

session with a chatbot, apart from at a superficial level. The reason for this is that language is complicated. We have cleverly invented words that have multiple meanings in our language, which presents real challenges for digital assistants/assistance. In any case language often only ever represents the 'headlines' of our thinking. Apart from this, humans are pretty good at understanding what others mean, even when communications are not expressed well. I am sure you will have noticed this when people spell entire sentences incorrectly and when the words are jumbled up. Machines are not currently as adept at such nuance, as you might have noticed when using autocorrect on your smartphone. However, some machines are smart and they offer us the opportunity to collaborate to advantage to do things that could not be previously done as this next example demonstrates.

Intelligent team collaboration

q-bot develops intelligent tools for the built environment, that turn difficult, disruptive and dirty jobs into clean, efficient and safe processes. The company was formed as a result of a 3-hour chance meeting on the Red Sea between Professor Peter Childs and Tom Lipinski, an architect, after Tom mentioned that he had a problem getting into tight spaces. It so happened that Professor Childs had been a locksmith in much earlier life and after some conversation it transpired that being a locksmith also required similar skills. He had experienced using lots of gadgets in the 1980s using bicycle cables to access difficult spaces and places. The conversation, over a bottle of wine, led to the drafting of six patents.

q-bot has been successful at getting councils engaged via a clever combination of market research and economic analysis. The company has persuaded several councils to offer what it calls 'Warmth on prescription' since it has demonstrated health benefits arising from warm housing, which is greater than remedial impact on Health and Social Services.

q-bot began its life in Imperial College London and has grown to 19 people as a start-up. Tom was interested in sustainable technologies. There are lots of things you can do to your home to make it more environmentally friendly, but one of the least known ones is underfloor insulation, which offers a much greater payback than what most people think are the best options, e.g. double glazing, boiler insulation, loft insulation, etc. Underfloor insulation is painful to do. You have to remove the floor, fill a cavity and if you do not fill it all it might not be that effective. q-bot's robots are single-task robots that perform tasks that humans cannot do, but do it completely and in ways that can be verified.

The principal market is retrofit of Victorian housing stock, which has a fairly small cavity, which is inaccessible by humans. At this time the company specialises in this area, although there are clearly many other applications of the q-bot technology, e.g. in hazardous environments, etc. With q-bot, a robot can be inserted through an air vent, deploy within the void and, without even the need to enter the property, apply insulation to the underside of the floorboards. This keeps the floor warm and dry while still allowing the ground to breath.

Although the main benefits are economic and environmental we noticed that many rooms show up to a four degree Celsius thermal gradient between the ceiling and the floor. This is why many people say that they experience 'warm feet' after the floor is insulated. This is an important side benefit of the process. The payback period is years and not decades. This is evident in significant reductions in energy bills.

Professor Peter Childs

Throughflow is important in terms of the number of exchanges of air per hour to avoid sick building syndrome through off-gassing of things we use on a daily basis.

The first q-bot prototype was made with wheels from a golfing trolley, which gave the company press attention. The basic design has been reduced in size by 75% since that time. The robots have vision so they can survey the terrain but also so they can verify complete filling of the cavity. This is an important benefit with respect to insurance and so on.

The q-bot example offers us insights into intelligent team collaboration using small cells of people and the augmentation of human capability to devise completely new services, which could not be performed by a human being. This offers us a vision that we will find new things to do with the advent of machines and AI. Teams need sensitive guidance and facilitation in order to gain the best from them and we next look at the subject of facilitating brainy teams.

MATHEMATICAL CREATIVITY

Rethinking the man/machine interface

- How could we augment human capability through robotics and so on as per the q-bot example?
- What elements could we remove as human functions to release time for more purposeful activities?
- How could we multiply our work or impact through the adoption of machines?
- How could we divide the time that our unimportant but essential tasks take through better or different use of machines?

CHAPTER 7

Team chemistry

To move from brainy atoms (individuals) to brainy molecules (teams) needs the skills of team chemistry, otherwise known as facilitation, sometimes by someone within the team, sometimes by an external agent (catalyst), if the degree of personal involvement or complexity of the issue demands it. Some think that facilitation is a fairly passive activity and that it merely requires the ability to write on a flip chart or hand some Post-It Notes out. I once sat in on a session where the facilitator more or less pointed out where the toilets were and mentioned timings for coffee and lunch. This is rather more like the kind of guidance given to you on an aircraft before take-off and gives facilitation a bad name. Equally bad is the type of facilitation I have seen within one or two otherwise great companies, where open-ended brainstorming sessions are run more like a question and answer session. Simply stated, bad facilitation is not worth having, but good facilitation can transform a situation beyond the simple signposting or didactic brainstorming approaches implied in our examples. How should we know the difference between effective and less effective facilitation? Well this comes down to how we measure the output of a piece of facilitation. There should be a very high ratio between thoughts and deeds after the intervention, and ideally no gap at all between talk and doing, i.e. 100% conversion of decisions taken into purposeful action.

> Great facilitation leaves no gap between thoughts and deeds.

A great team facilitator will adopt a range of styles that are consistent with the need, shifting shapes in response to the evolving need across the entire spectrum of behavioural styles available to them. I especially like John Heron's model of intervention styles, since these cover interventions across the spectrum from directive to non-directive and flag the many roles that a great facilitator must cover:

Prescribing (directive): Essentially a 'tell' style. For example: "Take these pills and you'll feel better." Prescribing is probably the quickest way to get someone to do something. However, the quickest way

116

is not always the most effective way. We know full well that we do not always take the doctor's advice if it does not accord with our own wants, whims and fancies as articulated by the Dunning-Kruger effect, where people of low ability tend to assess their own cognitive abilities as being superior to experts and vice versa. It is perhaps for this reason that the other styles exist, since we are not that great at taking direct advice if it is dissonant with our prevailing paradigm.

Informing (directive): Neutrally passing on information, ideas and knowledge. For example: "I can tell you that your team scored minus 25 on risk taking." This gives people the chance to make their own minds up without feeling pressurised or manipulated. Informing does not draw a conclusion. It simply provides neutral information, leaving the recipient to draw their own conclusions and formulate actions. However, one then needs a lot of time for team members to process the information provided to them and come up with options and actions to address the need. There is, of course, always a risk that the information will be processed but no action will result or possibly the 'wrong' course of action. While informing might be more effective in the long term, it requires more time and processing power than prescribing.

Confronting (directive): Involves challenging viewpoints and requires the examination of motives. For example: "You said that you wanted to devise a creative strategy, but I've noticed that every time we try to do this you want to talk about what the company is doing about the Christmas meal." Confronting should not be confused with aggression – it can be done with a soft pillow as well as a hard edge. Confronting is, however, one of the more difficult interventions that a facilitator can undertake as it usually results in some level of cognitive dissonance, where people are held to account or get 'found out'. Done with skill, it can be very effective and relatively quick, but once again the Dunning-Kruger effect applies and people can become actively defensive or, worse still, passively so, which is harder to spot.

Non-directive interventions usually take longer than directive ones. After all they are literally less 'direct'. However, they can be very effective in more troublesome situations. They also require greater levels of skill and sleight of hand techniques to make them work. The TV detective Columbo is a great place to study these interventions used in a particular direction. Columbo rarely confronts his suspects, using a series of much more subtle but clever interventions to smoke the culprits out. Far from a simple piece of entertainment, I discovered from the Metropolitan Police Diplomatic Protection Group that they use Columbo at Hendon Police College to train their top detectives for similar reasons that I have described here, contrasting the approach with some less effective approaches from other TV copumentaries.

Cathartic (facilitative): Interventions that enable people to 'get things off their chest'. For example: "Can we spend some time exploring what it feels like for you to lead this project?" Catharsis can be extremely powerful as a means of allowing people to relieve tension about things that are hard to express in more direct terms. One example of this is the use of extended metaphor, where the facilitator asks the team to describe the issue under discussion in metaphorical terms. Sometimes this level of detachment allows people to say hard to say or unsayable things. See also our discussion on 2nd and 3rd positions from NLP in Dialogue I.

Catalytic (facilitative): Providing a sounding board and helping others to come up with their own solutions. For example: "Would you like to explain more about the opportunities for business improvement?" Catalytic interventions build on the idea of catalysis in chemistry. A catalyst is used in small doses to promote a reaction, but is itself not involved in the actual reaction and remains unchanged at the end of that reaction. It is once again a detached position to take for the facilitator, giving others space to reflect, consider novel ideas and rethink old approaches.

Supporting (facilitative): Feedback to staff in which they are actively listened to and encouraged in what they are doing. For example: "I can understand why you would feel that the company is benefitting from your strategy to encourage innovation from what you have told me." Supporting is often of great value when using the more challenging interventions in the facilitator's toolkit. It provides the essential positive assets in the 'bank balance' between the facilitator and the team to draw on when dealing with more challenging elements of the team's agenda. In general it is always wise to use plenty of pull strategies if you are also pushing for change and a sensible ratio is at least 2:1 pull:push. It is also important to consider the 'rhythm' of your interventions. After all, facilitation is like a dance at some level and keeping in step with those you are attempting to engage in the dance of change is important if you are to maintain a high conversion ratio of thoughts into actions.

Great team facilitators are both well prepared and also great improvisers to follow lines of enquiry, balancing the need for direction with the need to facilitate thinking and action within teams. Here are ten starting questions to ponder next time you are called to facilitate a team:

1. Why are we doing this in terms of the higher purposes for the team and the enterprise?
2. What are the needs of the situation I am working with (outcomes)?
3. Who are the people? What are their individual needs in terms of outcomes and the journey toward those outcomes?

4. What are the team's wants as a collective (routes, journeys, environments)?
5. How can I design a process that engages with team preferences (wants) without prejudicing the outcomes (needs)?
6. What information must be made available to the team before, during or after the intervention?
7. What techniques or combinations of techniques are most expedient to have as a starting plan, given the answers to the above questions?
8. Where are we planning to meet? What environmental considerations are important in terms of physical or psychological environment?
9. How much time is essential in order to do a good job? Is there any implied order or sequence of the issues that must be tackled?
10. What facilitation styles do the answers to the above questions demand of me and how best might this be conveyed to the team?

An important dilemma is deciding on the bandwidth of styles that you are able and willing to use. This requires that you know yourself. A key factor in determining how you will facilitate a team is your own personal preferences. This is what Charles Handy has called a 'proper selfishness', what Daniel Goleman calls 'emotional intelligence' or what the Swedish pop group ABBA called 'Knowing me, Knowing you'. If the group need is outside your personal preference range, you have several choices to address this:

> **Act as if you can**: Adopt the desired behaviours until they become part of your repertoire. Practice does of course make perfect, although this is not a strategy to use in areas of critical need for your team. This strategy is much better used with self-disclosure for authenticity.
>
> **Change the raw materials**: i.e. get someone else to do it. Use a specialist to deal with a specialist need rather than attempting to 'fake it till you make it'.
>
> **Use self-disclosure**: Tell the team that this is not your forte and ask for their help/tolerance/forgiveness. Although this sounds like a 'weak' strategy, it has the side benefits that it is (a) very authentic and (b) ensures the team takes some level of ownership and gives you the support you need to succeed.

Above all else, it pays to have an awareness of your personal preferences with respect to facilitation. This allows you to make a conscious choice as to whether you feel able and confident to flex your style. All of the above assumes that you are working with an intact team of employees. But even this is under review in an age where team membership is transient. In some cases the team might be composed of people off the payroll or freelancers. How can you make teams work in such circumstances?

The gig economy and teams

I asked Professor Charles Handy what he thought would become of large organisations and enterprises at the launch of his book *The Second Curve*. As is becoming of Charles, he simply shrugged the question off casually and said, "Oh, that's easy, they will just become irrelevant". In conversation with Peter Cheese and a group of CIPD leaders we concluded that while this was a trend, it was unlikely that our enterprises would disappear completely, yet we all agreed that they would need to reform structurally and culturally if they are to remain relevant. In particular, the declining half-life of knowledge, globalisation and the development of the gig economy make it much more likely that we will be working as portfolio workers in the future. We will also see much more floating team membership as a result of the gig economy whereby team membership will be at least transient and, on occasion, might be a single assignment or task. Individuals will need to learn how to join and mesh with teams rapidly. Leaders will need to learn how to form and reform virtual teams rapidly around shifting priorities, multiple geographies and with differing motives for participating in those teams. To make agile virtual teams work leaders must:

- Spend time clarifying goals that align the enterprise's purpose with individual talents and how these talents can combine for effective teamwork. So much time and energy is wasted in unformed teams, yet the remedies are simple if leaders go slower at the outset to enable them to go faster when it counts and ensure new members are inducted quickly and effectively into the team.
- Create a climate/culture where virtual collaboration is natural, including the rituals and routines that support cohesion and talent sharing. In real teams, we can easily detect nuanced communications through body language, facial expression and other signals to gain insights into small but vital information on the health of our team. In a virtual team it is different. Much of the time there is no facetime. This means that leaders must judge the health of their team in other ways. Leaders must become adept at reading the minimal cues people give out across virtual communication devices. The good news is that the lack of a visual stimulus can actually help in terms of really listening to what is said and what is not said. I learned this directly when tutoring as an MBA student where much of my contact with students was by phone. What I lacked in specific knowledge about them was counter-balanced by 'meta-knowledge' of how they spoke. I could usually detect if there was something deeper that they wished to tell me if they called to discuss general progress and this work on the phone was an excellent arena for deliberate practice of Heron's six facilitation styles.
- Manage differences and diversity. Requisite diversity is a fundamental business issue if you seek innovation and not a nice-to-have addition to the HR department's remit. We explore this further in the section 'Opposites attract' coming up.

- Structure their teams organically so that they can quickly reform and regroup around changing priorities. Paradoxically this requires the development of stronger team norms in terms of Tuckman's model of forming, storming, norming and performing. So many dysfunctional teams I see these days are not 'mature' in terms of this model, with disastrous consequences for collaboration and performance. Although high turnover of team members can be stimulating, continuity and effectiveness are the casualties. Leaders make entry, exit and re-entry seamless and efficient.

- Develop rewards and recognition based on coopetition where all win for audacious results and great efforts, regardless of whether they succeed. The best teams and their leaders play the game of reciprocity really well. This is the 'give and give' game rather than the 'give and take' game. It is the 'win-win' quadrant of our Man-Machine grid where men/women and machines are maximising their coopetition. There is a virtuous circle of reinforcement going when teams use such strategies and the smart leader ensures that the circle is unbroken and fast flowing from purposeful action to reciprocity and reinforcement.

- Build support systems around teams, not the other way round. While humans are hugely adaptable, if we want enterprises that engage heads, hearts and souls, we need to give due consideration to the adoption of systems by people. Support systems at work should be light touch and not high maintenance. We have all had the experience of deciding not to use a system because the effort somehow outweighs the benefits.

- Leaders as synthesisers. Synthesis is the art of bringing diverse ideas together in a way that makes more sense and value than the individual ideas alone. The synthesiser sees connections between disparate items of information, provokes others to make these connections and signposts people on the systemic connections between where they have been, where they are, and where they might want to go next, so that people can see the wood and the trees. Good synthesis can identify issues people agree upon, issues that still need investigation or ones of inherent uncertainty.

How then do multi-disciplinary teams actually work in the knowledge age? We went to Arthur D. Little to find out. ADL have perhaps above all else been first movers in the knowledge economy. Here Greg Smith and Carl Bate share their views on how ADL harness collective intelligence to address VUCA problems.

> In 2007, technology was an integral part of all projects as part of Arthur D. Little's People, Process and Technology approach. Yet 90% of tech enabled projects failed to meet expectations. We reflected that either we were poor at doing them, that they are indeed difficult or that we were doing something wrong. We decided to explore the last hypothesis and evolved a number of unique features that set us apart from the crowd:

- We 'bake in' human factors to our work at the outset. All too often technology projects undertake the tech implementation and then do the change management, which leads to adoption problems. This includes how we go about individual selection and the way we set our teams to work on client problems and opportunities.
- We are more concerned with what C.K. Prahalad calls 'next practice' rather than 'best practice', which is more to do with keeping up. Benchmarking can be seen as a 'keeping up with the Joneses' approach to strategy.
- We realised that we were conflating a complicated system with a complex system in terms of what we learned from the differences between Dave Snowden's Cynefin approaches of simple, complicated, complex, chaotic and disorder. Snowden defines and describes four primary domains with the direction of drift in enterprises from complicated to complex:

  - Obvious. The relationship between cause and effect is clearly identifiable and understood by all.
  - Complicated. There is an identifiable relationship between cause and effect, but the relationship needs to be discovered through analysis or investigation.
  - Complex. A relationship between cause and effect can be identified in retrospect, but not in advance.
  - Chaotic. There is no identifiable relationship between cause and effect.

- We fundamentally start with gaining a whole system definition of a project, testing to destruction the various hypotheses that people come up with about what they consider the problem is. We challenge the 'specious certainty' of the 'problem-solution' paradigm: placing too much certainty on the capacity of new technology to deliver operating-model change; setting unrealistic expectations and outcomes and creating long-term plans that aim to deliver in the future what is actually required today; and having blind faith in immutable, up-front specifications and then failing to re-assess regularly enough whether to further invest, pivot or stop.
- Rather than leaping to solutions, we spend a long time with our project teams getting to the heart of a given problem using what we call 'pattern breaking' and 'pattern matching'. Essentially these are a playbook of techniques that enable us to test hypotheses and converge on the one from which all others flow.
- We start with the end in mind, thinking about jobs to be done more than technology per se. This focus on ends means that our teams are smoother and faster with implementation.

Because ADL are problem-led rather than solution-focused, they have not sought to scale the operation in the same way that other larger technology consulting houses have done. In the case study below, Greg and Carl explain how they put these principles to work, using a team that came together at BA and eventually ended up working at Arthur D. Little.

Flying without lights at BA

British Airways have all the resources they need and, therefore, they do not necessarily need external help. We therefore took the approach of asking them for an intractable problem to solve. One such wicked problem was that of the snow in 2014, which shut down the airline during the early days of the new London Heathrow Terminal 5. Since BA were responsible for the terminal passengers blamed them rather than BAA for the failure. Arthur D. Little were told that they had five months to develop a solution that worked to make BA fit and fast. This would have been impossible in the steady state operation, due to the complex procedures and protocols, so Arthur D. Little insisted on moving the development into a technology start-up environment, where five months would be sufficient to do what was required. BA CEO, Willie Walsh made a public statement and this triggered a number of strategic actions: "Next winter, we will fly if it snows."

The main difficulty in realising a technology-based solution to the problem was around information provision, which was late, imperfect and often difficult to interpret. In the first six weeks we concentrated on building credibility and plausibility within BA that a solution was possible. It was not possible to develop the solution in this time but there had to be something which people could touch that developed confidence in the system. Once this had been achieved there were 14 weeks to develop an MVP (Minimum Viable Product). We aimed to iterate the product every four weeks, thus building in the possibility of 4 × ROI (Return on Iteration). The product went from being a crisis management tool for 80 people to a situation awareness tool for 15 000 people. In doing so, we had to work with the people in the unit rather than picking people who were attuned to the solution and then undertaking a change management project to gain adoption. This produced a certain amount of realism, which was valuable for the project. We were assisted by the mandate from Willy Walsh and we considered that we had a finite number of architectural exemptions and that helped us gain acceptance for the project. Negotiation was reserved for absolutely critical requirements to make the system work.

Don't take the cheap shots as they can turn out to be the most expensive ones. Don't pick fights just for the sake of it. It requires a fine balance between confidence in what we were recommending plus humility to get people to sign up to it.

Storm St Jude provided an opportunity over two days to test the system and between 12 000 and 14 000 people reached their destination who would normally not have managed to do so. When BA stopped cancelling flights all the other airline's performance improved and the press stopped bashing BA.

We used an old school approach – instead of using predictive analytics, we used descriptive analytics in near real time, which allow people to affect the outcome. We persuaded BA that prediction of unknowable incidents was a waste of time but the ability to help people make the best decision with real time data offered real possibilities of addressing the presenting problem.

In the event, this required Arthur D. Little to put together a team of diverse people in record time to deliver the project, combining specialists, generalists and gig workers into a team that could focus on the goal in a seamless way. Requisite diversity demands that leaders are good at bringing opposites, and even misfits, together in a collective effort and this requires that they are excellent at managing conflict.

Opposites attract

Gone are the days when a lone individual could envision and develop all the ideas to conceptualise and execute an innovative product or service. Innovation is now a team game and one where cross-disciplinary thinking and working are essential. In pharmaceuticals, we combine apps with traditional treatments as 'Healthware'. Remote medicine is not far away. In financial services, Fintech may replace traditional banks that have always been interested in automating functions to reduce costs, provide better audit control, such as our example with CaseWare and improve customer access. Even the United Nations can no longer recruit weapons inspectors who are PhD physicists or chemists alone. They must be skilled in computing, biotechnology, physics and so on to function effectively and work as an effective team to face the complexity inherent in modern weapons and warfare. How then shall we combine our intelligences for SCA?

I wrote the title of this section and almost as soon as I did, Prime Minister Theresa May used the phrase to describe her potential relationship with President Trump. Nonetheless I am compelled to continue writing . . . Diversity is not a nice-to-have fluffy concept for the HR department to run events around and proclaim at every watercooler, washroom and website. It is a crucial business issue that separates the sheep from the goats in organisational life. Should diversity be distributed across the whole enterprise or concentrated in areas such as the R&D division? This is a hard question to answer with certainty, as it is highly situational and culture dependent. However a mathematical comparison gives some clues. A study was made on the innovation structures at Apple and Google and some differences observed.

- In ten years Apple produced 10 975 patents from a team of 5232 inventors.
- Google produced 12 386 from a team of 8888.
- However Apple's core shows a group of highly connected super inventors at the centre.
- Google's structure is more dispersed, empowered and networked.
- The researcher Bernegger points out that there is more connectivity and collaboration at Apple with the average number of inventors listed on a patent as 4.2 as compared with 2.8 at Google. This translates into an ROI (Return on Innovation) of 9 at Apple compared with 4 at Google.

This example teaches us that requisite diversity is valuable for innovation, but also that where there is diversity there is a need for connectivity and collaboration as well, however this is organised. Context matters in terms of what works in a given culture. We explore the structural ramifications of this later on and in Dialogue III.

However, opposites are hard to tolerate in business unless you work really hard to hear ideas that do not accord with your own. The barriers to profiting from diversity are many and include a digital versus analogue approach to decision-making. What I mean by this is an on/off approach to making decisions rather than an approach that relishes contemplation and delay. Sometimes it helps to have a common language to describe differences and I have found Dr Meredith Belbin's approach to this helpful and durable over many years.

Belbin was fascinated by how management teams worked or did not work. He summed up some of the concepts in his first book *Management Teams: Why They Succeed or Fail*. Belbin said, "Nobody is perfect but a team can be". We must manage differences in biodiverse teams and a first step toward this ambition is to understand the raw materials you are working with. He identified eight roles in an effective team. These broadly break down into four higher-level functions, which offers a greater level of simplicity. Idea generators comprise the plant and resource investigator roles. Plants tend to be the pure idea generators, sometimes solitary and often untrammelled by current constraints. The resource investigator is the person that will get out and find someone or something that can realise an idea. Leaders comprise the coordinator, who makes sure there is good participation in a team, and the shaper, who nudges, cajoles, tells and sometimes manipulates to stop the team procrastinating. The third pair of roles are the checkers: monitor-evaluators are the arbiters of quality and good judges, whereas the completer-finishers are detail-conscious people who will plan to deliver a high-quality job. Finally the do-ers comprise the team worker who listens well, harmonises conflicts and supports the team, and the implementer who is stoic, getting on with the work. If a team has an obstacle preventing it from working then these general principles adapted from Belbin's approach help it to succeed:

If eight roles are too many for your team, I find that the Disney Creativity Strategy is another 'pracademic' model that helps teams focus on the roles needed in an effective team. The Disney Creativity Strategy is based on the adoption of typical roles seen in creative teams, allegedly from Walt Disney's own observations of what made a team succeed or flounder:

- **The Dreamer**: whose thinking is unconstrained by limitations, conventions, etc.
- **The Critic**: whose role is to examine potential constraints to achieving the dreamer's ideas. (Note: this does not mean they criticise – they employ critical thinking which is a subtle but important difference.)
- **The Realist**: whose job it is to synthesise the Dreamer's dreams with the Critic's constraints to come up with novel ideas that can be implemented.

There are many ways to use the Disney Strategy in teams: in sequence; in parallel; in situ; over time, etc.

Team development follows a time-honoured process and leaders would do well to understand, manage and respect the process. A team does not

TABLE 7.1

Situation	Potential remedy
Team round in circles?	Add plants to generate new ideas
Idea development too radical or too many?	Add monitor-evaluators to check them out
Too much cleverness creates arguments?	Add coordinator
Insufficient execution?	Add implementers to get things organised
Are things being done to high enough standards?	Add completer-finishers
Is anyone communicating with the outside world beyond the team?	Add resource investigators
The team has lost its direction?	Add a shaper to bring energy to the team
Internal conflict?	Team workers facilitate dialogue in teams
Does the team lack knowledgeable professionals in key areas?	Add specialists

just form overnight. It needs to be nurtured and goes through a series of rites of passage, whether or not the membership is permanent or temporary. Usually, a team is not effective until it has passed through its forming, storming and norming rituals. Only after the storm do team members normally work out exactly how their roles interlock and support one another. Once a team is at the performing stage the atmosphere becomes quietly productive, with occasional meetings to fix problems and check on progress. New members can help you renew, or a new problem can reinvigorate the team. In modern teams some of the members are transient and this can mean that the team never forms properly without deliberate intervention by the leader.

GROUND CONTROL

Balancing head, heart and soul

To what extent do you attract similars or opposites in your working life? Does this differ in your private life?

How do you challenge your viewpoints and beliefs on a regular basis?

CHAPTER 8

Connecting collective synapses

The idea of an intelligent team brings up the question of who owns intelligence, individually, collectively, corporately and in communities. Google have a different answer to the Chinese in this respect. Google is currently estimated to process 3.5 billion requests a day. The *Guangzhou Southern Metropolis Daily* reported that the Chinese state not only collects personal data about its citizens, but it also sells the data. It seems that one can gain access to data about people's movements, borders crossed, who they met, driving offences, pictures, location, etc. for small sums of money without any questions. The Chinese Government also plans to give each citizen a 'social credit' score, which will rank people's trustworthiness from their online behaviour. Of course, we are already used to such things on e-bay, Experian, but the difference here is that we opt-in to such things whereas the Chinese way assumes the state own the data. Might total transparency be such a bad thing? It is something that we explore in the epilogue and here is a preview:

> *Work is flexible. Julie works the hours as needed by a complex coordination of her client's needs, her family and herself. Her personal digital assistant Rover looks after all the mechanics using a set of algorithms that Julie agreed about various priorities for her work/life balance. There are no more days when she makes a plan then to be let down by cancellations or conflicts as everyone decided to 'choose life' when they elected to receive a basic income in exchange for full employment, fewer hours worked and the opportunity to earn more by discretionary contribution to the collective net worth through the IGOK (International Grid of Knowledge). Julie has young children so she contributes with one-third of her time to IGOK in exchange for a set of family orientated benefits via her PSP. She has planned to store up some of her contribution for a life-changing trip to Mars in 2050 with Virgin Celestial, which offered its first commercial flights to habitable planets from 2040.*

In the context of teams, we need to reform the ways in which people are engaged, encouraged and rewarded if we are to see a genuine flow of knowledge between team members for the greater good of the enterprise. Gone are the days when Harry Beck received five guineas and a plaque on Finchley station for his groundbreaking design for the London Underground map. Harry's design became an international standard for metro maps due to its resonant simplicity and rule breaking from the generally held principles of cartography.

Apart from the issues of who owns intelligence and how that is recognised and rewarded, there is the question of practice to reach peak performance. Great teams in any field do not just rely on natural abilities to reach high performance. They supplement natural talent with deliberate practice in areas of strength and, more importantly, weakness. At the same time as team cohesion we need also to look at disrupting groupthink in a VUCA world. Teams are great when they reach the high-performance stage of development and they provide huge benefits in terms of feeling part of something and the camaraderie that goes with belonging. Yet the downsides of groupthink are cults, cabals and cliques, which are unhelpful in a fluid and agile workplace. Aside from that, we expect the new world of teams to be populated by teams that form, perform and reform rapidly around need. How do we get teams to work in a world where team membership is often temporary? How do we reach high performance when freelancers and transient experts work alongside staffers?

Paradoxically some of the most effective strategies are the simplest to do. They are often overlooked due to busy-ness in business. A good beginning often leads to a happy ending with the middle then looking after itself. As with most things preparation is the mother of innovation.

Good beginnings

It seems almost pointless and mildly insulting to say this but, as a school governor, I watched in horror when the chair brought new people to the team and then did not give them an opportunity to find out the other people's names, what they did and so on. It took me some months to find out all the names of governing body members! You might be forgiven for thinking this is just a feature of the education sector, but I have seen it happen in some great companies as well, so it really is worth repeating. It is all very well bringing cakes and so on to team meetings but all rather pointless if people do not know each other's names! Then, of course, they need to know what they bring to the team, what they will be expected to contribute and so on. Although it seems strange to ask, I always make a point of asking people something about their hobbies when forming new teams, as this can be more revealing than their job description if you are to get discretionary effort from them.

Dear AA,

Many thanks for agreeing to attend our innovation summit. We are delighted to have you aboard what promises to be an event that is both inspiring and game changing for our company.

  All great things rely on great preparation. To this end, I need you to give me four items to help us prepare. Please supply the following items:

1. A recent head and shoulders picture of yourself
2. Your job in no more than seven words
3. Your personal passion or hobby
4. Your favourite piece of music or a work of art/literature that you love

You will find a copy of the latest book by our lead facilitator for the event. Please read a couple of relevant articles in the run up to the event:

  Page 82–90 – The Beatles and Creativity

  Page 163–170 – The Innovation Factory

  Page 225–231 – On Reinvention

Best regards
Laurence

A good beginning to a team deals with questions of 'us' (the individual), 'them' (the team) and 'the work' as a bare minimum. Here is a specimen invitation covering the bare essentials as applied to a global innovation meeting where hardly anybody knew one another and there was a need to reach peak performance in a limited amount of time. The information we gathered was used systematically with the team over the two-day summit to great advantage. We also spent the entire first evening on team formation in a social setting via a combination of structured networking, games and what the professionals call 'cross-functional social underlay', more usually referred to as 'food and drinks'.

1. **Us:** Each team member must know what they are expected to contribute and something about the norms regarding contributions.
2. **Them:** Teams need to know each other's knowledge, skills and experience at the outset.
3. **The work:** People need to understand the task before them and expectations regarding the delivery dates, amount of work and collaboration patterns, etc.

The middle

While beginnings and endings are vital elements in terms of setting the tone for the work and whether more work will happen after the work is finished, the key point of work is . . . er . . . the work! Great songs have a great beginning and a supreme end but of course the song itself is the main point of the song. Brain Based Leaders can ensure that the work proceeds well by managing people's differences and, of course, the progression of the task or the project, solving problems as they arise through structured divergent and convergent thinking and helping the team deal with the unpredictable. Ultimately the Brain Based Leader helps the team to help itself by installing the values, beliefs and behaviours needed to manage its journey, rather than acting as a rescue service, which builds in dependency within the team.

Happy endings

In the art world, we know when a great piece of music or literature is about to end. Listen to a Mozart symphony, for example. There are clues within the movements, cadences and ornaments that let the listener know when they are expected to applaud and so on. So, the leader can be considered to be the conductor of a project, marking the start, keeping progress through-out and marking the end of the work in ways that provide closure and value to the team.

1. A team cannot move on without completing its unfinished business and endings matter as much as beginnings. If a project or venture has gone well there is much to learn from it. If it has not gone well, there is even more to learn.
2. Then there is the question of celebrating success, irrespective of how well the project has gone, there should be some act of closure that lets people know that the project has come to an end.
3. There is also the question of ensuring that the team has profited from the neural network that has assisted them in delivering the project. This means that people are able to access and utilise each other's skills in other projects in the future via an update of the company 'Yellow Pages' database or similar.

Open source teams

The Johari window is a classic model that helps us understand ourselves in concert with others. As such it can usefully be adapted to the world of data, information, knowledge and wisdom. Devised by psychologists Joseph Luft and Harrington Ingham in 1955 the Johari window took its name from their first two names Joe and Harry. Here we apply the model to the ques-tion of sharing knowledge within and between teams. As always, nobody does it better that Professor Charles Handy, who offers us an eminently sim-ple way of understanding the Johari window as a house with four rooms. The first room is our open source, the things that we and others know about ourselves, for example, our height, approximate age, LinkedIn profile and so on. The second is our hidden area, the things we know about ourselves but others do not, for example medical history, relationships, etc. The third area is our blind area, things that others know about us but we are unaware of, for example, at a trivial level, whether someone has placed a sticker on our back, whether someone has said something bad about us in private to them and so on. Finally, there is our unknown or unconscious area, the things that neither we, nor others know about us, for example, our futures.

> *Julie is able to communicate her thinking directly to others via an interface in her brain that allows people to access her thinking as and when needed. Access is on several levels: an open source region for work associates; a private region for friends and family and a personal region which contains Julie's thoughts on love, life, etc. only accessible with express permission. She has a closed region of her mind, which is totally restricted even to her, although she may ask the interface questions about this area for the purposes of self-discovery and personal development.*

The hallmark of intelligent teams will be that the open source area will be maximised for maximum shared value. We have become progressively used to people knowing personal details about us through social media. However, work is normally different as our professional knowledge is sometimes at the heart of our salary. Yet innovation arises from shared knowledge and wisdom. We must, therefore, find ways to encourage a gainsharing approach to team collaboration if we are to realise the open source dream. Sometimes enterprise structure can be an enabler of knowledge transfer.

Machinery, machine bureaucracies and enigma machines

We traditionally think about organisation structure and teams in terms of two-dimensional industrial metaphors such as machine bureaucracies, organograms, unitary management, vertical hierarchy and so on. However human beings and teams are flexible organisms capable of much more than purely digital responses (up-down, on-off, one-zero, one dimensional thinking, etc.) In the Man-Machine age, I argue that we need to reform the industrial machinery model toward one based on more intuitive and natural biological metaphors, if man and woman are to collaborate intelligently with machines rather than become enslaved by them. What has driven this need?

Master and servant

Over the last 30 or so years, teams and enterprises are no longer defined by the people that you own. Teams might comprise people who are transient members and ones that are not the 'property' of the enterprise, e.g. customers offering valuable knowledge and insights into your products and services, perhaps as participants of crowdsourcing innovation projects. This raises the question of how you gain commitment from people you do not 'own' via a pay cheque or some other 'master and servant' relationship that obliges obedience rather than ideas, initiative and intelligence. Control without ownership is a burgeoning problem for leaders and those people who have to gain results through people. There is much to learn from voluntary organisations and charities in this regard, although the learning might have to be adapted to fit enterprises where there is a less obvious relationship between its *raison d'être* and the employee's psychological contract.

Welcome to the jungle

Another change driven by globalisation and the advent of social media is the sheer number of connections that many of us have. This, together with modern global communications systems makes it possible for us to combine capabilities for innovation, independent of geolocation. Many of us now have many more connections than Dunbar's magic number of 150, an estimate from anthropology of the maximum number of people that can effectively maintain stable relationships within 'tribes', yet many teams, cells or scrums operate with between four to six members at maximum efficiency. For teams to work effectively we know they must reach the performing stage of development. We discuss Bruce Tuckman's model for team effectiveness shortly. Finnish game company Supercell uses autonomous 'cells' of four to six people and they find this enables them to be nimble and innovative. In such small teams it is possible to have autonomy and alignment, unlike in monolithic teams. To ensure they align on purpose they have an agile team coach. They set a lot of store by hiring correctly, especially around team behaviours. A good team member is both self-directed and collaborative (what Professor Charles Handy called a proper kind of selfishness). Supercell is more concerned with progress than the accumulation of power per se. Information is distributed so that people can get on with work without waiting for decisions in a self-service information culture. This is a good example of what we dubbed the open source Johari window approach to knowledge management.

I developed a system for qualitatively valuing and improving the value of team relationships at work based on some ideas from my chemistry lessons at school. To be effective at making a network work you need to *know*, *like* and *trust* the people in your network. By the way 'like' does not necessarily imply agreement with your peers' views or values. To develop high-performance teams requires tolerance or even encouragement of difference and diversity. This simple empirical system allows you to ascribe values to the depth of your connections by considering the strength of the chemical bonds you have with each person, as follows.

SINGLE BOND

I KNOW THIS PERSON

DOUBLE BOND

I KNOW AND LIKE THIS PERSON

TRIPLE BOND

I KNOW, LIKE AND TRUST THIS PERSON

A single bond signifies someone you simply know something about. You might think of them as acquaintances in everyday terms. Many Facebook friends are merely acquaintances under this classification and some social media contacts might have virtually zero bonding using our model. In other words, you are connected but might know little more than 280 characters about the other person if they are a Twitter connection. This can help to account for the frequent misunderstandings that take place between 'Facebook friends'. A double chemical bond is someone that you know and like. It is much more likely that you will have some kind of interactions with someone you are double bonded to in a business context. A triple chemical bond will likely be someone you have worked with or faced some challenge with, since trust usually emerges from some testing of a bond between people. Only at this point is it likely that mature collaboration will take place. Many business relationships and transactions taking place on the Internet cannot be considered to be mature under this classification, sometimes with disastrous consequences. It is important to note that the idea of 'like' and 'trust' does not imply that you agree with the values and behaviours of your network colleague. Smart people surround themselves with disagreeable people that they trust as well as inhabiting 'echo chambers' with 'similars'.

When working in India some years back, I had wanted to travel to Agra to see the Taj Mahal before my return to the UK. I took advice from the Managing Director of the factory I was working at. He told me to simply arrive at Bombay (Mumbai) Victoria train station, hand all my worldly goods and my money to the first person that approached me and all would be well. I did as he said and 20 minutes later the man arrived with my ticket but no luggage, explaining that the luggage was on the train. I assumed he was telling the truth. He was. This is the meaning of trust. I seriously doubt that the experiment would work so well at London Victoria train station and my Indian friends tell me that, sadly, times have also changed in India. I like to remain optimistic, however. Much the same thing happened when I missed a flight to Nepal, due to the plane being overbooked on Indian Airlines. My MD friend had expected this might happen and instructed me to ask for the 'airport captain' and show him my tickets. Again, I did as he asked. The captain took my tickets and told me to come back here tomorrow at 10 a.m. and all would be well. I said, "Do I need any receipt or document?" He replied, "You have my word". Sure enough, I arrived the following day to find myself booked on the flight to Kathmandu. This is the essence of trust, not a pre-nuptial agreement, a 360-page tender document or an affidavit. I am not saying that we should not write things down, just that extensive documentation is a symptom of a lack of trust and we might need to relearn some of the basics.

GROUND CONTROL

Balancing mind, body and soul

1. Map out all the people you feel you 'know' on a very large piece of paper. These are your 'single bonds'.
2. Link those that you know and like with 'double bonds'. Note that you need not agree with the other person to like them.
3. Link those that you know, like and trust. These are your 'triple bonds'. If you find the decision hard, ask yourself the question "Who would I give my cheque book to without condition?" or "Who would I trust to give my worldly goods to?"
4. What do you notice about the differences between each category?

One of the problems I notice time and time again in the current age is that people try to play together as a team when the team psychology is not 'mature' and the bonds between people are either at 'zero' or 'one'. You cannot 'cheat' by attempting to short circuit Bruce Tuckman's fundamental team development cycle from forming, storming, norming and performing as we discussed earlier. Sending a few e-mails and texts with a mission statement is not sufficient, as the human condition remains unchanged. Teams must have laughed (or perhaps cried in triumph and/or adversity) together to have the necessary cohesion to live through good and bad times, even if membership of the team is transient and part of a network rather than a geolocated business unit. This point is not well understood by busy leaders and managers, who want their teams to hit the ground running with little or no 'foreplay'. Like all things in life, preparation is the mother of innovation.

What part can 'knowledge farmers' and 'boundary crossers' achieve in bringing people from different disciplines together then? In the following story of a voluntary activist group set up to improve democracy in the UK there were some significant opportunities missed and I have highlighted them.

Herding cats

As part of my personal contribution to Corporate Social Responsibility within my business I helped to organise a group that campaigns against the naked populism behind our bipolar referendum to leave the European Union. This culminated in my attendance at a conference inspired by Gina Miller, the woman who single-handedly took the UK Government to the Supreme Court to improve our democracy, facing threats of beheading and gang rape into the bargain for her attempt to preserve our sovereignty. The conference was organised rapidly but some significant opportunities were missed to extend the impact of a great event, featuring 'talking heads' such as former Deputy Prime Minister Nick Clegg, Sir Bob Geldof, the philosopher A.C. Grayling, Michael Gove, Jarvis Cocker of Pulp and Gina Miller herself. Here are three crucial missed structural opportunities that limited the effectiveness of the event to network intelligence and collective action from teams:

1. **Participation lesson 101**: The conference was organised with the assumption that the only important people in the room were those on the stage. This manifested itself in a number of ways: limited access to the talking heads; limited and inadequate opportunities for people to contribute. Some simple remedies were available but missed: offer a limited number of bookable appointments with such people based on a 'pitch'; offer improved collaboration and lobbying opportunities within each session (one microphone at the front was insufficient for meaningful conversation from a ratio of 2000:1 and led to unhealthy competition between the attendees).
2. **Participation lesson 201**: Conference organisers expected that people would naturally 'find the needles within the haystack' and form the appropriate action groups from the 2000 or so people present. Some simple networking remedies would have improved matters: provide a delegate list; simple devices such as a 'would like to meet board'; improved delegate management during and after the conference.
3. **Participation lesson 301**: Conference organisers believed that social media activity would be sufficient to form the various relationships needed to continue the work beyond the conference itself. However, a Twitter hashtag was insufficient to bring people together. A simple remedy would have been to make it possible for people to collaborate online before, during and after the event so that they could extend their influence.

As a consequence of this, a massive opportunity was lost to engage and network the heads, hearts and souls of around 2000 activists seeking to extend their influence and who could have turned the fortunes of this movement through grassroots activity. None of this was done wilfully. It was simply the product of people doing this for the first time, combined with a fair amount of pressure to deliver the event, which meant the urgent items outweighed those things that were more important. Nonetheless these are valuable structural lessons for anyone operating in the knowledge economy.

Structuring knowledge and relationships

We must think fundamentally about the real value of relationships and knowledge if we are to have workable strategies for leveraging knowledge in Brain Based Teams. If knowledge is a major currency of coopetive advantage in the modern age, then we need to incorporate that into our structural arrangements at work. Knowledge-management structures serve our need to incorporate greater levels of thinking into enterprises as products and services become more 'intelligent' and less labour intensive. A knowledge-management structure needs to provide the following outcomes:

- Who knows what? – allowing people to access islands of knowledge and wisdom.
- Who knows who? – the passive network, which allows the soft relationships and networks to operate.
- Who is doing what with whom? – the active network, which allows people to build on current collaborations and extend their value.

Most companies are able to reach the first 'level' of this list, often through 'Yellow Pages' type approaches, which codify knowledge, competence and experiences and the owners of these things. Subsequent levels are much more difficult to codify and are essentially the 'underground map' of the company, although modern business networking platforms such as LinkedIn clearly offer some views of your personal reach via your network, but not how well you know people and can access their time, etc. Here we have an arena where companies could gain advantage.

The 'Yellow Pages' type approaches to knowledge management are all about the conversion of tacit (unconscious, located within individuals) knowledge into explicit (conscious, decoded and shared) knowledge. Nonaka and Takeuchi have pointed out that there are other possibilities. These are summarised in this model, which I have adapted to look at different knowledge sharing strategies:

The obsession with tacit to explicit knowledge results in the production of instruction manuals, protocols, standard operating procedures, etc. and processes such as ISO 14001 and their international equivalents. In other words, to 'download' unconscious knowledge into a form that others can copy. There is nothing wrong with this as far as it goes. However, there are other strategies, some of which are more effective for teams trying to learn from each other rapidly.

1. The act of codifying and commodifying complex knowledge can make it rather cumbersome to adopt or adapt. Imagine having to codify the instructions on how to ride a bicycle? The procedure would likely be thousands of pages long and would be unnecessarily cumbersome in terms of the nuance needed to learn the skill. It would be insufficient to just say '1. Get on. 2. The ride. 3. Get off'.
2. There is an assumption that knowledge is transferable to different contexts. The extraction of knowledge and its codification produces 'protocols', 'standard operating procedures', etc. These are fine in a 'standard world' but of dubious value if we are seeking to introduce

STRUCTURING KNOWLEDGE AND RELATIONSHIPS

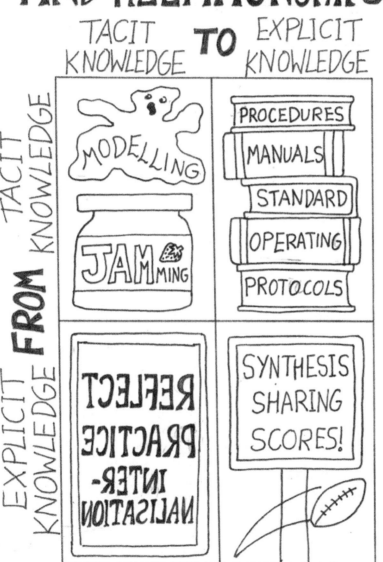

Source: Adapted from the work of Ikujiro Nonaka and Hirotaka Takeuchi

variation for competitive advantage. Simon Warren of CaseWare discusses this issue in terms of overcoming taxonomy problems in accountancy through machine learning:

> Data exchange can be a very simple and logical process, a 'Slot A into Tab B' environment where there are lots of logical rules to apply. However, to take this to another level of complexity two systems could describe identical things in very different ways, Turnover/Fees/Income being an example. One method of solving this issue of labelling was XBRL technology (Extensible Business Reporting Language), which sought through means of a common dictionary ('Taxonomy') to label similar things with the same name. It is tricky to apply the solution however, and despite technology companies' success in getting this to work very well it was undermined entirely by one thing. Every accounting body and national standards group decided they would accept the concept of a common dictionary, but applied different national characteristics, words, terminology, etc. to their taxonomies, thus destroying the very commonality the technology set out to achieve.
>
> So, machine learning could solve these issues by being able to 'learn' from the behaviour of users. If people manually link a certain item of information to the same destination regularly it could well be the case that the machine will offer this as an automatic data association on every subsequent occasion, and allow the user to make a correction if it goes wrong. This means that a given system could 'learn' about a huge number of links between numerous disparate systems, effectively building its own 'taxonomy'. CaseWare is doing this with its core cloud platform, under the name of 'Automapping'.
>
> Simon Warren, MD CaseWare

3. There is an assumption that knowledge management is about 'knowledge'. The world of invention and innovation is mostly about specific skills and non-linear insight and wisdom. These things are notoriously difficult to codify using conventional means.
4. The conversion of tacit knowledge into explicit knowledge is an intellectually tough and inefficient process. Imagine the earlier example of trying to write detailed instructions for riding a bike. Apart from the problem of length, it also introduces a major potential error in 'translation', since 'average' individuals might not be able to exactly understand and then reproduce the strategy.

When we examine knowledge management from the perspective of leading innovative enterprises, a number of different assumptions apply:

1. The knowledge-management need is more in the areas of tacit to tacit learning, creation of transferable wisdom through explicit to tacit learning and synthesis through explicit to explicit learning. An example of tacit to tacit learning would be the situation of two cooks working closely together in the same kitchen, making omelettes or some other concoction that is apparently simple, but which requires a great deal of 'feel' for success. Through the process of demonstration and 'getting a feel' for the subtleties of each other's style, different 'recipes' are shared and new ones arising from a combination of each other's talents generated. Matsushita literally applied this approach by sending apprentices to work with the head baker to learn how to make a better bread-baking machine. This resulted in a machine that could add a 'twist' to the dough and a product that sold in record quantities in its year of launch.

   Improvisation also allows for tacit to tacit and explicit to explicit learning. This is why music is a robust model for learning about creativity and innovation. We focus in on transferable lessons from music in Dialogue III.

2. Knowledge, skills and wisdom are shared through active engagement, the use of 'codified' knowledge where appropriate (recipes) and unconscious learning. This approach allows for 'context related' learning to be understood and incorporated into the repertoire. For example, in our cookery illustration, one cook might use a little extra salt when using a particular type of cheese in the omelette.

3. Knowledge transfer mechanisms include modelling (tacit to tacit), reflecting on one's own practice and dialogue (explicit to tacit) and sharing recipes (explicit to explicit) rather than learning procedures (tacit to explicit).

4. Synthesis (explicit to explicit learning) is an interesting area. Just as a musical synthesiser allows you to mix a range of similar or different waveforms, synthesis of ideas can involve consolidation, such as what might happen when two experts get together. It can also involve a more dissonant approach, such as what might happen when an idea generator meets a marketing person or a venture capitalist. In Belbin's terms, we have to work hard to get plants to work together with shapers, for example, even though both types almost certainly need each other badly.

The dark side of knowledge management

Knowledge is easy to lose. Unlike many other resources we possess, some business knowledge has an incredibly short half-life. Just consider how short the half-life for information is within financial markets. In an enterprise, sometimes knowledge is stuck in a silo, people take it with them when they leave, there are no 'prizes' for sharing it, or, worse, there might be reprisals.

The company might not have the skills to search the silo effectively or it might lack time or resources to conduct such exercises. A fundamental limitation of an intelligent society is the well-tested idea that knowledge sharing suffers if knowledge = power. The fundamental transformation dynamic we need to address here may be summed up by the following equation:

$$A \text{ shift from: } K = P$$
$$\text{Knowledge} = \text{Power}$$
$$\text{To: } KSU = P^2$$
$$\text{Knowledge Shared and Utilised} = \text{Greater Power}$$

The distribution of formal power is intimately connected with the dark side of leadership and leaders. Do leaders withhold information? Do they restrict access to their networks and so on? Leaders play a vital role in setting the tone for what others will do in terms of their own attitudes to sharing knowledge. For knowledge management to succeed there must be an alignment of these power sources in favour of sharing knowledge, skills and wisdom. There are things that leaders can do to set the culture. Then there are systemic things that help to oil the wheels of intelligent teams and enterprises:

Leadership interventions: Leaders design reward and recognition systems that positively encourage the sharing and successful utilisation of knowledge, skills and experience while actively discouraging the opposite of these behaviours. They also develop people in the art and discipline of 'creative swiping', i.e. the adaptation of knowledge, skills and experience to suit different contexts.

Structural interventions: Knowledge champions and learning guides can be very helpful as catalysts. These people will assist with the type of knowledge transfer that is needed, i.e. modelling, reflection, sharing 'scores', etc. Some of this activity can be conducted using electronic media but much is through body-to-body contact.

Systems interventions: Enterprise-wide knowledge-management systems must offer significant valued advantages over informal networks for them to gain acceptance. Word of mouth is still often more valuable than word of web. Good knowledge-management systems do, themselves, help overcome the problem of information overload. Good systems are coming to the market every day and it is worth considering the cost of drowning in data versus the opportunity of having access to the right information.

Environmental interventions: The built environment is just as important for the transfer of knowledge, skills and experience. As we move to more virtual organisational forms, this aspect of life in companies will have to be increasingly managed.

▨▨▨▨▨▨ MATHEMATICAL CREATIVITY ▨▨▨▨▨

Rethinking structure

- How could we add simplicity to the structures in our enterprise?
- How could we remove complexity from our structures?
- How could we multiply structural elements of our enterprise so that people can flow and fit more easily into different parts of the structure through rotation and other approaches to organisational agility?
- How could we divide monolithic structures so that they behave more like tribes, able to focus on a goal untrammelled by distraction?
- How do we identify 'connectors' to make divisional boundaries work better, both within and outside the enterprise?

Pollinateurs, intrapreneurs and agitateurs

Every new idea in science, politics, art or any other field, evokes three stages of reaction:

"It's impossible. Don't waste my time."

"It's possible, but it's not worth doing."

"I said it was a good idea all along."

Clark's Law of Revolutionary Ideas

In leading across teams, across the enterprise and beyond, more than ever we need the kind of enterprise skills that exist in the small business sector within companies, or what are usually called intrapreneurs. Sometimes these people have the luxury of greater levels of funding than they might be able to access as an entrepreneur. However, depending on the company culture, they might not always be afforded the same freedoms as an entrepreneur. The intrapreneur must therefore be skilled in the art of navigating barriers to the conversion of an idea into a sustainable innovation. To do that they often need to draw on the skills of people who will cross-pollinate the idea across the enterprise and people who will agitate in a good way to secure the necessary resources to advance the idea and improve the ROI (Return on Iteration). What then are the typical barriers to getting your idea off the ground inside an enterprise?

Selling your idea

Novel concepts are, by their very nature, fragile and must be communicated clearly and potently to those who must sponsor them. If your concept is complex, it is of vital importance that you communicate the concept simply to those who will advance funds, people and time to develop the idea. We frequently see how complex concepts fail in the TV soapreneur programme *Dragon's Den*. Of course, the show is not real life and you are normally given more time to pitch your idea at work. Nonetheless, simplicity, brevity and potency are key to capturing the interest of your sponsors. Try the seven words test. Can you explain the raw essence of your idea in seven words or less? If you can do that, then getting five minutes to explain your idea, its unique qualities and long-term benefits is going to be much easier.

So many times I have encountered people with great ideas but without the emotional intelligence to communicate them in a way that engages their target sponsor. I did some work for an innovative company in California working in the surf suit business. Their ambition was to gain endorsements and sponsorship from Sir Richard Branson. After some enquiries it turned out that they actually did not know what type of wetsuits he used, among many other gaps in their intended communication strategy. It was not difficult for a small child to gather the required data from a quick Internet search. I was somewhat surprised that they did not already know Branson's 'inside leg measurement' among other intelligence about his interests in surf wear necessary if they were to have had a chance of making an intelligent pitch. Aside from this, gaining an endorsement is quite different from gaining sponsorship and they needed to be much clearer on their goals to have a chance of success. Needless to say the project did not progress as well as they might have hoped, and, indeed hope is not a strategy when you have a limited window of opportunity to present an idea. To communicate an idea, as we have discussed, the bare minimum you need is:

- A potent message, expressed in your intended target audience's language and values. Too many times I see entrepreneurs and intrapreneurs working inside their own heads and comfort zones such that their messages do not reach their intended target. The NLP skill of 2nd position is an essential skill for someone wanting to convey his or her idea to others in ways that persuade.
- The right messenger to deliver the message. Sometimes this is not the ideator, who might lack the communication skills for their idea. In some cases they could be so passionate that this hinders their objectivity in presenting the idea in a way that persuades. Evangelism can be a real turn off when selling an idea and many times a more balanced approach is more persuasive. Oddly enough the passion that many entrepreneurs have must be tempered for a dispassionate approach when selling an idea.
- The right combination of communications channels – there are many, some are impersonal such as e-mail and some better for a dialogue such as face-to-face encounters. The selling of an idea is usually a discursive process and face-to-face contact is usually better when dealing with a dialogue when questions/objections may be raised rather than an asynchronous approach. Elon Musk adds weight to the notion that you should use the right channel for communications and not just the one that gets you into the least amount of trouble:

There are two schools of thought about how information should flow within companies. By far the most common way is chain of command, which means that you always flow communication through your manager. The problem with this approach is that, while it serves to enhance the power of the manager, it fails to serve the company.

Anyone at Tesla can and should e-mail/talk to anyone else according to what they think is the fastest way to solve a problem for the benefit of the whole company. You can talk to your manager's manager without his permission, you can talk directly to a VP in another dept., you can talk to me, you can talk to anyone without anyone else's permission.

Moreover, you should consider yourself obligated to do so until the right thing happens. The point here is not random chitchat, but rather ensuring that we execute ultra-fast and well. We obviously cannot compete with the big car companies in size, so we must do so with intelligence and agility.

- The receiver of the message must be awake, alert and receptive. This often points to a series of preparatory strategies rather than a single shot, especially if your access to the final decision-maker is limited. Preparation really is the mother of innovation.

In any situation of selling an idea it is also wise to identify the different stakeholders who might be involved, from the gatekeeper, whose job it is to allow you into the situation of influence (or not), the influencer who will want to study your idea in detail and could be the person to ensure your idea is accepted, and the decision-maker who signs the cheque. Each of these different stakeholders requires different treatments from you in the idea selling process.

Never give up

Spence Silver took 15 years to convince 3M that his idea for 'a glue that wouldn't stick' was a winner (the 3M Post-It Note). Ken Kutaragi nearly lost his job at Sony Corporation when he worked for Nintendo in his spare time developing what became the Sony PlayStation. Kutaragi found a product champion in the form of Norio Ohga, Sony's CEO, who recognised his creativity, when most of the senior management team saw his project as a distraction rather than a serious piece of new product development. By 1998, the PlayStation provided 40% of Sony's profits. The lesson here is to play the long game. Overnight success as an intrapreneur is the exception, not the rule. However, the type of persistence we are talking about here is not the 'If at first you don't succeed, try and try again' type. I call this head banging. In other words, 'doing the same thing over and over, expecting a different result'. I prefer the maxim 'If at first you don't succeed, try something different'. This is persistence plus creativity and it requires emotional resilience. In other words, this is your ability to bounce back from setbacks, having learned and incorporated this into your wisdom.

Tight fit or misfit?

Many enterprises are stuck in the groove of using time-honoured MBA concepts of suitability, feasibility and acceptability, pioneered by Johnson and Scholes, to judge novel ideas. Suitability is about fit with the business environment, the opportunities and threats therein. Feasibility is about whether the enterprise has the resources and capabilities to realise the strategy. Acceptability is about the return on risk for stakeholders. By their very nature, novel ideas often appear to be ill-fitting and therefore fail the test of suitability. They might require resources and capabilities that are currently unavailable to the enterprise and therefore seem unfeasible. They might also, therefore, have a high risk profile and therefore be unappealing to shareholders and key decision-makers, thus failing on acceptability. Johnson and Scholes' criteria are also often inappropriate for judging new ideas. The NAF criteria are often better (novelty, appropriateness and feasibility).

Much new product and service innovation succeeds because the product or service augments or is consonant in some way with existing approaches. We have already discussed consonance and dissonance earlier and these terms correspond to market pull and product push in the field of innovation. So, you can increase the probability of adoption of an idea that is somewhat dissonant by demonstrating how it fits in. When Akio Morita introduced the Sony Walkman, he considered the lifestyle compatibility issue by making shirts with a pocket designed to hold the device, thus solving the problem of 'where to put it'. Always think about the way in which your idea will be used and ensure that it fits in with the social and technical systems, which will improve adoption. If you are attempting to diffuse a 'misfit' into the market, then it is essential to build a bridge between the known and the unknown lest cognitive dissonance sets in, which will undoubtedly kill your brilliant idea even if it does not deserve to die.

Timing and time

Timing in the innovation game is everything. Da Vinci 'invented' the helicopter several centuries too early! Newspapers were arguably two decades too early going online, Google + (too late?) and AskJeeves – "Ask who?" you might ask? In research on innovation across 200 companies, timing was the most important factor in terms of impact on innovation success (42%), then team/execution (32%), the idea itself (28%), the business model (24%) and finally access to funding (14%). Google and Facebook are good examples of companies that got the timing right.

I was privileged to work for Sir Trevor Jones at The Wellcome Foundation in my early days, a philanthropic not-for-profit pharmaceutical company that was devoted to innovation. Trevor was a feisty and passionate scientist who unusually also understood the importance of advocacy and working across and outside the enterprise. He had a number of exceptional habits to help him keep his eye on the ball of long-term strategy while dealing with today's priorities. One neat trick was his 'too difficult' in-tray, for ideas that people had submitted that could not be implemented due to various issues including timing. He systematically recycled the items in the 'too difficult' pile so that they could be launched when timing favoured their introduction.

The other vital issue is securing sufficient time to work on your idea, in order to convert it into an innovation. Pharmaceutical company Roche take the view that intrapreneurs must be allowed time to innovate, and have applied the '20% bootlegging principle', originally developed by serial innovators 3M. Basically, this allows intrapreneurs to spend 20% of their time on non-job-related speculative projects.

Synthesis

Leading intelligent individuals in teams requires a style of leadership that is more directive in terms of setting a direction and rather more facilitative in terms of engaging the team on that journey. This, of course, is a generalisation and on occasion it is important for leaders to consult those they lead in the creation of a direction for the enterprise. Brain Based Leaders also respect and celebrate the diversity within the team.

When facilitating intelligent teams, leaders need the full range of facilitation styles from directive to non-directive. The Brain Based Leader masters facilitation to get the best out of the people they lead in teams.

As opposites attract so there will be conflict among diverse teams. The Brain Based Leader is skilled at handling conflict, applying the full range of strategies from head on inter-team confrontation through to skilful accommodation to address short-term concerns while keeping an eye on the long-term wellbeing of the team and the enterprise.

Brain Based Teams use a range of strategies for the transfer of knowledge and intelligence, ranging from the more familiar conversion of tacit knowledge to explicit knowledge (essentially a download-upload approach) through to more nuanced methods such as modelling, internalisation and so on.

To make cross-functional teams work, cross-pollination is needed to oil the wheels of enterprise by dealing with interface management. Such people are fluent in the different business languages of the different divisions and especially able to deal with differences.

DIALOGUE THREE

Brainy enterprises (global intelligence)

CHAPTER 9

'Video Killed the Radio Star'
Continuous disruption

Early synth pop duo Buggles were the first band to have their music played on MTV in 1981 with their song 'Video Killed the Radio Star'. This became a defining moment in changing the way music was consumed and changed other music TV programming forever. The title of the song has never been truer in terms of its wider meaning for Darwinian change in business. Yet the notion of disruptive change is not exactly new. Canals in the 18th century, railways in the 19th, and fireplaces, have all played their parts in transforming our lives. Fritz Haber invented the Haber process for making ammonia for use as a fertiliser in 1908. Up to this point potassium nitrate (saltpetre) had been used. Almost overnight, ammonia replaced the need for saltpetre and allegedly trains full of saltpetre were left half-way en route to their destinations as the value of the chemical plummeted. More recently, Kodak, Blockbuster and Betamax all discovered the power of disruption to their peril. Satellite navigation devices were thought to be a standard addition to a car until Google Maps arrived and the market fell off a fiscal cliff edge.

The idea of large corporations might also be up for disruptive change. In a conversation with Professor Charles Handy, he put forward the idea that large corporations will cease to exist. However, Peter Cheese at the CIPD was not so bullish about this possibility:

> Will we still have large organisations as some fundamentals prevail? Advantages of scale, the even greater need for collaboration, notions of strategic partnering. However, with the emergence of networked enterprises will come more organic, more accountable, more transparent organisations, which are porous in terms of who considers that they 'belong' to the enterprise and who receives a pay cheque and a permanent job there. The idea of hierarchy is a more questionable idea into the future. A quick look at the FTSE and Dow Jones shows that the half-life of organisations is in decline.

Looking further into the future, the Netherlands has mooted the idea of banning new petrol and diesel cars from 2025. This will be a game changer for the automobile industry. Given the declining half-life of businesses in the Fourth Industrial Revolution one can ask unreasonable questions such as, "Will Facebook exist in ten years time?" and "Will Amazon be disrupted?" The lesson for BBEs is "Be a disruptor or be disrupted". Disruptive change comes from the unknown and the unknowable in some cases. How then should we conduct strategic reconnaissance in unexpected places, spot weak signals of change before others do, continuously reinvent, collaborate with competitors and so on to create SCA?

The term disruptive thinking has had a mixed reception, possibly because the word disruption can imply breakage or loss for some people. Yet the term as originally coined by Professor Clayton Christiansen does not require careless behaviour, more a careful analysis and response to missed opportunities to change a sector or an entire industry. Yet we have seen the longevity of companies in free fall over the last century, often because something disrupted their world and/or they failed to notice the early warning signals of decline. In the last 15 years from 2000 some 52% of S&P 500 companies have disappeared, with the average lifespan of 61 years in 1955 versus 17 years in 2015. Darwinian change is nothing new in business or life. Leaders must then also ask themselves whether strategy itself is being disrupted. Should they throw away the underlying ideas of strategy and planning as sacred cows in business? A number of shifts are in play, which make the life of a leader more demanding than ever.

TABLE 9.1

Strategic shift FROM	Strategic shift TO
Strategy = long-range planning.	Strategy = anticipation, responsiveness, planning and improvisation.
People management = acquiring and deploying assets.	People management = developing agile employees who can learn rapidly.
Finance = looking backwards and extrapolating forwards.	Finance = extrapolating forwards and seeking funds to manage emerging scenarios.
Operations = fixed assets, e.g. factories, plant.	Operations = the ability to assemble and reconfigure manufacturing operations rapidly.
Information management = drowning in data.	Information management = swimming with information.
Marketing = push and pull.	Marketing = pull and push.
Environmental management = CSR.	Environmental management = strategy.
Innovation = R&D.	Innovation = Core business.

CHAPTER 10

Strategy is dead. Long live strategic improvisation

> Perplexity is the beginning of knowledge.
>
> Kahlil Gibran

On 13 July 1985, just as Live Aid was beginning, I flew out of the UK aboard Aeroflot, to begin a tour of Russia lasting several weeks, spanning the whole continent. Despite the very strict rules on photography on the railway network, one of the more surprising sights I took away was spying a missile on a launch pad in the middle of Siberia as we ambled past on the Trans-Siberian Express! What was perhaps more revealing was the fact that the Soviet system of rigid five-year plans led to waste, hardship and bizarre Monty Pythonesque practices, such as having to keep the under-floor heating on in our apartment in Irkutsk at the height of summer. This required me to stand on one foot at a time in the shower and dance like a Prussian flamingo with matches under my feet! The experience of rigid plans that were totally out of phase with actual need was mirrored in trips to Bulgaria, Poland, Hungary and, worst of all, Romania, where central planning and manic control by Nicolae Ceausescu seemed to have left most people with basic subsistence but without resilience. Such things were not confined to the Communist world. In the early days of the European Union we saw butter mountains and other products of centralised long-term planning that was somehow disconnected with real life. You might well say that long-term thinking is dead in a disruptive business world, but what are the alternatives?

Strategy through the ages

Strategy is the process by which an enterprise examines its external and internal environments and makes choices that maximise its purpose, whether

153

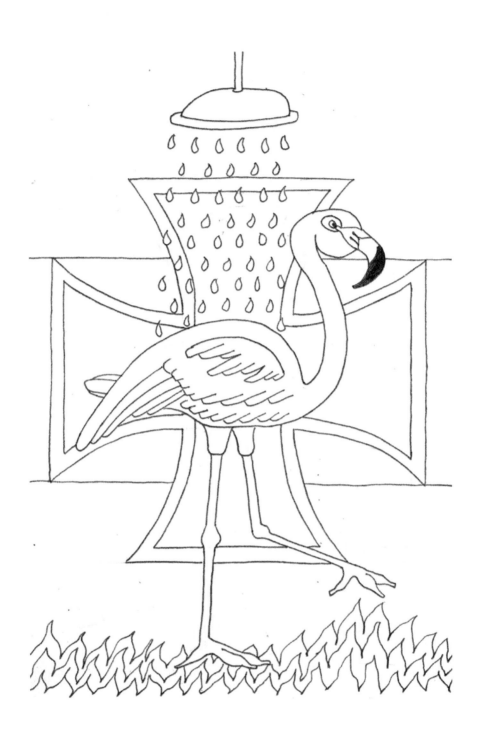

that is measured through profits or some other good, e.g. impact on society. Typically it involves some formal analysis, although some businesses develop strategy more intuitively, perhaps by experimentation in their marketplace. Typically strategy operates at three levels: The corporation; business unit level; functional level, e.g. HR strategy, marketing, etc.

There are several schools of thought on strategy. Here are some of the main thinkers in the field of strategy and their views condensed.

Competitive Strategy was epitomised by Michael Porter in his seminal book *Competitive Advantage*. Porter has now revised his views along the lines of our concept of SCA. Porter's essential contribution was to look at the enterprise in systems thinking terms around five forces. A complex systemic interaction between:

- **New market entrants** who can disrupt your existing foothold on power simply by dint of their newness or perhaps by competitive pricing strategies and other approaches.
- **Product and service substitution**, which can also take a market by surprise. Quite literally, video killed the radio star!
- **Customer bargaining power**. Think of Tesco or Amazon dictating the terms of business and prices offered to their farmers for 'grazing' and their authors for 'information grazing'.
- **Supplier bargaining power** with larger suppliers traditionally holding sway over the terms of business. Think of Tesco or Amazon dictating what the public can buy based on what they decide to stock in their stores.
- **Industry rivalry** with different players jockeying for position through different elements of the marketing mix from product to price, promotion, PR, etc.

Porter's thoughts fit in with the more general idea of deliberate strategy, which is analytical, structured and deterministic. Devices such as Vision and Mission Statements, SWOT analysis and MBO (Management by Objectives) are all products of a more deterministic approach to strategy. These are, of course, dreadfully attractive to those people who like to feel in control of their destiny and that of their enterprises.

Emergent strategy was the contribution made by Henry Mintzberg et al. Mintzberg and his followers made a distinction between deliberate strategy and emergent strategy. Emergent strategy results from the interaction of the organisation with its environment. Emergent strategies exhibit a kind of convergence in which ideas and actions from multiple sources integrate into a pattern. Authors such as Peter Senge tend to fit in with Mintzberg's ideas in so far as they see a need for continual organisational learning. This seems increasingly relevant in a world where information

EMERGENT STRATEGIES

NON-REALISED STRATEGIES

INTENDED STRATEGY

DELIBERATE STRATEGY

REALISED STRATEGY

is a major source of sustainable competitive advantage. For example, the founder of Wal-Mart built his stores close to his first store in rural settings rather than in big population cities, because it was easier for him to manage. He perhaps unwittingly stumbled upon a winning strategy. He found that there was less competition and people in the countryside would travel miles for discounted items.

Grant looked at strategy from the inside out, based on internal resources in what came to be called resource-based strategy, something that many smaller enterprises or voluntary ones operate by. Resources were defined thus:

- **Valuable**: A resource must enable a firm to employ a value-creating strategy, by either outperforming its competitors or reducing its own weaknesses.
- **Rare**: To be of value, a resource must be rare by definition. In a perfectly competitive strategic factor market for a resource, the price of the resource will be a reflection of its rarity.
- **Hard to copy**: If a valuable resource is controlled by only one firm it could be a source of a competitive advantage. More often it is bundles of resources that make a strategy hard to copy.
- **Non-substitutable**: Even if a resource is rare, potentially value-creating and imperfectly imitable, an equally important aspect is lack of substitutability.

Often these factors, when combined, lead to the notion of a USP or Unique Selling Proposition. Some niche businesses swear by this approach to strategy, others swear at it, believing that they control all the resources they need. A resource-based strategy can be a pragmatic step for enterprises that can combine elements of strategy in ways that build a unique position. If they can then brand that, their position can be sustainable.

Other views include strategy as agility and strategy as execution. Companies like Toyota, Nokia and Virgin pride themselves on being nimble and quick to respond. Nokia has mastered the chameleon principle, starting as a paper mill in 1865, moving through rubber boots to power generation and mobile phones. It remains to be seen how agile it remains under Microsoft's stewardship. More provocatively, author and speaker Tom Peters suggests that strategy *is* execution. In other words, plans are nothing without action. This implies that strategy is made up on the ground and occasionally adjusted midstream in a chaotic business environment. Even large companies such as Unilever must consider the idea of flexible execution as customer moods and tastes change rapidly and brand loyalty is weaker. A relevant parallel to consider is the idea of improvisation in business and music. Here we examine the artform of improvisation in its many disguises and consider its application to a BBE.

The perils of free improvisation

As I write, we live in an age of greater spontaneity. A visible example of this is the recent sea change in our international affairs, where Donald Trump appears to have no time for rigid plans and stodgy committees, procedures and processes, preferring 140 characters rather than depth of character to make policy decisions. I must say I also have no appetite for petty bureaucracy in business. Yet Trump has adopted a pendulum 'bipolar' reversal, creating a war on plans and planning, where strategy is made on Twitter one day and reversed the next. In my experience, this free improvisation or 'making it up as you go along' approach to strategy is equally as unhelpful as long-range planning as exemplified by Shell in the industrial age and Communist Russia. To take a parallel lesson in music, in my time as a musician I have observed that freeform improvisation in music is often exhilarating for the musicians involved but it does not always attract or engage an audience. If I mentioned the musical artists Can, Stockhausen, Henry Cow et al., I am quite sure that only a few of you would have copies of their music in your collection. In extremis, free improvisation is an internally focused artform where the musicians are almost quite literally playing to themselves. Freeform guitar improviser Derek Bailey says that free improvisation is "playing without memory".

In business, free improvisation, or what Professor John Kao calls jamming, is the realm of some start-up lifestyle businesses that are essentially serving themselves, sometimes with disastrous consequences. I must therefore take issue with Donald Trump over his free improvisation approach to strategy, although in doing so I may of course have missed the next wave. Time will tell. Undoubtedly we live in a disruptive world, but it does not follow that we should change our strategy as often as the ebb and flow of ladies' hemlines in the fashion world, although it seems to be a modus operandi for strategy in the case of the 45th POTUS.

The perils of rigid plans

I must also take on the mighty Nassim Nicholas Taleb, author of *Antifragile* and *The Black Swan* on one particular matter. In *Antifragile*, Taleb criticises the idea of what he calls corporate teleology or, simply stated, planning. He says that everything he learned in business school was babble, although he also mentions that he never bought any of the books or paid attention to his tutors! Citing the examples of Coca-Cola, which began life as a pharmaceutical product, and Nokia who started life as a paper mill, Taleb dismisses the notion of planning. For me this is just too much of a generalisation and I must therefore challenge his generally brilliant thinking in this particular area. Rigid plans are certainly problematic in a changing world, yet I frequently experience the poverty in the complete lack of planning in smaller enterprises and start-ups, who often subscribe to the view that 'planning is for dummies', sometimes because they lack the skills to do so or because they prefer to run a lifestyle business. Managing by drifting might be a lifestyle choice for some but it rarely leads to sustainable success. Some structure/discipline is usually needed to scale an enterprise without placing a stranglehold on that business, its owner and the people. In many cases the old adage 'Fail to plan, plan to fail' is borne out by extensive experience.

Taleb cites the example of AZT as one of the few pharmaceuticals that resulted from deliberate planning to justify a complete dismissal of the importance of planning. Yet the drug Zidovudine (AZT) was discovered in 1964 as part of a project to discover potential anticancer drugs. AZT's activity in HIV/AIDS was only identified and then licensed some 22 years later, due to the routine screening that pharmaceutical companies give to their store of novel compounds. This is clearly not an example of deliberate strategy, except in the sense that the deliberate screening of compounds against new diseases is a logical and systematic approach used by all pharmaceutical companies in the search for remedies. I was proud to help bring the product safely to market in record time so I have some insights into the process.

Viagra (Sildenafil) was also not the result of a planned approach or a deliberate strategy. The compound was synthesised originally for expected activity in the area of hypotension but it demonstrated none. However, nurses noticed that it had side effects of penile erections during clinical trials. Scientists examining the data picked this up. It also needed considerable effort by a woman working in Pfizer's marketing division to persuade Board members to embrace this new area of medicine, which was not taken seriously initially. It is a fantastic example of the systematic use of planning *and* analysis, without which we would not have Viagra. Taleb seems to misunderstand the improvisational nature of early stage drug discovery. We need to harvest the benefits of planning *and* agility to profit from a disruptive world, so let us next look at what can be learned in business from the field of improvisation in music.

Not only strategy but also improvisation

Bad improvisers block action, often with a high degree of skill. Good improvisers develop action.

Malcolm Gladwell, *Blink*

Improvisation is a mystery. You can write a book about it, but by the end no one still knows what it is. When I'm improvising and I'm in good form, I'm like somebody half sleeping. I even forget there are people in front of me.

Stéphane Grappelli

The word improvisation is derived from *lila*, a Sanskrit word for divine play, which conveys the meaning of improvisation in terms of the creation of newness in the moment. Another way to think about improvisation is the French word *bricolage*, which means making do with the material at hand, perhaps like the notion of resource-based strategy and our thoughts to come on the power of constraints in business. The *bricoleur* is an artist of limits, the nearest equivalent thought being that of do it yourself or DIY. Improvisation is a product of *bricolage* but when people talk of improvisation they often think of music, dance and comedy, rather less business. Yet all of us practise improvisation every day in conversation and in a sense much of life is improvised, where we are testing thoughts out with others, sometimes in an open search and on other occasions a closed one, where we are seeking a more limited set of options or answers. Improvisation in my professional life started at an early age. At the tender age of 25 I was sent on my first international assignment for six weeks to start up a new pharmaceutical factory in Indonesia. The culture shock was palpable to say the least, having barely travelled further than Calais on a ferry to France before this 17-hour trip to what seemed like another planet where I was warned that there were frequent shootings of foreigners! There was nothing in the way of what we would call mentoring or detailed planning and much of what I did to respond to this challenge could therefore be called improvisation. I remember the mixture of confusion and terror as I had a short meeting with the old grandee who looked after international support before I set out from the UK. Rather than giving me a business briefing, he reminded me to get my cholera and typhoid jabs done, but his best advice was that I should make sure I took a jar of Piccalilli and a bottle of Drambuie for Harry, the ex-pat factory manager. It turned out that these items were impossible to get in Jakarta. As I was about to walk out of the office, he added dryly "Harry does not really want you there. He thinks he can do the job himself". Being thrown in at the deep end is one way to learn to improvise and I think I profited hugely from this and many experiences like it, but there are others . . .

Improvisation is ubiquitous in life and business due to the inherent entropy in the human condition. As pearls are formed when a piece of grit slips into an oyster shell we improvise spontaneously all the time from shopping to photoshopping, from sailing to emailing . . . and more deliberately during iterative design and new product development. Even in those jobs we might casually see as non-improvisational walks of life, for example surgery. Talking with surgeons it becomes apparent that, although they have a model of the body in their head from their training in anatomy and so on, each patient they are working on is slightly different to the model. Thus a skilled surgeon will improvise around their mental model to conduct their work with flair with obviously dramatic effects if they are successful or otherwise. Jacopo Martellucci undertook detailed studies on improvisation and surgery, concluding that surgery shares certain parallels with jazz improvisation, such as:

- simultaneous reflection and action;
- simultaneous rule creation and rule following;
- patterns of mutually expected responses;
- use of shared codes and signs; for example, people sometimes tap their head to signify that the band needs to move back to the motif (the 'head');
- continuous integration of the known with the novel; and
- a heavy reliance on intuitive grasp and imagination.

He states:

> As surgeons, we spend endless hours tying knots with one hand, practising with a piece of string over the back of a chair, building homemade simulators, or looking for other creative methods to learn surgical tricks. As musicians, we practice scales until they become automatic.

Healthware enterprise Touch Surgery is helping surgeons develop sufficient deliberate practice such that their reliability when dealing with real surgery patients improves. CEO Jean Nehme explains that they use cognitive mapping techniques, AI and 3D rendering technology to codify surgical procedures. Touch Surgery also work with leaders in virtual reality and augmented reality, working toward a vision of advancing surgical care in the operating room.

Henry Mintzberg characterised improvisation in business as a kind of 'guerrilla management activity'. He wrote on how managers cover up intuition with apparently rational activity. I have noted on many occasions that much great thinking in business is often 'flimsy' in so far as it occurs in the bath, the bed and the bar. Yet managers feel that they need to dress their ideas up in PowerPoint, spreadsheets or graphs in order to persuade hardbitten decision-makers that an idea is 'oven ready' and 'pressure tested'. In some enterprises, the culture allows and encourages speculation as a means of accumulation. For example, 3M allow time and money for employees to improvise by developing new ideas and products outside the company's current bandwidth for many years. Google allowed employees to operate on a 70/20/10 basis: 70% of their time on designated work, 20% of their time on projects and innovations linked to that designated work, and 10% of their time on 'free' innovative activity. This has produced innovations, such as Google Maps and Gmail, although Google have reviewed this policy now. Yet the term improvisation is relatively poorly understood in business circles, as it implies 'making things up' when nothing could be further from the truth. Improvisation in music offers unique insights into understanding improvisation in business. I have met the good, bad and ugly of improvisers in my time and it is wise to learn from the best.

As Mintzberg points out, improvisation is a natural phenomenon in most business situations. Just consider this 'day in the life' story taken from a colleague's direct experience as a change agent. The facilitator (hereafter called Jane) starts her day at 5.00 a.m. with a light breakfast. After all, she has a 50 km journey to her client's site. On arrival, Jane finds that the e-mails she sent regarding room layout and other important details have been mostly ignored. Just as well that she is there by 7.15 a.m. Jane fixes the various items that seem unimportant to the event organisers (but wonders why they asked her to e-mail all of this in the first place). Anyway, she continues to ensure that everything looks 'swan like' (graceful on the surface, with great amounts of turbulence underneath) by the time the client arrives at 8.45 for coffee. The client (Michael) throws in a few new surprises. Of the 20 people invited, it turns out that eight of them have been sent to another equally important meeting. "No matter," says Michael, "I've invited a collection of office staff that may well find the meeting interesting, even though they have no real interest in or knowledge of the topic under review. You did say it was important to have naive people in the room, and these people know nothing about the product or why we are here today." It turns out that Michael did not even send them the invitation, which explained the reason for the event and what was expected by the end. Jane smiles and sighs inside. "Ah well, this is one of the reasons why they hired me", she says to herself. Jane reminds herself of some useful knowledge she picked up when working in an improvisational theatre company. If an unplanned obstacle, such as a chair, appears on stage, the rule is to make sure that you 'use the obstacle'. She quickly ensures she gets round the new people to introduce herself, the purpose of the day and what is expected of them before the start time. At the start, she asks for one or two members of the group to explain the purpose of the day to the newcomers and asks the newcomers to ask questions until everyone is at the same starting point. Not only has she 'used the obstacle', but the exercise has additional value, as some of the previously invited people had not read the invitation anyway! Turns out that two of the administrators have sociology degrees and had wanted careers in marketing and sales. Another secretary is an avid collector of garden gnomes and spends some time explaining their virtues to Jane while she is trying to set the projector up. We can learn well about improvisation from the arts so let us look at the relationship between order, structure and creativity, improvisation in business through the ears and eyes of music.

Business improvisation lessons from music

> The very act of putting my work on paper, of, as we say, kneading the dough, is for me inseparable from the pleasure of creation. So far as I am concerned, I cannot separate the spiritual effort from the psychological and physical effort; they confront me on the same level and do not present a hierarchy.
>
> Igor Stravinsky

Improvisation in music has been recognised ever since Mozart, Beethoven and Chopin's activities showed that improvisation was viewed as an acceptable alternative to the performance of compositions from notation. A modern day example of structured improvisation in action is the music polymath Prince. Prince was highly disciplined about his work, using structure as well as improvisation to achieve a seamless performance, leading the band using a series of codes that signal musical changes which the whole band understands. For example, when he says "On the one, bass," the whole band stops playing except the bass player on the first beat of the next bar. This requires extensive practice of a repertoire of hundreds of songs, from which Prince would draw down some 20–50 or so on a given night, sometimes without prior warning. I have interviewed several members of Prince's musical collaborators, such as George Clinton, Marcus Anderson, Sheila E and his wife Mayte Garcia. One of the standout moments was an interview with Ida Nielsen, Prince's bass anchor for his last six years. She had some practical observations to ground the subject of skilful improvisation at the highest levels of performance with masters of their art.

Ida is a living example of the idea of 'deliberate practice' as proposed by K. Anders Ericsson. Deliberate practice requires the systematic extension of one's repertoire beyond one's comfort zone. In our experience, some musicians reach a plateau of competence, due to re-rehearsing that which they already know. To master an instrument requires practice outside of the known regions of your competence. Ida related a story about learning 'Donna Lee' by bass maestro Jaco Pastorius that was way out of her competence range at the time. She pointed out that by setting the bar very high, eventually difficult pieces become easy. In my own case, I consciously switched from playing rock music to gypsy jazz in order to move my playing skill up a level through seeing and hearing things anew after I had plateaued in an existing genre. This concept applies in many fields of human achievement. The parallel notion in business is that of extending your competence beyond familiar behaviours or even familiar markets in order to master new approaches. The degree to which you decide to do this of course depends on your enterprise's risk profile.

Ida respects and learns from great innovators in her field, like so many masters of their art, fusing their insights and inspirations into her own unique style. Her influencers include Marcus Miller, Victor Wooten, Bootsy Collins, Steve Bailey, Rocco Prestia, Jaco Pastorius and Esperanza Spalding. She cites Larry Graham as a key influence. Larry is credited with the invention of 'slap bass playing'. This occurred out of the constraint of not having a drummer in the band, which required him to develop a more rhythmic way of playing the instrument. We explore the role that constraints and *bricolage* play in the improvisational process shortly.

Ida also spoke with me on the relationship between mastery and agility/improvisation when working with Prince himself. Ida had to learn more than 300 songs in order to have the flexibility to vary a given performance, sometimes on the fly. This is quite different from performing with most professional musicians, who prefer to hone a set and perform this as a set piece on all dates of a tour. This level of agility gave Prince and 3rd Eye Girl the ability to personalise their music to a given audience every night. To do this requires mastery at the individual and team levels, with everyone paying close attention to each other's performances. This is IQ, EQ and SQ working in perfect harmony in the context of a team performance. Mayte also testified to the fact that Prince was a workaholic and a perfectionist in a counter-intuitive observation to what most people would think about people who are improvisers. Prince put much more than the so-called 10 000 hours of deliberate practice into his work in order to set himself free to improvise. His blend of order and creativity was exemplified down to the last detail. Mayte pointed out that all of his clothes were arranged in separate colours in his wardrobe. In their 10-year relationship, Mayte performed an estimated 129 shows, not including after shows, music videos, jam sessions and award shows and the work was of prime importance. Prince studied James Brown's way of working and adopted a disciplined approach to the work:

> We all worked for him. Whilst on tour I was not doing enough activity to keep in shape and Prince docked my pay and whilst he was very encouraging, he also expected discipline and the entire band knew that. It was a wake up call. Any dancer or ballerina that wants to be great knows that it requires hours of blood, sweat and tears to be your best. Nobody sees it.
>
> Mayte Garcia

Prince's sax player Marcus Anderson is a rare breed in so far that he is an improvising musician who is also classically trained. Sometimes one discipline drives out the other unless you are a master of your art, which Marcus is. He also gives testimony to the value of mastery or what Mihaly Csikszentmihalyi called the state of 'flow'.

> Although I can read music and therefore understand the 'mathematics' of jazz, the real skill of improvisation comes from using your ear/intuition, paying attention to the other band members, feeding off them and finding a flow that moves the group performance up to the max.
>
> Marcus Anderson

The insights we can take away from Prince's example is that improvisation is largely about 'prepared spontaneity'. This aligns well with the idea of anticipation, which also has transferable value for businesses. Scott McGill, an improvisational musician who has worked with John Coltrane's teacher talked a lot about anticipatory skills when improvising. McGill is also influenced by Ericsson's findings. Ericsson noticed that the fastest and most accurate typists are the ones who can quickly anticipate the next move: "In sum, the superior speed of reactions by expert performers, such as typists and athletes, appears to depend primarily on cognitive representations mediating skilled anticipation rather than faster basic speed of their nervous system."

Ericsson suggests that deliberate practice requires individuals to set performance goals beyond their current level of achievement, thus leading to repeated failures until eventual mastery is achieved. He also insisted that performing at the highest level depends on the quantity and quality of that deliberate practice. The concept of setting performance goals that are higher than one possesses but that are not too far from one's present abilities agrees with other concepts such as Vygotsky's Zone of Proximal Development. The Zone of Proximal Development (ZPD) is defined as the distance between the actual developmental level as determined by independent problem solving and the level of potential development as determined through problem solving under guidance, or in collaboration with more capable peers. If we are to swim rather than sink in the information age, we all need to:

1. Learn to stretch beyond our comfort zones and completely switch genres on occasion to improve our value and relevance in a changing world. You might wish to seek out a challenge in order to grow, even something you would naturally avoid.
2. Tolerate, learn from and even enjoy mistakes and occasional failures, recovering rapidly.
3. Learn how to improvise and ripen our ideas so that they produce ROI (Return On Innovation).

If you are to improvise, it follows that there will be occasional mistakes. Improvisation is also based on having certain rules (constraints) and freedoms and it requires us to embrace the unfamiliar (dissonance). We next explore these as the breakfast of champion Brain Based Leaders.

GROUND CONTROL

Deliberate practice

- Start by setting yourself a stretch goal that is within your ZPD.
- To learn skills more rapidly observe others who excel at your goal.
- Make incremental changes each time you practise and note what works and what does not.
- To move toward your goal more quickly, get feedback from a friend, mentor or coach or use video to improve your performance. Use an app or a diary to record your progress.
- Systematically work on weak areas, not by repeating them but by visualising ways to overcome them and then practising strategies to reach your goals.

The power of mistakes

Do not fear mistakes. There are none.

Miles Davis

If enterprises are going to improvise, then it follows that there will be mistakes and occasional downright failures. How we respond to such things is therefore critical as leaders. The history of innovation is littered with mistakes and failures. We would not have penicillin without Fleming's tardiness in leaving his culture plates unwashed while he went on holiday. Roentgen's discovery of X-rays was thanks to careless handling of a photographic plate. I interviewed psychedelic rockers Hawkwind who were innovators of their age, performing with highly volatile VCS3 analogue synthesisers that would break down frequently or go out of tune due to the temperature. I asked them how they managed to reproduce their sound and the randomness with Apple Macs and they did admit that they had to consciously work at introducing failure into work in order to give it their characteristic strangeness and charm. The digital world is currently not as prone to analogue mistakes as the human condition and this makes it especially important for us to nurture our mistakes in the future if we are to produce things that take people by surprise.

When I worked in novel pharmaceutical development at The Wellcome Foundation we had an urgent and important problem on the pathway to the delivery of the world's first HIV/AIDS product that came to be known as AZT/Zidovudine/Retrovir. We needed to make the very first products for clinical trial. The product was presented as capsules in blister packs. During the packaging process one in a million or so of the capsules would burst. You might think this is not a massive problem, yet a burst capsule in a production line would mean that hundreds and possibly thousands of capsules would have to be rejected due to powder contamination in the blister packing machine, which would mean that the machine would have to be completely cleaned and thousands of packs rejected due to poor sealing. Supplies of the drug were scarce and this obviously had massive implications for our ability to deliver this drug to patients in time and all efforts were directed to finding out the cause of the problem. All minds were applied to the problem and various 'theories' emerged. The most prevalent paradigm was that the machine was somehow damaging the capsules and a vulnerable one would break occasionally. High-speed video cameras were deployed and I recall spending hours looking for the source of the problem like a modern day Sherlock Holmes of drug development. All efforts were diverted to improving the handling of the capsules until I decided to study the gelatin capsules themselves, against the advice and hectoring of my bosses to "stay focused on the packaging machine and simply stake out the production department until I'd figured it out". I did as I was told . . . and decided to do some other things . . .

PENICILLIN

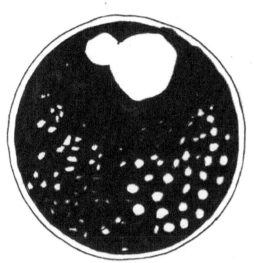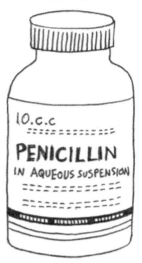

X-RAY

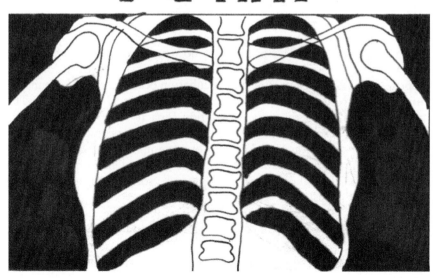

I developed a set of elaborate experiments to test the capsules for rigidity and therefore potential fragility under stress during packaging. We had just introduced tamper-evident sealing of capsules due to concerns arising from the Johnson and Johnson Tylenol incident where people died from the introduction of poison into the capsules in 1982. Our tamper-evidence system required that each capsule would be filled with powder, the cap applied and then a liquid gelatin seal applied around the middle of the capsule. I hypothesised that this made the capsule much more rigid when shocked and may have contributed to the problem. I set about trying to replicate the 'painting of hot gelatin' on the capsules with an artists' paintbrush. I started to notice that this did make capsules more rigid, but needed to find a way to test my hypothesis. Talking with my friend and colleague Jim Coghill, one day I 'found the answer'. For some reason, unknown to anybody including me, I used to have a small bust of Lenin that I bought in Russia on my travels at that time. It sat staring menacingly at any bosses that wanted to speak with me in my office cubicle. I needed something to test my theory about rigidity and the bust of Lenin fitted the bill perfectly.

Jim and I started smashing capsule samples while discussing the rigidity/flexibility properties of ones that had the tamper-evident seal (banded) versus unbanded. Jim remembers picking Lenin up and smashing a capsule with him. V.I. Lenin burst this banded capsule, which resulted in a jet of toxic powder all over my desk. But Vladimir squashed the unbanded ones. On inspection, most of the powder was retained within the intact but deformed unbanded capsule shell. This was our 'aha' moment!

To create happy accidents we need both techniques/discipline and freedom from techniques/discipline. In this case, our 'technique' was not a spreadsheet or a machine but a found object, which allowed us to see the problem more clearly. True intelligence involves surrendering ourselves to the possibility that we will succeed if we open ourselves up to making a mistake in order to learn. This is especially so when you are stuck. Successful people allow space and time for free play/improvisation with the obstacles to progress. What I call ripening and incubation occur when we have mental and physical freedom to reflect and learn about obstacles to progress. This may be done in an active experimentation capacity, as our bust of Lenin shows. It may also take place in more passive contexts, such as the 3 B's: in the bed, in the bath, in the bar. In our example of the capsule breakage problem, we felt we had the freedom to play and experiment with the bust of Lenin. This is how problems come to be solved, and not necessarily through sheer persistence.

As a result of these experiments, my attention switched locations to the department where the capsules were manufactured rather than the building where they were packaged. It turned out after much investigation that one of the process operatives would sometimes leave the gelatin roller running during lunchtime whereas others did not. On those occasions a small deposit of gelatin would build up on the rollers and one or two capsules would then

get a marginally thicker seal as soon as production started in the afternoon. These capsules were the rigid ones that would be subsequently susceptible to breakage during packaging. All of our intelligence had prompted us to look in entirely the wrong places for the answer to the problem and it was counter-intuitive intelligence that eventually solved the problem.

The point here is that analytics and therefore machine learning/AI did *not* solve this problem. A machine would *not* have thought to smash the capsules with a bust of Lenin! We must embrace mistakes and failures if we are to learn faster than our competitors.

The power of dissonance

One thing I know, that I know nothing.
This is the source of my wisdom.

Socrates

People talk eloquently about the need to hire disruptors, but corporate life can all but squeeze the life out of those valuable free radicals of free enterprise. A good disruptor must be comfortable with and capable of managing what psychologists call 'cognitive dissonance'. Turning to music to draw a simple parallel, musical dissonance occurs when two notes conflict together, due to them having frequencies that interfere. The effect is for the sound to somehow jar in your ear. In musical terms notes that are one, two or six intervals apart can cause the most interference effects that we experience as musical dissonance. In contrast, consonance is when those frequencies add together for a generally pleasant effect such as experienced in what are known as third part harmonies such as The Beatles, The Beach Boys and consonant four part harmonies in Barber Shop music. Listen to the beginning guitar phrase to 'Paint It Black' by the Rolling Stones just before the drums kick in to hear two dissonant notes, just one semitone apart. Speaking from the world of physics, the notes 'interfere' in a joyous way and give the song a distinctive motif. Other examples include Jon Lord's keyboard solo on 'Flight of the Rat' from 'Deep Purple in Rock'. The glorious clashing of guitars and viola on 'Venus in Furs' by the Velvet Underground is another good example. The best example of unbearable musical dissonance is Lou Reed's classic album 'Metal Machine Music', which consists of 64 minutes of white and pink noise, which to most ears is quite unlistenable (and of course to a few is pure joy). Reed observed somewhat pompously on the album sleeve 'My day beats your week' in a rather carefree attitude to the record company who had wanted a repeat performance of 'Walk on the Wild Side' from his best-selling album 'Transformer'. Heavy metal pioneers Black Sabbath are also masters of the universe in terms of using dissonance to great effect in their music, typified by the title track of their first album 'Black Sabbath', which uses the 6th interval as the signature motif. The 6th interval was considered so powerful that the Catholic Church tried to ban its use in the 16th century, long before our understanding of physics developed to the point that we understood that you cannot simply 'ban' electromagnetic radiation!

Yet many great earworms are the result of using unusual combinations of notes, which quite literally make the music unique. Dissonance can make musicians millions, so where is the useful parallel in psychology and business? Gerry Johnson offered us valuable insights about cognitive dissonance in his classic work on this topic. Businesses have a range of responses to disruptive external changes, ranging from ignorance, consonance or dissonance. Internal politics can kick in which usually results in conflict and then attack/defend spirals or referrals to committees. Worse still is denial.

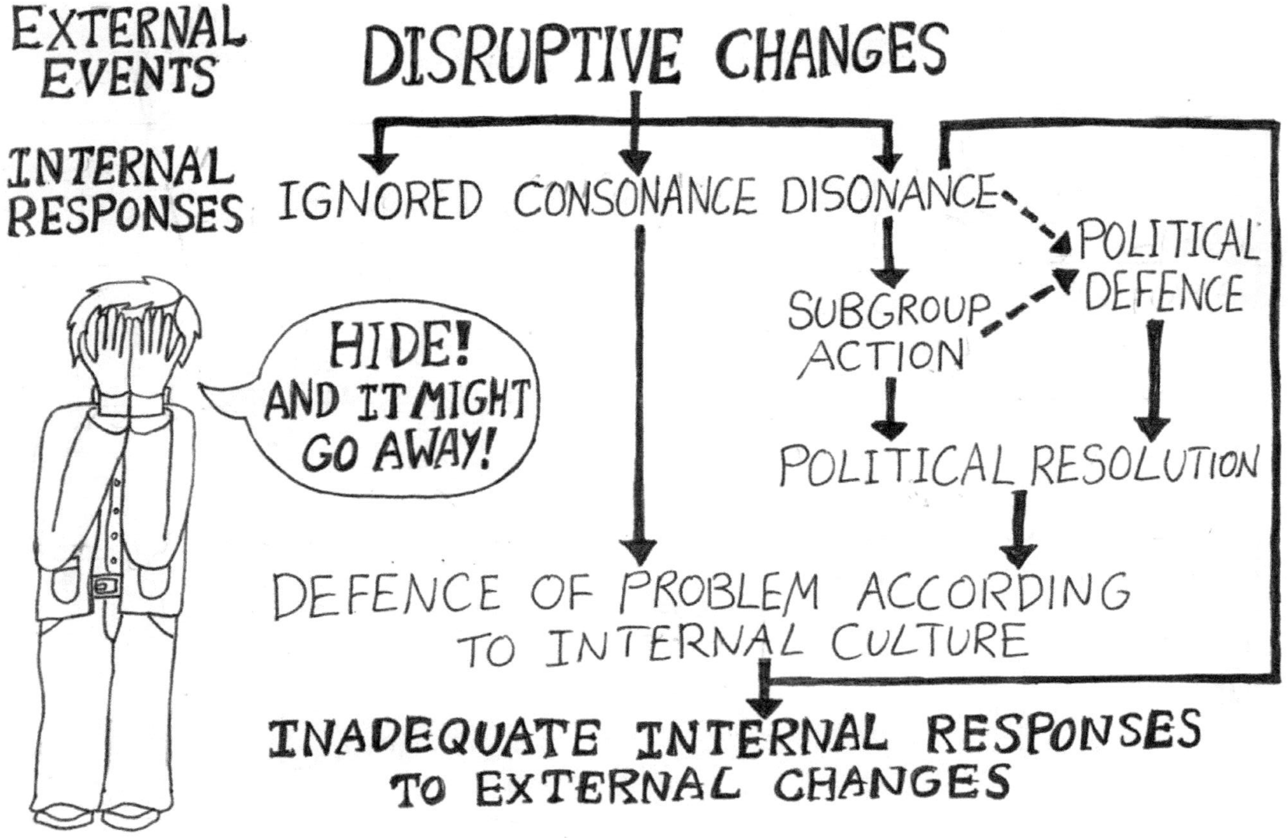
EXTERNAL EVENTS
DISRUPTIVE CHANGES
INTERNAL RESPONSES
IGNORED
CONSONANCE
DISONANCE
POLITICAL DEFENCE
SUBGROUP ACTION
POLITICAL RESOLUTION
HIDE! AND IT MIGHT GO AWAY!
DEFENCE OF PROBLEM ACCORDING TO INTERNAL CULTURE
INADEQUATE INTERNAL RESPONSES TO EXTERNAL CHANGES

In all cases this leads to an inadequate response to external opportunities or threats with the consequence that the business fails to capitalise on external change. This might account for why Kodak did not see the Polaroid camera on the horizon, and why they failed to predict the impact of digital photography on sales of photographic paper.

A typical situation of cognitive dissonance in business is with ill-formed or dysfunctional teams at a meeting. Everyone says agreeable things. On leaving the meeting room everyone privately criticises the meeting, the views and even personalities of the people present. Unlike our musical example, cognitive dissonance can cost millions and even billions, as Pfizer found out with their inhalable insulin product Exubera. Leaders must get used to hearing ideas that do not accord or strike a chord with their own. The successful innovator is a master of gaining people's attention to hear dissonant ideas and embrace them. There are different types of innovator:

- Conformist innovators accept the dominant values and relationships within the business and attempt to demonstrate how their activities contribute to the enterprise's success criteria.
- Deviant innovators act by working toward organisational success in their own way, demonstrate that their contributions provide a different yet better set of criteria for change, thereby gaining acceptance of their ideas.

Elon Musk is a good example of a deviant innovator, having set up Tesla Motors in 2004, opening up all his patents and changing the dynamics of patent control by saying "We will not initiate patent lawsuits against anyone who, in good faith, wants to use our technology". Tesla Motors also broke with tradition by selling direct to the public rather than via showrooms.

Greg Smith of Arthur D. Little sees the need to address cognitive dissonance as a business-critical issue when analytics do not match people's mental models or beliefs.

> We tend to hire young minds. The more senior some people get, the more people can become successful by what they know rather than their ability to find an answer. The more we define ourselves by knowing the answers, the more unsuitable we are in facing unknown and unknowable problems and challenges. A lot of seniority is based on knowing the answers rather than being able to find answers. The CEO should be the Chief Don't Know Officer even though there are clearly times to be more knowledgeable such as when presenting to shareholders.
>
> As consultants we are taught to deal in certainty and yet the best answers are often "I don't know". The dualities of one-zero, in-out, on-off are a limitation in finding ingenious solutions to problems as much innovation springs from the spaces in between these polarities.

GROUND CONTROL

Dissonance and consonance

Write down a number of your strongest held beliefs. These could be things about the world around you, your principles, expectations of others and so on.

Now reverse these beliefs in a radical way. Don't just say "I don't believe x", think of a serious antithesis. For example, if you feel you get the best out of people by being nice to them, imagine that you believe that you get the best out of people by ignoring them or abusing them in some way.

Try 'living with these beliefs' for a few days and note how you feel about them over time. Ask questions of them from time to time.

Review your findings to see if you can extend the repertoire of your behaviours and beliefs as a result.

CHAPTER 11

Corporate agility
Enterprise-level learnacy

One of the best examples of almost perfect enterprise-level learning in humanity is the Indian 'Tiffin' system of lunchbox deliveries. I learned directly from the street about this amazing piece of human ingenuity when working in India many years back, having dabbled with the idea of riding on the train roofs to experience the Indian Railway system as a commuter. I watched in wonder at the clockwork precision of the Tiffin system as chaos abounded all around at railway stations in Mumbai. The *Financial Times* stated that from 80 million deliveries per year there were no more than 300 errors or 0.0000000375%, a figure that compares favourably with any computerised Six Sigma operation. Experienced *dabbawalas* attribute the achievement to their own organisation (33%), the bicycle (33%) and the train network (33%), leaving 1% for serendipity!

However, the Tiffin system is a purely human enterprise with no computers currently involved, which makes it even more remarkable. We discuss beehives as complex adaptive systems later, but the Tiffin system has been a gold standard of complexity management for 125 years that most organisations struggle to beat. Even FedEx visited Mumbai to learn from the Tiffin system about how to improve their own excellence.

The Tiffin system is a complex web of relationships that delivers home prepared food via *dabbawalas* to some 130 000 workers in the centre of Mumbai, right first time, on time, 365 days a year. But what are the secrets of the Tiffin? It comes down to having a very simple but effective system of identifying the boxes using numbers, letters and colours, a simple process that all follow, supreme time-management skills (collections are timed with great precision, which is remarkable in itself for a city that is not known for precise time management) and great people who follow the rules but are also flexible in terms of local adjustment when necessary. The Tiffin system is the ultimate example of human ingenuity and intelligence to adapt and learn inside a structure. It is also an exemplar of mass personalisation, long before the term was coined in business circles. To achieve such seamless efficiency requires the democratisation of intelligence and the freedom to utilise it to adapt service delivery to the individual.

If individual learnacy is relatively easy and team learnacy more difficult, then networking the intelligence of a whole enterprise is the greatest challenge facing a BBE due to the nature of complex adaptive systems and the difficulty of achieving alignment in a disruptive age. In this section we merge ideas about social approaches to learning with that which comes from machines – a kind of 'cybersocial' approach to learning. As well as a thirst for learning, is there a case for us to become 'comfortably numb'? In other words, in a world where we consume 48 Gb of information every day in our leisure time, is there a time for 'social loafing' in order to reflect and renew? Is there an absolute necessity to shut down in a business world that never stops 24/7/365? What oasis points can leaders offer in order to help with personal and corporate renewal?

Peter Senge's seminal book *The Fifth Discipline* was more than 25 years ahead of its time. In the book Senge described the concept of a 'learning organisation', an enterprise that continually transforms itself. Building on the work of Argyris et al., expounded in their book *Organisational Learning*, the concept has now properly come of age in an era of digital disruption. In an age where the half-life of learning is in free fall, Senge's concepts of 'unlearning' and 'relearning' become more important for enterprises, especially ones that have strong embedded cultures. What strategies, assumptions and mental models in the business world are up for unlearning and challenge in the Man-Machine age?

Sacred cow # 1. First-mover advantage

Traditional 'taken-for-granted' thinking suggests that being first to market with your product or service confers advantages in terms of market penetration and ultimately dominance. For example, Sony was able to make a success with the Walkman and preserve market share for some ten years due to superior design skills, marketing skills and the Sony brand. However, this did not translate into similar levels of success in video recorders. Similarly Hoover gained first-mover advantage through incremental improvements over 30 years. Starting in 1908, the first upright vacuum cleaner was slow to diffuse into the market with only 5% of households owning one by 1930. With further design innovation Henry Dreyfuss produced a streamlined model, which became a dominant design until James Dyson disrupted the market with his dual cyclone cleaner in 1993. By that time the word Hoover had replaced the word vacuum as a verb, further solidifying Hoover's market dominance.

In the Man-Machine age, however, what Michael Porter called 'barriers to entry' are often relatively low. Just take the example of crowd funding giant Kickstarter. I had cause to use Kickstarter to fund a cancer project a little while back. All was going well, but then I started to receive reports that people were being refused when trying to pay through Kickstarter's payment wall. I investigated and discovered that this was a well-known problem at the time.

On contacting them I faced denial that the problem existed by Kickstarter's corporate immune system and an insistence that people should simply try harder. They seemed not to appreciate that once you get a letter from your bank suggesting that you have attempted the F word, i.e. fraud, people tend not to try again. Despite my protestations at the highest level, I got the same response. My hunch is that Kickstarter have been so successful that it mattered not if a few people are unable to get through their payment wall. Yet, in the wired world this is a dangerous assumption. When compared with a shipyard with huge physical assets and hard-to-find skills, Kickstarter's net assets, crudely put, are 200 kids, 200 laptops and a brand. Once word of web gets around, there are very few barriers to entry for a competitor to enter the market and improve the service. So, first-mover advantage can work when you have a chance of branding your product/service/enterprise so that it effectively prevents people looking elsewhere . . . for a while. But migration is much easier to do for customers these days. I sincerely hope Kickstarter takes note, as every other aspect of their service is excellent.

In other cases, the short half-life of some technology innovation demands first-mover advantage in order to gain the full value of the product before extinction. Netscape would be a good example of a pioneer technology that spurred the age of Internet browsers, although in Netscape's case the massive growth in the market they pioneered meant that it was extremely attractive to large players such as Microsoft, who threw huge resources at the opportunity. Eventually Netscape arranged a sale for $10 billion to AOL. If you choose first-mover advantage it is imperative that you then brand and protect your brand in a fast moving market.

TABLE 11.1 Core competences compared

The Industrial Age – Chatham Dockyard	The Information Age – Kickstarter
Large-scale premises 1.6 m²	A rented office
Complex large-scale machinery, some of which is not available on a proprietary basis and some highly specialised items 'invented' by the enterprise	200 laptops
10 000 skilled and trained artisans	200 kids with programming, IT and marketing competences
400 years of laid down brand protected by laws that prevent competitors	A brand made on the Internet, open to competition and with few barriers to entry
Funded over the long term by taxes	Funded on an ad hoc basis by customers

Speed in business is thus an inviting concept to gain first-mover advantage. It is exciting and gives us a rush of blood to the head. Most businesses are controlled consciously or otherwise by a 'rhythm section'. Sometimes this will be a function of leadership, in other cases it might be the speed of the slowest division via the theory of constraints, regulation or internal/infernal 'red tape' that impedes innovation velocity. Consider for a moment what would happen if your company was working to a tempo like a piece of music and started playing 'dance music' at 126 beats per minute (bpm), rather than a 'blues' at say 98 bpm? Try using a metronome or listening to different music to get a feeling of the differences in energy between these tempos.

The attraction of speed in business is easily demonstrated:

$$126 \div 98 \times 100 = 29\% \text{ performance improvement}$$

If it takes three years to get a new product to market, this translates into:

$$3 \times 0.71 = 11 \text{ months reduction in time to market}$$

Some industries have fast product development cycles. In aerospace, development times can be as long as 20 years. Imagine the impact that this would make to the bottom line. It could also contribute to increased competitive advantage through gaining first-mover advantage where this is of value. In the pharmaceutical industry an enterprise can spend $1.6 billion to introduce a new drug to the market, taking 12 years and involving the screening of some 2 million compounds. Any improvements to the cost and speed of screening through automation can make a major impact on the cost of this process. Getting the enterprise to up its tempo by a few beats without losses can be a very attractive notion.

The blockages to higher speed change over time. For example, it was a popular assumption that the main barriers to faster product development in the pharmaceutical industry are all about resources and organisation. This has driven a number of initiatives such as introducing project management approaches to companies. Yet a major emerging barrier is the ability of these companies to convert data into information. The average number of clinical trials required to satisfy regulatory authorities of the safety of a new drug has almost doubled in ten years. This translates into approximately 1 million individual observations that must be converted into information that can be interpreted. Clearly this has a very big implication for the information processing capacity of firms operating in this sector.

So speed is all about efficiency. It might not always be effective. Just consider the story of the hare and the tortoise and its relevance to business. Contrary to popular belief, it is not always an advantage to be first to market. The first-mover advantage is based on assumptions such as:

- It is possible to convert all customers to a particular product, service or brand.
- It is possible to keep these customers through continuous incremental or radical improvement and branding your enterprise/products/services to make them the default choice.
- It is possible to stop customers migrating through patent protection and/or the erection of other barriers to entry.

▒▒▒▒▒▒ MATHEMATICAL CREATIVITY ▒▒▒▒▒▒

Making the first move

For your next innovative product or service launch, ask yourself:

- What could we add to the strategy that would increase the probability of first-mover advantage?
- What could we remove from the strategy that would increase the probability of first-mover advantage?
- How could we multiply our footprint/branding so as to secure our place in the market?
- How could we divide other entrants in some way to maintain our position?

Sacred cow # 2. From competition to coopetition

Another one of Michael Porter's 'sacred cows' is the notion of competitive advantage. Porter's famous five forces for competition are about driving costs down, driving prices up, locking in customers, locking out competitors and new entrants. In a flat networked society, the notion of competition is augmented by cooperation as a means of accessing the multiple talents necessary to innovate. In such a society the idea of coopetition might be more useful, in other words a merger of cooperation and competition between enterprises, to deliver a superior service or complete a customer value chain. Enterprises such as Google, Uber, Airbnb and Facebook are great coopetitors.

As long ago as 1766, Adam Smith mentioned ethics as a prerequisite of sustainable business. Trust has now become a major strategic issue in enterprises in a world where we transact business with people we might never have met face to face. Barbara Brooks-Kimmel, CEO of Trust in America demonstrated superior returns from companies who exhibit high levels of trust, showing that America's most trustworthy companies have produced an 82.9% return versus the Standard and Poor's 42.2% since 2012, so this is not just a nice-to-have part of your enterprise value chain.

At the same time people have been moved to rage against the capitalist machine. We see this manifested through seismic shifts toward populism in Europe and the USA. I believe capitalism has some questions to answer in a world where the perceived gap between the haves and have-nots is growing and the visibility of this gap becomes more visible through social media. The big question for capitalism is not:

> Should an enterprise make a profit?

But rather:

> How much profit should an enterprise make?
> To what purposes should it put that profit?

In a coopetive world, we know that what gets measured and rewarded gets done. Enterprises need to reform the measures and rewards to encourage coopetive behaviours, especially as these may run counter to the human condition, so voluntarism is unlikely to deliver the expected results in this regard. Table 11.2 shows some ideas on how we might go about these shifts.

TABLE 11.2

Coopetive strategy	Measures	Rewards
Sharing knowledge	How quickly knowledge is shared from across the enterprise	PSP contributions (Personal Sanity Plan)
	How quickly knowledge is converted into products and services that people want or need	Financial rewards for successes
		Recognition for good tries
Sharing work	Speed to market and ROI	Meaningful collaboration
	Examples of jobs shared	
		Sustainable businesses
Sharing customers	Reciprocity – how many times contacts and contracts are passed between enterprises and to what value	Resilience
		Antifragility

Sacred cow # 3. From strategic alignment to strategic drift

The CEO's dream enterprise is one where everyone points toward the same goals, values and behaviours naturally within the context of doing their job. In extremis however such a culture prevents corporate curiosity and the agility needed to respond to opportunities. Much more than ever, CEOs need to encourage at least some divergence from the path and, in some cases, to encourage departure from strategic goals. To some degree enterprises can have their cake and eat it by encouraging internal entrepreneurs or intrapreneurs.

Sir Richard Branson's Virgin Group is a very good example of a group of companies that are built around strategic drift and intrapreneurship. Richard might live on Necker Island, but he gets out all over the world to look for ideas. In the same way, it is no good behaving like you are an island as an intrapreneur. He is also skilled at encouraging others to do the scanning for him with people pitching ideas on a constant basis. You need to diffuse and spread your ideas widely in the company to build up support. Get out and talk to people who can help you spread your idea. Many companies use innovation champions to support intrapreneurs and we explored the idea of cross pollinators in Dialogue II. A champion will help you diffuse your idea within the company and could help you when the night is darkest.

Sacred cow # 4. From learning to unlearning and relearning

> We cannot solve our problems with the same thinking we used when we created them.
>
> Albert Einstein

> Anyone who stops learning is old, whether at twenty or eighty. Anyone who keeps learning stays young. The greatest thing in life is to keep your mind young.
>
> Henry Ford

Unlearning is not forgetting. It is about conceiving of alternative ways of doing things and crucially relies on creativity. When we learn, we add new skills or knowledge to what we already know. When we unlearn, we step outside the mental model in order to choose a different one. Unlearning takes place at a simple level every time I travel by car to Europe. When my awareness is high I am normally very good at 'reversing' my driving pattern, changing gears, driving around roundabouts the right way, etc. Thirty miles (or kilometres) inland it is quite easy to forget. Anyone that has been to Weight Watchers will be able to relate similar stories in terms of managing their diet and exercise optimally.

The same thing happens in business. 3M and Nokia are supreme examples of enterprises that made unlearning their modus operandi. In 3M's case, the company was built on a glorious mistake, having bought some mountains with the intention of mining corundum but which actually produced very little of the mineral. This set the tone for much of what has contributed to 3M's success in the innovation game over many decades. One-third of 3M's products were invented within the past five years. Nokia started life in 1865 with a single paper mill. At one point Nokia made toilet paper. Nokia subsequently transformed themselves through rubber tyres to being the market leader in phones over a decade. It remains to be seen if Microsoft will preserve Nokia's 'agility gene'.

Unlearning requires a recognition that your mental model is past its sell by date before you can do anything about it. Without processes or routines to increase our awareness of the need to change, we are doomed to repeat ourselves. I will just say that again. At the moment of recognition that there is a point of inflexion, the search for a better option can begin and, most importantly, the new approach must later on be embedded as business as usual. When working with companies trying to unlearn I have found that they find some kind of intellectual model helps them make the process a conscious activity rather than relying on serendipity. This helps people become conscious of their mental models and ambidextrous in their thinking. The process is moved from one of pure serendipity to planned luck as well.

I asked Simon Warren of CaseWare to speculate on the question of how humans might respond to developments in AI, what capabilities they would need and what 'unlearning' might need to be done:

> Despite prophecies of doom it is not likely that AI will completely overtake the professional world in a short space of time. That means that the human element of the overall 'machine' is still essential, but professionals and those that employ them will need to adapt.
>
> First, it is becoming essential that users become properly adept at using technology. One might think that a professional would be fully expert in their use of IT in the same way that a master carpenter or plumber is at one with their tools. In my experience this is very much not the case. We see time and again users who learn the bare minimum, who either lack the curiosity or (more probably) are not encouraged by their seniors to 'waste time' experimenting with technology. This is a particular problem in the professional world, caused by the 'curse of the timesheet'. This approach will almost certainly spell doom for a future worker, and they will have to exploit their technology toolkit to the full.
>
> Another challenge facing professional businesses is the looming training gap. Take, for example, a young lawyer who spends their early years becoming expert in the field of contract law by reading and analysing contracts. This process is being replaced by machines

that can read contracts and, with AI and machine learning tools, highlight problems and suggest changes. Now our lawyers are being asked to review and give an opinion on potentially only the trickiest and most taxing parts of a contract, but how will they develop the skills to get there? Will a firm, under fee pressure, continue to do these things manually for the long-term 'greater good', or go for the profit and competitive advantage?

There is of course another threat here too. Contracts will be automatically drafted in the first place, to ensure they pass through automated readers because that is the most cost effective way of getting through that part of a new business relationship. So not only will we not need lawyers to read contracts, we might not need them to draft them in the first place!

So, businesses will have to learn whole new ways of training their people, imparting the job experience in other ways or perhaps changing the very nature of their professional training structure. After all, young accountants are taught bookkeeping as part of their foundation, but what happens when every transaction is via a closed system like 'touch and pay'? The bookkeeping is done, the internal audit AI carries out all the necessary checks with 100% accuracy, and passes the data onwards through the system. What then for bookkeepers?

HMRC are moving toward their 'Making Tax Digital' destination, removing us as middlemen and linking straight to bank and other data. Ernst and Young recently reported that large companies are starting to invest more heavily in internal audit and anti-fraud automation. Why? Because in one of their surveys of FTSE company employees, a significant number stated they would not 'whistle blow' on a colleague out of loyalty to their peer group. Now that is a very real concern indeed to complex businesses where they rely extremely heavily on whistle blowing to expose what can be very well hidden and complex fraudulent activity. The humans are being treated as the weak points in the system.

Humans in the professional sphere will have to learn their trades in a new way, and possibly at a more advanced level from the start. Firms will require fewer staff, competition for those training contracts will get stiffer, and selection processes will become harder. It might also mean there will be fewer higher earners, with the corresponding impact on government tax-take, which is why people like Bill Gates are urging governments to look at the concept of 'tax the robot' not the employee. If the former becomes the more productive engine of industry it makes sense to tax the higher producer, not the lower. Exactly how you do that is not clear, but it is being discussed in certain circles as an important future consideration.

Alongside learning and unlearning, the concept of antifragility is also an alluring one here. The basic idea is that something when stressed becomes stronger rather than more fragile. Who would not want that in their personal and business lives? Hitherto, the concept has been mostly reserved for biological systems but we are starting to see the emergence of anti-fragile materials in the form of the earliest signs of self-healing materials. Professor Stuart Rowan at Case Western Reserve University developed a polymer-based material that repairs itself in response to an intense beam of ultraviolet light. He says: "What you can imagine is essentially a paint coating on your car that you can heal whenever someone has rubbed a key down the side of it."

What then is the self-healing enterprise? Perhaps the answer lies in working hard on resilience in a disruptive world, where competitive advantage on one day could be ancient history the next. Enterprises can increase their resilience through strategic rehearsals, learning to improvise and scenario planning among other approaches. The design of enterprises that learn, unlearn and relearn is the domain of great HR strategies and tactics and it is to these issues that we next turn.

CHAPTER 12

HR strategies that liberate minds, bodies and souls

We begin with a visit to the future:

> *Julie's day in 2030 is different than it was in 2015. Each day is broken into thematic segments called mind, body and soul, work, family and leisure. The day begins with mind, body and soul then some family time before work begins. Work is broken into four 45-minute sessions with short physical breaks punctuating the day, then a longer period of leisure/family time. Julie's working week is 20 hours long. Everyone agreed to work shorter hours in exchange for improvements to their lives in 2027.*

HR can act as a huge enabler of a company culture that multiplies its collective intelligence or a massive obstacle to such things. All too often I have seen great companies disabled by bad HR, having sat in far too many meetings at HR institutes where such things have been discussed in terms of reputation management and so on but too little action has followed discussion. Yet, great HR is a transformational force for an enterprise that learns. What then can HR people bring to the table to encourage enterprise-level learnacy? How can HR encourage people to collaborate in areas outside their professional expertise or comfort zones? How can it embed such strategies and practices to create a culture of curiosity and collaboration within and outside the boundaries of the enterprise?

If you have not got several years to study an MSc in Strategic and Operational HR, here is the shorthand of HR Strategy and Practice, based on my tuition of one-year MBA SHRM programmes over many years.

HR strategy unplugged

A great HR strategy responds to the business strategy by encouraging beliefs, capabilities and behaviours that are consonant with that business strategy, while minimising or extinguishing those beliefs, capabilities and behaviours that are dissonant with the strategy. This is a 'best-fit' approach. It does this by the setting of a culture and structures that enable the enterprise to deliver. The underlying philosophy is that you can design culture rather than culture being the sum of the collective beliefs and values of the people. If you are to design culture into an enterprise, there will be a heavy emphasis on recruiting people with values that fit the desired culture rather than training people to fit in. Companies such as Virgin, Innocent Drinks and Metro Bank place great emphasis on recruiting the right people rather than trying to mould people to fit the culture and I concur that for every pound you spend on HR you are better off spending it on recruiting good people rather than trying to fix people that do not fit your company. However, the paradox here is that most innovative companies need some 'misfits' in order to maintain a certain level of 'edginess' in their business strategy. Nothing is black and white when we are talking about people. People are analogue misfits and to try to digitise them is to miss out on those things that make them both special and occasionally infuriating.

Other enterprises are fond of adopting the 'best-practice' approach, simply bundling together those HR practices that have been shown consistently to be 'good things' and applying them to the enterprise. These include things like careful selection, good training and so on. Public sector organisations are quite fond of importing best practices in HR and there can be a case for doing so when adequate performance is sufficient to serve the enterprise's needs. Often best practice is nothing more than 'keeping up with the Joneses' and, at best, it allows an enterprise to stay in the middle of its peers with respect to performance. A best-practice approach is generally less helpful when we need exceptional performance.

In both cases the HR relationship is usually one of service. In other words the HR strategy serves the business strategy. There can be arguments for a reversal of this order, especially in industries where people are the only source of advantage. This is essentially what academics call a 'resource-based strategy' or what I call working with the raw materials that you have to create your unique offering. Some charities are rather good at making the best of what they have as an HR strategy. In some cases it is their only choice.

Finally there is the question of designing the enterprise as one that learns continuously. It would seem that this is a staple element of any BBE's HR strategy and practice and we have discussed this at length previously.

HR tactics unplugged

At an everyday level, HR operations are about an alignment of business and HR strategy with the so-called 'HR Six Pack', in other words Recruitment and selection, Assessment and appraisal, Reward and recognition, Training and development, Career management, Succession management. Alignment

TABLE 12.1

HR Six Pack elements	Strategies	Tactics	Outcomes
Recruitment and selection	Recruit for experience and attitudes more than knowledge.	Use networks for recruitment more than cold interviews.	Agility.
	Recruit for ability to apply knowledge.	Use valid selection techniques that target skills and attitudes over knowledge per se.	Organisational renewal.
	Recruit for track record of rapid learning and agility.		Innovation.
	Recruit people that are brighter than yourself.		
Assessment and appraisal	Assess for successes and mistakes with a view to developing learning and renewal capacity and capability.	There are no failures, only interesting mistakes.	Resilience.
		However, repeating mistakes is for dummies.	Growth.
			Tolerance.
Reward and recognition	Reward success.	Reward knowledge transformation into innovation.	Diversity.
	Reward collaboration.	Recognise well-intentioned failures.	Teamwork.
	Recognise effort.		Encouragement of intrapreneurship.
Training and development	Focus on what makes people unique but also part of a cohesive team.	Train to enhance EQ and SQ.	Corporate capabilities.
	Look for opportunities to harmonise man/woman/machine.	Work itself is the source of continual knowledge-based learning.	Teamwork.
		Develop staff in teams.	
Career management	Assistance to find your career direction.	Careers based on continuous rotation in and out of professional expertise areas.	Reinvention.
			Organisational renewal.
Succession management	Leaders are the people who contribute the greatest growth and change to the enterprise rather than the greatest short-term performance.	Hire gamechangers.	Reinvention.
			Organisational renewal.

and integration are often discussed at great length, yet mathematically we are trying to achieve coherence between eight things. This is, of itself, a complex task, especially when you consider that these elements are about ultimately variable things, i.e. human beings. It is not, therefore, resolvable as a mathematical or cybernetic equation as some HR academics might suggest. At best we can hope to reach a sense of coherence and eliminate the worst contradictions of strategy and tactics.

GROUND CONTROL

Balancing HR strategy

Consider the HR strategy for your enterprise for a moment.
Name one thing that would make people want to work harder for the enterprise. What is stopping them doing this? What can you do about it?
Name one thing that is preventing people from working harder. What can you do about it?

HR strategy 2030

I engaged in a dialogue with Peter Cheese, the CEO of CIPD and a group of opinion formers: David D'Souza, Head of London; Warren Howlett, Head of HR Content and; Ruth Stuart, Head of Strategy Development to discuss some of the impacts of these questions on the way we run BBEs in 2030. Here is a summary of the rich dialogue that ensued.

The future's already here. It's just unevenly distributed.

William Gibson

The CIPD takes the fundamental view that work is not only a platform for a successful society, but also that work is a means through which people as individuals derive (and create) value and meaning, and make a wider contribution. Work is a part of being human and we must take time and care to shape that well. The employment relationship will be different as is the role of the HR professional in such a world. More than ever it is important for us to decide what we would like work to be like in 2030. In making such decisions, it is clear that the outcomes from work in a human and social sense have not always been good. We know from CIPD surveys that problems with well-being and mental health have been by-products of modern pressures from work. Inequalities in wages and opportunities have also grown. If we do not address these things then we will be in a worse place, as will our enterprises.

In 2014, 90% of US workers were doing jobs that already existed 100 years earlier. Some economists estimate that up to 47% of American workers could lose their jobs due to automation. The World Bank puts that number closer to 57% with particular emphasis on industrial robots affecting manufacturing jobs thus far, which might help to explain the disaffection of blue-collar workers in the Rust Belt of America who largely voted for Donald Trump as their saviour.

> In 2030, a hallmark of a great place to work will be the ability to navigate difficult (what we call VUCA or wicked) problems. Fons Trompenaars' work on reconciliation is a useful starting point in this regard and this points towards the adoption of higher-level communication skills such as David Bohm's idea of dialogue and Peter Senge's concept of Systemic Thinking. In a world of work that has become more complex we need such things even more than ever.

CIPD are increasingly working across functions and disciplines to address the principles of what they call 'Good Work'. More humanistic approaches to work are not new. The Victorians recognised that if you look after the people then the business looks after itself. Talking in a seminar, Tom Peters was also clear that if staff are looked after, shareholder interests are also served. It is encouraging that many more business leaders now also wish to discuss such things. Unlike the past where business leaders have expected HR professionals to prescribe rules, there is currently an active thirst to engage on these topics and discuss principles from which good work can evolve. As a result of this dialogue, CIPD have identified a set of professional principles for better work and working lives. HR professionals must lead by principles, which are also evidence-based and outcomes-driven, to deliver better workplaces. The skill of a great HR professional is helping people navigate the tensions and contradictions between these principles to come up with ones that best fit the context of a given enterprise.

> Better decision-making will flow from a system-wide and economy-wide view. Good decisions combine inductive reasoning and deductive reasoning, in other words we don't have bad decisions or decision avoidance, i.e. the wilful blindness approach. Better decisions will be characterised as: more balanced; more transparent; the ability to speak truth unto power and so on.
>
> David D'Souza, Head of London, CIPD

All good HR strategies are tied to the ground by HR practices that reflect the broad vision down to the last small detail. In our next visit we examine what 21st-century recruitment might look like where people chemistry is determined by the body of evidence from our everyday behaviour through the application of big data.

TABLE 12.2 CIPD professional principles for better work and working lives

Theme	Principles
Work matters	• Work can and should be seen to be a force for good; for organisations, workers and the communities, societies and economies they are part of. • Good work is purposeful; it is designed to help everyone use their skills and talents effectively and find personal meaning in the work they do. • Good work is safe and inclusive; fairly recognising contribution and valuing human connection. • Good work exists for the long-term benefit of individuals, organisations and society. It balances economic needs with social accountability.
People matter	• People are fundamental to businesses and organisations; they are unique and worthy of care, understanding and investment. • People should have access and opportunity to work and be provided with the support, development and resources to be effective; in turn, individuals have a personal responsibility for their work, development and behaviour. • People deserve to be treated fairly and have a meaningful voice on matters that affect them, in addition to their rights and protection under law.
Professionalism matters	• Being ambassadors for the profession by acting with integrity and championing better work and working lives in all we do. • A commitment to continually develop and to make decisions that are principles-led, evidence-based and outcomes-driven. • Bringing our expertise on people, work and change, together with our understanding of how business creates value for all, to balance the risks and opportunities inherent in any organisation. • Understanding the implications of our decisions beyond the interests of our own organisations, for the good of wider society.

HR practice 2030

I also visited The Chemistry Group, a leading edge recruitment firm who are inventing the future of HR practice, blending analytics, AI and automation with great HR skills, working in collaboration with the University of Cambridge to give them rigour and sustainability. Gareth Jones leads The Chemistry Lab, a disruptive business within the business, to invent Chemistry's future organisation.

In the past HR would attempt to glean information about your knowledge, skills and experience from quite crude tools such as an interview, a CV, an assessment centre and so on. All such techniques put the interviewer into what could be described as 'clinical trial conditions' and are therefore relatively poor predictors of the person's overall job performance as they are effectively a 'laboratory animal'. Gareth observed that we now have the potential to corral masses of big data across many fields, e.g. social media, face tracking and other tools, to produce a much more rounded picture of the individual, their behaviour across many situations and their habits. This increases the reliability and validity of the selection process many times over, as used by SAP, Telefonica, Diageo and so on. As he points out, "Every time you ask a question in an interview, you are leading the witness. It is better to study people's everyday behaviour to see the whole person".

The inspiration for the Chemistry Laboratory came from the world's largest language and personality study. This suggested that a comprehensive scan of people's social media activity would provide a personality profile as accurate as a 5 Factor Psychometric profile. It is rather like tapping into the world's largest focus group on you. Chemistry studies five factors – Intellect; Values; Motivation; Behaviours; Experience – to build a rounded profile of a person. This is a much better approach to building a picture compared with some of the amateurs in the field. Experian are a case in point. I was astonished to find out that they rated someone I know as a high risk when he had been in business for 25 years, had no debt, no mortgage and had built his business on cash, yet another colleague was rated more highly when they had bankrupted their business in order to avoid paying debtors. Their defence was that they had just copied and pasted data from Companies House and therefore they were not responsible. I would agree with that, as reputations are made on good or bad data.

In conversation with Gareth, he explained the Chemistry's purpose in setting up the lab was threefold: To prove the use of AI/big data in real experiments and not just in theory; to demystify the use of these technologies in the HR world; and to spin out a new business from it.

> To do this we stack the data and look for connective patterns. We look for points of intersection within the data – if we have proved these points of intersection across large data sets, we can pick out correlations without having to go back through the big data search. This means that we are able to make much more accurate predictions about people without all the usual HR tools.
>
> Science hangs its hat on causation whereas big data has legitimised the idea of correlation. We can see patterns if we stand right back and look across vast amounts of data. A good analogy is that

if we stood in the Sahara we would say the world is flat and made of sand. If we viewed it from another planet, we would say it is round and we would see a number of land masses and so on.

In practical terms, Chemistry is transforming the recruitment funnel so that it is filled with more of the right sort of people for a given position, making recruitment more satisfying for the individual and more efficient for the business. In Gareth's words:

> "If you pour sh*t in the top of the funnel, sh*t will come out."

SAP have pioneered this by building the Company DNA into the personas, words, narratives etc. in their company branding and their recruitment funnel. Chemistry built SAP an app that integrates SAP's brand DNA into their Facebook page, websites etc. so that the very first touch by a potential hire helps them to find a fit between themselves and the business. It does this by scraping the applicant's social media profiles and then recommending particular job families within the company if appropriate. SAP wanted to give potential candidates a great initial experience by helping them to understand their potential while also helping to guide them into particular jobs at SAP if they fit the profile. Chemistry also developed a 'serious game' to help candidates find out aspects of their style.

The tools that Chemistry Lab are developing will be of wider application in helping people to understand their potential to switch careers as jobs are displaced. This will be tremendously important for people who do not understand their transferable talents in the age of machines. Gareth concluded by saying that there is no war for talent, but there is a war for achievement. We started this book by asking the VUCA question "What Do You Want from Life?" At Chemistry they now have the tools to help people get better answers to the question.

Human competences for 2030

Given the plasticity of the human mind, it is possible that humans have the capability and capacity to adapt to the challenges of an automated world. At the same time, we are creatures of habit and our active engagement will be needed to change the habits of a lifetime if we are to remain relevant in the age of machines. So, whether we adapt and survive or ossify and decline comes down to willpower more than ability. I have already indicated that emotional and spiritual intelligences will be in massive demand, perhaps more so than formal IQ. Intelligence will become the ability to use knowledge more than simply store it in our brains.

Frey and Osborne's research indicates that cognitive automation or augmentation can replace almost any job without one or more of these characteristics:

- perception and manipulation of things requiring high manual dexterity and discrimination between different objects in a complex environment, e.g. a hairdresser;
- creativity and originality, e.g. a classical musician; and
- social interaction/intelligence, e.g. social workers, primary school teachers, and mental health nurses.

In his book, *The Fourth Industrial Revolution*, Schwab describes examples of jobs most likely to be automated as telemarketers, bookkeepers, insurance assessors, referees, secretaries, hosts, estate agents, couriers and so on.

Frey and Osborne went on to say that jobs least likely to be automated are "generalist occupations requiring knowledge of human heuristics, and specialist occupations involving the development of novel ideas and artifacts". Schwab's list of jobs least likely to be automated includes specialist social workers, choreographers, physicians, psychologists, HR managers, computer systems analysts, anthropologists, marine engineers, sales managers, CEOs and so on.

So, what does that mean in terms of competences we will need in 2030? In a connected world, Schwab suggests we will need cognitive abilities, systemic thinking, complex problem solving, content skills, process skills, resource-management skills, technical skills and physical abilities. I asked thought leader and leadership consultant Jennifer Sertl for further comment on Schwab's analysis. Jennifer is CEO of Agility 3R and Strategy Leadership and the Soul. She discusses 3R's that are necessary for a connected world: Resilience; Responsiveness; and Reflection. Jennifer offers ten elements to mobilise your potential:

1. Our coopetive advantage is how quickly we learn. Knowing has lost traction. Our power is in velocity and depth. We are all students of the Fourth Industrial Revolution. This era asks us to build these skills.
2. Our coopetive advantage is the power of our peer community. There is a discernable value shift from organisational power to that of organised peer communities aka P2P Production.
3. Our coopetive advantage is how we participate within our teams. Google has spent a lot of time and research studying thriving teams, and their research points to Dr Deci's Self Determination Theory. He suggests that these three attributes must be present for a person to thrive in a team:

- Competence: a belief that he/she is capable to contribute what is necessary
- Autonomy: a belief that he/she has freedom to make choices that impact the work
- Connectedness: a feeling of belonging

We tend to overplay competency and autonomy in Western culture. However, feeling part of something bigger than oneself and a clear understanding of how one's contribution supports the collective is something that algorithms have yet to find the magic sauce for. We are moving from an attention-based ecosystem to an intention-based platform.

4. Our coopetive advantage is how well we govern our work groups. In an era with so much collaboration and value centred work. It is important that we keep in circulation the wisdom of Nobel laureate Elinor Olstrom. People put a lot of time and effort into designing output. We need to invest more time in how we work, how we collaborate, how we build community. There is an art to governance and we need more capability here. Here are eight principles for managing work groups:

- Define clear group boundaries.
- Match rules governing use of common good to local needs and conditions.
- Ensure that those affected by the rules can participate in modifying the rules.
- Make sure the rule-making rights of community are respected by outside authorities.
- Develop a system, carried out by community members, for monitoring members' behaviour.
- Use graduated sanctions for rule violators.
- Provide accessible, low-cost means for dispute resolution.
- Build responsibility for governing the common resource in nested tiers from the lowest level up to the entire interconnected system.

5. Our coopetive advantage is how well we leverage cognition. Ginni Rometty, CEO of IBM reminds us that machine learning is about the cooperation and coordination of smart individuals and smart machines. Human interaction in conjunction with technology enables insight. Data is data. What turns data into information is context. She says: "Ultimately your coopetive advantage is being cognitive. The advantage will go to those who will go and extract insights from the data we all talk about."

6. Our coopetive advantage is being able to offer value beyond an algorithm. Scenario planning needs to strengthen as we see the horizon. We are adaptable and will continually learn new ways to create value. Denial is not a strategy.

7. Our coopetive advantage is how well we educate our youth. I am not talking about 'inform' and skill build. Let us go back to Latin ēducāre, to draw out.

> If you want to build a ship, don't drum up people to collect wood and don't assign them tasks and work, but rather teach them to long for the endless immensity of the sea.
>
> Antoine de Saint-Exupery

8. Our coopetive advantage is how well we share information.
9. Our coopetive advantage is the power of our questions. We keep inviting the categorical imperative as defined by Immanuel Kant. We inquire about belonging and ensure humanity transcends the gadgets.
10. Our coopetive advantage is equal to our curiosity. Intelligence is given too much credit. Innovation comes from either pain or hunger. Perhaps our greatest hunger is to experience life in a way that gives us goosebumps. Living with curiosity always finds the sunlight in darkness, the pathway in a trap, and the flaw in an algorithm. May we find our 'awe'.

We further assert that organisations, every one of them, have their own soul, the internal, intangible yet extremely present and powerful set of inner beliefs that make the organisation one of a kind. We believe that recognition of this has immense value, and alignment of this 'soul' factor across customers, employees and business partners is a fundamental necessity for success. Following on from Jennifer's work here, I assert that the notion of a collective soul is effectively the company culture. If your collective soul encourages intelligent action you have no need for the other HR devices such as tools and techniques.

CHAPTER 13

Cultivating intelligence
Cultures that liberate minds

A strategy document might give direction but culture determines what people feel able to do and be at work. Specifically in a BBE the culture should encourage the liberation of individual minds, creative collaboration in teams and enterprise-level learnacy. When we experience cultures that liberate minds as a consumer of the enterprise, our experience is often via the inferred signs, signifiers, myths, stories and legends, in other words, what we think the enterprise stands for. For example, people see Virgin as a challenger of other businesses, a consumer champion and the stories that surround it are often related to adventure via the stories that exist about its leader Sir Richard Branson. When we actually work for the enterprise, the culture is usually about the more obvious behaviour, any explicit values and control systems. If the enterprise is truly authentic there is no gap between how people see the enterprise from afar and how it is experienced on the ground. In other words, the external brand is the same as the employee brand. Motivation and brand loyalty arise when there is a happy marriage between external and internal views of the culture.

What then do you have to do as a leader to establish a culture that encourages people to bring their brains to work and use them in pursuit of superlative performance? Leaders who encourage brainy people make positive assumptions about their capabilities:

- They focus their minds on the 'destination', while giving them 'seven degrees of freedom' in their self-determination of the 'journey', consistent with the costs of each option. Unlimited freedom in the intelligent management of brainy people can be very costly although the extent to which you offer a hands-off approach depends entirely on the stakes involved and the propensity of each individual to diverge constantly.
- They encourage openness, especially about obstacles and failures. Such things cost time and can ultimately ruin a project if not caught early and addressed. Sir Richard Branson is especially good at being open about the mistakes he has made amid his successes, and this is the hallmark of an emotionally intelligent leader.

- They assume that brainy people have all the sources they need to deal with the project or task they are working on, but they check in periodically to see if they are managing, connecting them to people and helpful resources as needed. They operate a light touch on coaching and supporting their people.
- They encourage some level of positive deviance while expecting sufficient adherence to the enterprise's values and processes. In the words of Einstein, these processes must be kept as simple as possible but no simpler.
- All of the above is not at the expense of accountability. Leaders exhibit a kind of 'tough love', expecting their staff to deliver on promises, but being kind to them to encourage the delivery of results.

One aspect of a culture that encourages brains is the duality between order and freedom. Two examples shine the light on cultures that liberate minds through this duality.

Cultivating brains: Pivotal software

Employees at Pivotal's 20 global offices are ready to start the day at exactly 9.06 a.m. At that precise time a bell rings, and all workers gather for a stand-up meeting that lasts for between five and ten minutes. Then the firm's programmers hit their computers, with no other meetings or distractions for the rest of the day. Pivotal's founder and chief executive Rob Mee says it is all about making the working day as efficient as possible. He says:

> I realised that programmers, if left to their own devices, may roll in at 10 a.m., and if they haven't eaten adequately they will be hungry by 11 a.m., so they'll stop for food, which then makes the afternoon too long. It is not very efficient. So we thought, "Let's provide breakfast for everyone". It gives them a reason to get here.

Everyone must leave the office at 6 p.m. Staff aren't allowed to work into the evening: "Programmers don't programme well if they are too tired, so we don't want them working late into the night."

I also know some programmers that tell me they thrive on sleep deprivation, but I sense Pivotal's application of structure is well founded if they are to avoid burnout in their programmers. In any case, the keen ones can obviously carry on programming into their leisure time! The micro case that follows is an old-school example of how one can bring these factors into play in a consistent manner. Kodak might well have lost their innovation mojo some years ago but that does not discount the value of relearning from their mastery when they had it.

Back to the future: Eastman Kodak

Eastman Kodak might be a bit old hat these days, having fallen from grace after failing to notice the advent of digital photography. Yet they did some amazing things so let us learn from their great achievements. They originated the idea of the 'Office of Innovation' (OI), which was copied by many of Fortune's top 200 US companies, e.g. Amoco Chemicals, Northwestern Bell, Union Carbide, etc. The OI is a cultural programme that draws on ideas from all parts of a company. The OI approach encourages maverick contributions and provides a high return on investment. Eastman Kodak estimated that in one year alone the harvest was $300 million (over lifetime of idea) out of an OI network of 19 offices whose cost was only 0.3% of potential revenue. The model works on an implicit 'formula':

$I = C + In + E$

Innovation = Conception + Invention + Exploitation

The OI concept facilitates the reduction of time taken at each stage. The philosophy is perhaps the most important aspect of the OI concept.

1. Ideas and inventors are fragile and they need nurturing. All ideas must be listened to. Ideas that have been developed and demonstrate potential should be brought to attention of management. This reinforces the need for a culture of idea development and sensitive selection of ideas to avoid disenfranchising staff who originate ideas that are not market-ready for some reason.
2. Originators of ideas often need help to develop them and market them and should be involved in that development. Both marketing and technical issues need be addressed. This serves to increase the ROI (Return On Innovation).
3. Differences between people are strengths of a healthy innovation climate, not a weakness and might need effective mediation. Requisite diversity and the facilitation of diverse teams become business-critical issues for a culture of innovation.
4. The most effective way to proceed is not necessarily the most efficient. We have echoed this point several times in this book and sometimes the tortoise is more effective than the hare when innovation is concerned.

It is one thing to introduce tools, techniques and processes to encourage innovation within your enterprise, quite another to make them part of the practice of everyday life, through installing a Brain Based Culture that harmonises interactions between man, woman and machine. That said, there is a role for structure to improve the efficiency of your BBE and we turn to this next.

CHAPTER 14

Networked intelligence
Structures that liberate minds

Culture sets the context for networked intelligence, shared direction, superior team collaboration and the thinking of great ideas that lead to sustainable innovations. Structure helps people organise, share and leverage intelligence, skills and energy. It is also responsible for the 'velocity' of the enterprise, its ability to respond and coordinate responses to meet unexpected requirements. It is no good having a culture that encourages people to do their best when there are no mechanisms to network their ideas, support them financially/emotionally, help beat a path to the market and seize the moment. While it is not necessarily true that good structures will assist a BBE, poor structures seriously hamper collective intelligence, action and speed and there are a lot of them around. Philosophically speaking, we see structure as a necessary but not sufficient condition for a BBE. Our conversations with the CIPD suggest that we will need to become much smarter at organisation design.

HR as organisation architects

> As HR have a declining influence on the mechanics of HR, they will create greater value as people who help design good jobs, good structures and cultures in their role as Organisation Developers. This will mean they are involved at the outset of new product/market ventures to help the enterprise design the organisation needed to maximise business opportunities. There is a massive opportunity to turn round disengagement and disconnection in the workplace, much of which relates to the question of trust and the psychological contract.
>
> Peter Cheese – CEO, CIPD, Personal interview

Here we examine structural strategies that liberate corporate corpuscles and collective synapses. Organisation structure is itself a wicked problem with no perfect solutions to the dilemmas inherent in trying to find mathematical answers to complex biological problems. Many good and great people have agonised for decades over attempts to find an ideal way to structure an enterprise. Therefore, we begin with six key questions for further dialogue:

1. *Does structure follow strategy, the entirely rational view as suggested by Chandler in 1962? Or does it follow the career whims of powerful individuals, the HR department's latest guidance on Organisation Development? Dare I suggest that structure might even follow management 'fashion' as determined by the latest airport business bestseller?*

Organisation structure should of course follow the enterprise structure in any rational view of the world. But rationality ignores biology and, in any case, there is no point in setting up an organisation structure that is hampered by the humans that must inhabit it. At best we can organise our enterprises according to the best blend of what head, heart and soul allow. We can expect improvements to the fit between structure and strategy in a world informed by greater levels of rationality, but only if we submit ourselves to the mixture of what machines can offer in terms of analytics, guided by an agreed set of values from the owners of a given BBE. So we may eventually approach Chandler's vision in the Man-Machine age.

2. *Are matrix management approaches better than bureaucracy? Do the complexities of horizontal strategy and multiple bosses outweigh those created by formal rigid rules and hierarchical control as outlined by Max Weber in his original treatment of the idea of bureaucracy? Do computers create more bureaucracy?*

In the last 50 years, business academics and managers have proposed and tried various reforms to the basic idea of Max Weber's concept of machine bureaucracy, typified by the structure of large entities such as the United Nations, The US Senate and UK Government. Weber's idea of bureaucracy has been corrupted over time, but in its purest form was about a number of worthy things such as recruitment based on merit, strict hierarchy, clear rules and protocols, impersonal authority, lack of politics and so on. Humans, of course, polluted Weber's concept and bureaucracy is now seen to be about politics, sex scandals and red tape in organisational life. One of the more popular reforms has been the idea of matrix working, which involves having more than one boss, the need to juggle and a focus on task and project management, which is a feature of many gig economy jobs these days. Matrix management was seen as a way of freeing enterprises from the traditional structures of machine bureaucracies, by installing what is essentially a horizontal strategy, getting people to work in teams across the enterprise built around projects across the value chain, rather than in functional silos. I was part of an early experiment in matrix working in the 1980s, some years before the term had been coined. For some reason I had two pharmacists as my bosses, one of whom worked mornings and the other afternoons. Yet my work was project-based in the sense that I would have 5–7 main goals, which I would pursue over many weeks, sometimes months at a time. I must confess a certain degree of naughtiness crept in at times, or what we might now call moral hazard. If I did not like one of the projects from the morning boss I would say I was busy with the afternoon boss's work and vice versa. Now I am sure none of you reading this would confess to such appalling practices but I would not mind betting you have on occasion decided to do the thing you *preferred* doing over the thing you *had* to do in life?

When you scale this relatively simple situation to a network structure with transient leaders and a multiplicity of masters the matter becomes complicated. As a portfolio worker I regularly juggle 4–5 projects at a time, although I must adopt a different approach to my customers from the one I used as a young man. Rather than delaying any one project, I must work through peaks and troughs to keep my customers satisfied, since they all expect me to treat their project as the priority. In extreme circumstances it is better to refuse to take work on or at least to refer it to others in my network organisation, rather than to attempt to fit too much into too little time. This is at least some proof of growth and learning with maturity on my part!

However, it is clear that some people like, and even need, bureaucracy and rigid structure in their lives. I am aware that some people find it extremely troublesome to work in the gig economy with no assurances of an income or the ability to plan over the long range as a result of such employment practices. Professor Charles Handy's notion of a 'stability zone', explained in his book *Understanding Organisations*, is a durable concept that leaders must bear in mind when designing structures that enable people to bring their heads, hearts and souls to work. Each and every one of us would do well to think clearly about what lies at our root or stability zone and seek to protect that which allows us to adapt and flex in our daily lives. For some it will be family, for others geography, others some kind of passion that drives us.

Most company structures evolve from what they currently have and there are no magic recipes for structure. Bureaucracies often move slowly, managers become 'desk jockeys' and get stuck in a role and in a rut. Matrix management can be a recipe for overload and the tyranny of too many bosses if not executed properly. Enterprises often move from one structure to another without a clear rationale, perhaps in response to the latest fashion. In such circumstances, it is no surprise that each structural rearrangement often fails to address the particular ills that it was designed to cure. Structure is indeed a wicked problem and it helps to get back to fundamentals. If we are to design a BBE that is agile as well as successful, it helps to consider what fundamental engines of organisation improvement are. Arguably a BBE is a *thinking* organism and a *doing* machine. If we see these domains of activity over time, i.e. the past, present and the future, we can map out a number of functions that an effective structure might enable (see Table 14.1).

TABLE 14.1

Dimension	Past	Present	Future
Thinking	Converting knowledge into wisdom Unlearning Reflective practice	Operational planning Continuous improvement	Strategic thinking Rapid learning and reinvention
Doing	Cost reduction Killing off dying products	Optimising processes Adding new elements that confer improved value	Implementing strategic plans Improvisation and innovation Rapid prototyping Adventure teams

Some enterprises split the 'brain/thinking' parts from the 'brawn/doing' parts as a design principle. The academic parts of a university are essentially a thinking function, while the administrators are seen as the doing function although some academics have to endure teaching, which is essentially a doing function and one that externalises its work to the world and thus makes it accessible to all. If our university example were composed solely of thinkers, it would never deliver anything to the market. So it is also with many other 'professional' services enterprises.

We also have to solve the tendency for unhealthy competition to become a by-product of organisational structure. Some years ago pharmaceutical giant GSK split their R&D into a number of profit centres in order to gain from healthy competition. These centres compete for funding from the corporate parent and with external R&D agencies. They also pay for shared services. Like most things in business, the degree to which it succeeds will largely depend on how GSK implements the structural, cultural and capability changes that will be needed to make the idea work in practice. Since this is a fundamental structural shift, it will also be impossible to observe the effects of the change for some years to come.

This example also illustrates the problem of size with respect to innovation. Structuring a small innovative company is different from a large institution. The problems are different, not any better or worse. Small companies often lack all the resources they need whereas large institutions have the problem of coordinating the resources they do possess. Communications is a central issue. Putting this into a domestic context, a square table is quite sufficient to get good communication if you are inviting four people to dinner, but a round one is necessary if you want similar results from eight people. Beyond eight people, we need even more ingenious approaches to maintain good communications. In business, various observers believe that 100–150 employees is a magic number beyond which a sense of community breaks down. It seems that GSK is trying to preserve the benefits of size with the flexibility of a small institution.

Our robotics firm q-bot has a network structure, sourcing its needs from specialists rather than building a large organisation. This enables it to be agile. Although the company is in the 'Brain Based Economy' it employs some good old-fashioned management tools to ensure its products are fully grounded. For example q-bot uses incremental systematic development via market research rather than intuitive leaps of faith as its main source of input for design. It remains to see how they will structure themselves as they grow the enterprise.

3. *How much of our enterprise should we centralise? When and what should we outsource to free our enterprise to do what it does best? What are our core competences? How can we preserve and enhance these?*

Through history, we have lurched through fads and fashions regarding what to outsource and what to keep in house. Pharmaceuticals became quite obsessed with outsourcing everything in last few decades, even going so far as to outsource their inventive capacity via R&D activity. In the Fourth Industrial Revolution a key question is can you contain intellectual property leakage? Or will ideas about patent protection be overtaken by the speed of innovation through knowledge?

4. *Does size matter? Can technology help us break away from learning from cavemen and anthropologists? If so, how can we be both large and flexible? If not, how can we structure ourselves in ways that model entrepreneurial businesses?*

Size does matter. Dunbar's number suggests that the maximum number of humans that co-exist is around the magic number of 150, yet most enterprises exceed this number many times. While we can probably buck the trend of Dunbar's number in business through intelligent use of communication and collaboration devices, ultimately biology is bigger than big data. Our need to commune in tribes is a basic human instinct and we ignore it at our peril. BBEs are also Heart- and Soul-Based Enterprises and the smart leader makes sure that team members know enough about each other to profit from that knowledge as we explored in Dialogue II.

5. *Is structure the enemy of creativity, innovation and change? Are creativity, innovation and change the enemies of structure and control? To what*

extent can creativity, innovation and change thrive in a company that measures everything? Is measurement the enemy of these things? If it is not, how often should we measure the corporate pulse, so as to mark progress but not to destroy value through an OCD approach to measurement?

There are two related questions here. The question of the relationship between structure/order and creativity/freedom. Also the vexed question of measurement in a world where we can measure everything and must therefore make good decisions about what matters most. We have already discussed the notion that measurement should be 'necessary and sufficient' in an age when we can measure almost anything. The question is not 'can we measure it?' any more. It is 'should we measure it?'

Aside from that, creativity needs structure. Structure needs creativity. I believe they are essential bedfellows. Too much of either and your enterprise ossifies either through endless deliberation (structure) or unfinished business (creativity). As someone who consults widely on creativity, people sometimes find it strange when I advocate greater levels of structure in a business in order to harvest greater levels of innovation and vice versa in enterprises that are wound too tightly. A case in point is an enterprise that produces data analytics and intelligent software for a variety of high-tech industries, which realises that it needs creative ideas to develop their business:

> Our staff are very pedantic and quick to point out flaws in ideas, so, rather than expanding and exploring a suggestion, they tend to shut it down.
>
> Anon

6. *How do we capture the structure of 'relationships' and 'knowledge' in a complex world of connected global relationships? Should we even attempt this? Is the HR division the real expert in structural design, or would this task be better left to a social architect, a humanistic physicist, an anthropologist or a tea lady?*

Every structure provides certain benefits but introduces a number of compromises. When people talk about structure, they are talking about a variety of potentially competing elements. These include the use of structure for efficient delivery of customer requirements, a functional structure that optimises resources internally and lets people know 'where they are in relation to others', a learning structure that enables knowledge, skills and wisdom to flow and be multiplied, and a career structure that allows people to feel valued for their contribution and progress within the company, etc.

Inevitably, structure is both a rational and emotional issue, since it must serve the head, heart and soul of the enterprise. This point is not always well understood by the 'professionals' in this field, who are mostly concerned with questions of reward, grade and fitting 'pegs' into 'holes'. As a rule, they are also only concerned with two-dimensional representations of structure and operate from a rationalist perspective, failing to notice that it is the 'music', i.e. the relationships, harmony and collaborations between individuals and groups, that produces enterprise value rather than the individual 'notes'. We therefore turn next to the world of biology to look for structural insights with applications to the world of economics and business.

The Man-Machine bio-interface

> If you want to do complex things, keep your organisation as simple as possible.

Biological structures also require biological behaviours to make them work. We must master complexity and multiple relationships. As things become more complex in the world of work, humans have a tendency to match the complexity by adding layers of complex process and procedure, when exactly the opposite is usually needed. I have previously talked about how insects are smarter at dealing with inherent complexity than humans although it is fair to say that many insects are 'single purpose' beings. For example, termites build the human equivalent of cities without Microsoft Project, a decision tree or a Gantt chart. As far as we know they use pheromones to communicate, for example to find food, reproduce, etc. Some use vibration to signal alarm, by bashing heads together rhythmically.

Bees also coordinate complex affairs and build hives comprised of honeycombs of rhombic dodecahedrons of precise mathematics without attending maths lessons, using blueprints, training programmes, Six Sigma beehive building courses, etc. Pappus observed that bees have a certain geometrical forethought: "The bees have wisely selected for their structure that which contains most angles, suspecting indeed that it could hold more honey than either of the other two."

The average beehive comprises 50000–100000 individual bees, significantly more than Dunbar's number of 150. Bees differ from humans in so far as their colonies have flat structures and therefore significantly more order than human systems. They have a single boss and a few specialised roles: workers; drones. They are thought to communicate either through waggle dancing or smell rather than the multiplicity of methods humans use. Time and time again, the insight comes through that if you want to do complex things, keep your organisation as simple as possible. We regularly break

Dunbar's number on social media these days, having many thousands of friends in some cases, although at best many of these will be merely acquaintances. Even in this field, we only succeed if we apply some structure on these networks, perhaps sorting people into groups such as sporting friends, music lovers, lovers, close personal friends, close impersonal friends, acquaintances, stalkers and so on.

In *Leading Innovation, Creativity and Enterprise*, I point out that no single bee wants to become Senior Vice President of Pollination (SVPP), CEO (Chief Ecology Officer) or Director of HRM (Honey Resource Management). Bees do not have marketing, HR, IT or corporate governance departments or extensive compliance divisions requiring every flower to be checked for PC (Pollen Coefficient). They do not use Gmail for communication, preferring Bmail. Frivolity aside, by contrast, humans have not yet managed to make flat organisation structures work as well as bees. We simply must be able to do better than bees with all of our supposed intelligence. What structural lessons then can we learn from the synthesis of biology and mathematics to improve enterprise structures?

> **Order, order**: If we learn one thing from nature's patterns it is that inherent order is needed for success in a complex world. The Fibonacci sequence is a design principle inherent in so many of nature's structures such as pine cones and tree branching structures, which ensure that leaves have maximum access to sunlight and water. The basic mathematics is that each number is created by adding together the previous two, so we get 1, 1, 2, 3, 5, 8, 13, 21, etc. The number of spirals on a Romanesco cauliflower head is a Fibonacci number with its ever-decreasing series of logarithmic spirals that resemble a fractal.

> **Simple, simple**: Biology often uses inherently simple systems to address a complex environment. Occam's Razor is a practical manifestation of simplicity that helps us improve the 'signal:noise ratio' in terms of selecting out what is important from the background in organisational life based on the selection of hypotheses with the fewest assumptions attached. Many underlying concepts of smart design are also based on inherent simplicity and enterprises would do well to study them.

> Steve Jobs gained 347 patents in ten years. Yet Google's Sergey Brin and Larry Page only produced 27 in the same period. Apple use centralised development, whereas Google has a more distributed, open-source structure for new product development. Simplicity has its benefits. Size is supposed to confer advantages of scale and efficiency, but in many cases size means slow and inefficient. Of course size is not the only factor at play here as proximity/chemistry also matter. Interviewing Tim Smit, serial entrepreneur and CEO of The Eden Project, he summed the issue of size up neatly:

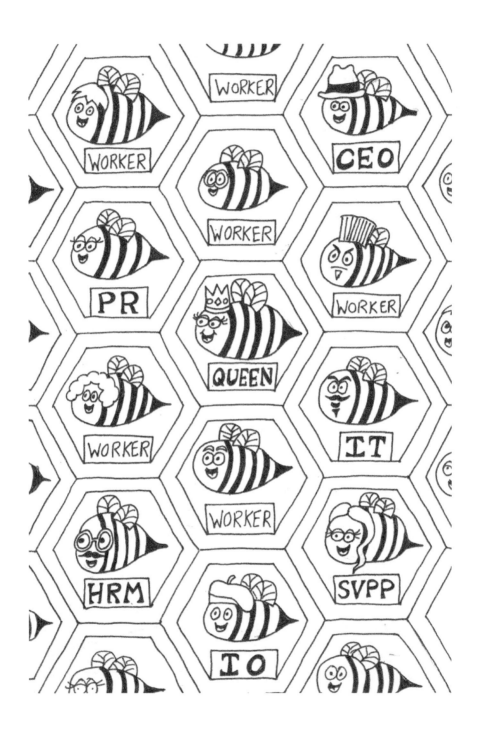

> My role as a CEO is to shake things up, to make sure we don't
> atrophy. As soon as an enterprise atrophies, as soon as something
> becomes a career path, you lose that sense of flux and excitement
> that makes the enterprise a great place to work.

Yet from my long experience of working in major corporations,
there is a tendency for larger organisations to lose their adaptive and
responsive behaviours that made them successful in the first place.
In a competitive world, this offers business opportunities for smaller
companies. What 'David' sized businesses can we learn from, then?
Bandcamp was founded in 2007 by Ethan Diamond and a bunch of
programmers and has succeeded in offering its customers superior
service and clear commercial advantages for the aspiring musician. As
a musician on Bandcamp, you can gain up to 90% of the income from
your music, whereas your royalty on a £0.99 single can be almost
nothing on the major download platforms and even less of nothing
from streaming services such as Spotify. Artists are paid immediately
when they sell their music. As a result of offering these clear advantages to musicians, Bandcamp grew rapidly. Artists like Thom Yorke
and Wolfmother all have their own Bandcamp accounts, alongside
notable indie labels, who make music from notable acts like Tom
Waits, The Black Keys and Spritualized. By simplifying the structure of their interaction with the customer, they have created a niche
offering for artists. Bandcamp's founder Ethan Diamond had the idea
after becoming frustrated trying to buy an album from a local artist
from their website.

Frustration is indeed a source of inspiration if it turns into action, as
Sir James Dyson found out while discovering that his Hoover really
did 'suck' as it did not suck. The frustration became the spur for the
Dyson vacuum cleaner and Dyson's way of structuring the company
was also based on simplicity and cell working rather than a traditional
bureaucracy.

Small, small: The abiding conclusions from years of experience
working in larger enterprises and also from academic research point
to the idea that if you want to do big things, keep your fundamental
units of organisation small. Team size crucially affects efficiency and
effectiveness. For instance, a team of two has one two-way channel.
With three members in a team, there are three such possible channels. With four team members, there are six channels. Adding one
person to a triad doubles the number of potential channels. With
larger team size, the number of potential dyads is $N (N - 1) \div 2$. To
do big things, look to the atomic units of your enterprise and the
small molecules.

GROUND CONTROL

Nature trail

Go on a nature trail in search of the following items (OK, you might have to visit a supermarket in some cases):

- A Romanesco cauliflower
- A pine cone
- A red cabbage cut in half
- A flock of seagulls
- A snail shell
- A shoal of fish
- Police controlling a riot

What do you learn about structure, order and resilience in your own enterprise?

Synthesis

Strategy is no longer about long-range planning. Rather it is about setting out a direction of travel, keeping your corporate receptors open and being quick enough to respond to life's opportunities along the journey.

Improvisation is a core skill for leaders in a disruptive world. We can learn about improvisation from textbooks but it is much easier to learn from deliberate practice. A rich arena of practice is that of improvisation excellence from the world of the arts, especially in music, where we can observe overt behaviour in teams.

Many taken-for-granted 'sacred cows' in business must be slain in order to succeed in a VUCA world. These include: the idea that being first to market is not the only strategy for success; the need for coopetition rather than competition in a connected world; the notion of strategic drift and a strategy; and the need for rapid learning, unlearning and relearning to develop an agile enterprise.

BBEs need supremely good HR strategies and practices to engage their people. This includes a culture of meaningful participation and one that encourages people to bring their heads, hearts and souls to work.

Biology beats computers when it comes to organisational design. That said we would do well to learn from the discipline of the digital logical world when designing our enterprises. We will have the opportunity to do both in the future and reach a point of convergence between what Chandler predicted in 1962 and reality, that structure should follow strategy.

We have all the potential in the world to do better at designing our workplaces if we think carefully about enterprise designs that engage people's heads, hearts and souls.

EPILOGUE

Future manifesto

Julie wakes up at exactly the optimum time to maximise her sleep, well-being and energy, to a vibration in her neck from her embedded wellbeing monitor. Some ambient music fills the room, bathed in soft purple swirling lighting and the smell of freshly brewed coffee percolates upwards from the kitchen. These are things she chose in her psychological contract with Rover. In a few minutes, Rover, her personal robotic assistant, brings coffee, water and fruit slices to her. It is time for Julie's early morning wellbeing session, led by her ever-faithful 24/7 digital guide, who has already ironed her underwear, run a bath, organised her bag for the day, checked her travel schedule, confirmed her appointments and so on. Rover also monitored Julie's vital signs and adjusted her personal exercise routine around her expected physical activity during the day, to maximise her balance of mind, body and soul. Rover is, of course, a robot and makes rational decisions based on an aggregation of big data about what is best for Julie's work, life and play. However, Rover has also integrated humanity by taking on board Julie's own personal values within the decision-making algorithms that Rover uses.

Rover also made breakfast and collected, collated and prioritised her overnight e-mails. Rover even took two video calls during the night to gather rainfall and other data and convert this into information needed for an agricultural project Julie is working on. She is not allowed to see any of the overnight work until she has had her workout and breakfast through the agreements she made with her clients and Rover. Mindfulness and physical exercise precede brainwork and the data from her morning routine is automatically fed into Julie's PSP. All of Julie's home appliances are enabled for her to speak to Rover anywhere in her house while he gets on with the housework. She talks to Rover via the fridge this morning, which gives her exercise class and meditation session.

Rover then conducts a business briefing and runs through the days' meetings and calls that Julie must make. This leaves Julie to do what she does best, although she has an agreement with Rover that she is open to challenge when her decision-making appears to be overly sentimental or not cross-checked with relevant facts. This level of structure and organisation allows Julie to be more agile and responsive to the various disruptions of business life in 2030.

Julie's day is different than it was in 2015. Each day is broken into thematic segments called mind, body and soul, work, family and leisure. The day begins with mind, body and soul then some family time before work begins. Work is broken into four 45-minute sessions with short physical breaks punctuating the day, then a longer period of leisure/family time. Julie's working week is 20 hours long. Everyone agreed to work shorter hours in exchange for improvements to their lives in 2027.

Julie cycles to work along a relatively empty cycle superhighway, since it was converted from a road after cars largely became a thing of the past. Even in winter she no longer fears riding in darkness as crime is now virtually eradicated, due to improvements in facial recognition, the ability to report crime in real time and receive remote assistance within minutes from Police enforcement drones and other general improvements in community policing. This also means that self-driving car sharing is a realistic option for those people who want to make longer journeys to work and this has dramatically reduced congestion. Julie's morning starts at 10.00 till 10.45 with a meeting and setting out her plans for the day. She then has two project activities and a wrap-up meeting to plot the course for tomorrow's work, with three further 45-minute sessions and a one hour lunch break devoted to learning and spiritual development while also feeding the body. She chooses to travel to work for reasons of wellbeing, EQ and SQ rather than there being any real need to geolocate. Julie is able to communicate her thinking directly to others via an interface in her brain that allows people to access her thinking as and when needed. Access is on several levels: an open source region for work associates; a private region for friends and family and a personal region which contains Julie's thoughts on love, life, etc. only accessible with express permission. She has a closed region of her mind, which is totally restricted even to her, although she can ask the interface questions about this area for the purposes of self-discovery and personal development.

Work is flexible. Julie works the hours as needed by a complex coordination of her client's needs, her family and herself. Rover looks after all the mechanics using a set of algorithms that Julie agreed about various priorities for her work/life balance. There are no longer days when she makes a plan then to be let down by cancellations or conflicts as everyone decided to 'choose life' when they elected to receive a basic income in exchange for full employment, fewer hours worked and the opportunity to earn more by discretionary contribution to the collective net worth through the IGOK (International Grid of Knowledge). Julie has young children so she contributes with one-third of her time to IGOK in exchange for a set of family orientated benefits via her PSP. She has planned to store up some of her contribution for a life-changing trip to Mars in 2050 with Virgin Celestial, which offers its first commercial flights to habitable planets from 2040.

Julie works as a project manager for a sustainable farming community based in a small village. She signs in for the day using her digital tattoo, which has replaced the multiplicity of passwords, freeing her mind to focus on what matters most in her life and work. She must plan the harvesting with a series of robots that are currently assessing the crops to determine the optimum time for the harvest. The robots work in tandem with a few skilled agricultural consultants, who advise on matters that are hard for robots to sense or accommodate into their plan.

Julie's clothing reminds her that she has not moved actively for 20 minutes so she is prompted to take a break. She takes a 15-minute nap to recharge her batteries. Refreshed, she then moves on to do some of her work while walking, using an augmented device in her arm. This allows her to operate a computer from a series of hand movements, which more or less equate to computer mouse movements, assisted by her voice. One of the great things Julie is able to do that she could not do before she was 'augmented' was 3D spatial design. This means that she is able to help people visualise ideas in space by using her body as a paintbrush – ideas that she creates using this approach can be 3D printed, which has significantly improved her ability to explain new ideas to others.

At the end of Julie's work she finds that she has a series of decisions to take in terms of her role as part of Citizen Government. She must express her views on matters ranging from the provision of community knowledge banks through to the reclamation of land in Norfolk as part of a project to address the loss of coastal areas as a relic of the industrial age now that sea levels are predicted to rise dramatically in the next 70 years. She does this by receiving a short, fact-checked briefing on each issue. She is expected to ask questions to test her understanding of the issue. She then responds using her augmented arm via a series of Likert scales in most cases rather than a simple Yes/No dynamic. This has been found to be a much better way to engage people in complex decisions due to the ability to aggregate big data and qualitative opinions into well-balanced decisions. Democracy has been reformed in the process and people's consequent engagement in things that affect their future has improved dramatically.

Julie has elected to do some voluntary work at weekends creating new knowledge, which is shared on IGOK. This work contributes to Julie's ROI (Return on Innovation) investment in what is effectively a collective bank of knowledge, which pays for holidays, healthcare and life's occasional luxuries. Everyone receives a basic wage and work becomes something that takes people further up Maslow's hierarchy of needs.

Julie blanks out an average of seven hours per day without computers to do human things. This includes childcare, family, leisure, sex, gardening, crafts. All the hardy perennials of being human. She also likes to have some unstructured time, which they often use to do old-school things such as go to the movies and play games together as a family. Julie's seven hours per day away from automation works well as it is also Rover's time to recharge (literally and metaphorically) and deal with the outfall of Julie's day without the need to interrupt her leisure and private time. Today she decides to

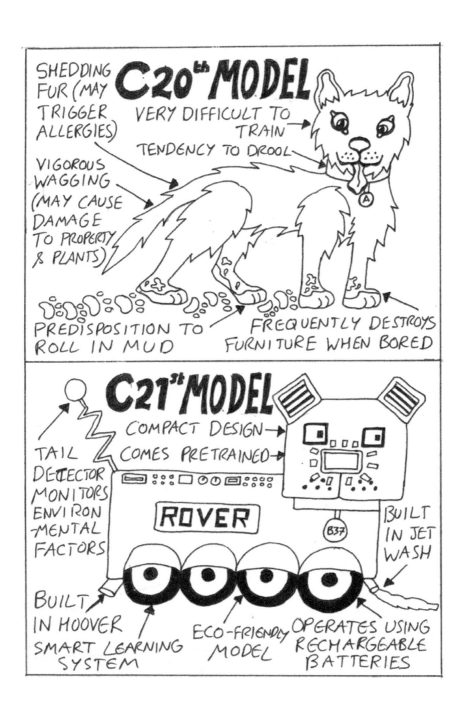

prepare the family meal with her children and Johnny. Although Rover likes to cook, so does Julie from time to time and it is also essential family time to build their EQ. She has delegated all the peeling and preparation jobs to Rover, leaving her with creative control of the cooking. Since food preparation consumes something like 50% of the time taken to cook, she saves about 30 minutes every day from this strategy, which she redirects into play with her children. Julie's husband Johnny is the major childcare expert and spends much of his day looking after them, although Julie elected to continue breastfeeding her baby girl Esmeralda and her sons James and Tom.

Julie wonders what life was like before the shifts she made to an economy in which people exchange brainwork for leisure and self-actualisation . . .

BIBLIOGRAPHY

Argyris, C., and Schön, D. (1974). *Organisational Learning: A Theory of Action Perspective*, Reading, MA: Addison-Wesley.

Ariely, Dan (2011). *The Upside of Rationality*, London: HarperCollins.

Ball, Philip (2009). *Branches*, Oxford: Oxford University Press.

Ball, Philip (2009). *Flow*, Oxford: Oxford University Press.

Ball, Philip (2009). *Shapes*, Oxford: Oxford University Press.

Barrett, F.J. (1998). 'Creativity and Improvisation in Jazz and Organisations: Implications for Organisational Learning', *Organisation Science*, Vol. 9, No. 5, 605–622.

Belbin, Meredith (2010). *Team Roles at Work*, Oxford: Routledge.

Belbin, Meredith (2011). 'Management Teams: Why They Succeed or Fail' (3rd edn), *Human Resource Management International Digest*, Vol. 19, No. 3.

Bell, Jason (2014). *Machine Learning: Hands-On for Developers and Technical Professionals*, London: John Wiley.

Berliner, P.F. (1994). *Thinking in Jazz: The Infinite Art of Improvisation*, Chicago, IL: University of Chicago Press.

Berns, Gregory (2010). *Iconoclast*, Boston, MA: Harvard Business School Press.

Branson, Richard (2006). *Screw It, Let's Do It*, London: Virgin.

Branson, Richard (2014). *The Virgin Way*, London: Virgin.

Burnard, P. (2012). *Musical Creativities in Practice*, Oxford: Oxford University Press.

Chace, Callum (2015). *Surviving AI*, New York: Three C's Publishing.

Collins, Jim (2001). *Good to Great*, London: Random House.

Cook, Peter (2006). *Sex, Leadership and Rock'n'Roll: Leadership Lessons from the Academy of Rock*, Carmarthen: Crown House.

Cook, Peter (2015). *The Music of Business*, Faversham: Cultured Llama.

Cook, Peter (2016). *Leading Innovation, Creativity and Enterprise*, London: Bloomsbury.

Csikszentmihalyi, M. (2013). *Creativity: The Psychology of Discovery and Invention*, New York: Harper Perennial.

Deci, Edward L. (1996). *Why We Do What We Do: Understanding Self-Motivation*, London: Penguin.

Dilts, Robert B., Epstein, Todd, and Dilts, Robert W. (1991). *Tools for Dreamers: Strategies for Creativity and the Structure of Innovation*, Capitola: Meta Publications.

Dimiriadis, Nokolaos, and Psychiogios, Alexandrios (2016). *Neuroscience for Leaders*, London: Kogan Page.

Drucker, Peter (2006). *Innovation and Entrepreneurship*, New York: Harper Business.

Dunbar, Robin (2010). *How Many Friends Does One Person Need? Dunbar's Number and Other Evolutionary Quirks*, London: Faber & Faber.

Ericsson, K. Anders (1993). *Protocol Analysis: Verbal Reports as Data*, Cambridge MA: Bradford Books.

Ericsson, K. Anders (2009). *Development of Professional Expertise: Toward Measurement of Expert Performance and Design of Optimal Learning Environments*, New York: Cambridge University Press.

Ericcson, K.A., Krampe, R.Th., and Tesch-Römer, C. (1993). 'The Role of Deliberate Practice in the Acquisition of Expert Performance', *Psychological Review*, Vol. 100, 363–406.

Festinger, Leon (1957). *A Theory of Cognitive Dissonance*, London: Pinter and Martin.

Frey, C.B., and Osborne, M. (2013). *The Future of Employment: How Susceptible are Jobs to Computerisation?* Oxford: Martin School, University of Oxford.

Gardner, Howard (1999). *Intelligence Reframed*, New York: Basic Books.

Gardner, Howard (2011). *Frames of Mind*, New York: Basic Books.

Ghiselin, Brewster (1985). *The Creative Process*, Berkeley: University of California Press.

Gladwell, M. (2006). *Blink: The Power of Thinking Without Thinking*, London: Penguin.

Gladwell, M. (2008). *Outliers: The Story of Success*, New York: Little, Brown and Co.

Gleick, James (1987). *Chaos*, London: Abacus.

Greenfield, Susan (2004). *Tomorrow's People*, London: Penguin.

Gundling, E., and Porras, J.I. (2000). *The 3M Way to Innovation: Balancing People and Profit*, Tokyo: Kodansha International.

Handy, Charles (1989). *The Age of Unreason*, London: Arrow Books.

Handy, Charles (1993). *Understanding Organisations*, London: Penguin.

Handy, Charles (1998). *The Hungry Spirit*, London: Random House.

Henry, Jane (1991). *Creative Management*, London: Sage.

Henry, Jane, and Walker, David (1991). *Managing Innovation*, London: Sage.

Heron, John (1989). *The Facilitator's Handbook*, London: Kogan Page.

Johnson, G.N. (1987). *Strategic Change and the Management Process*, Oxford: Basil Blackwell.

Jones, Chris (2012). *The DNA of Collaboration*, Charlotte, NC: Amberwood Media.

Kahneman, Daniel (2011). *Thinking Fast and Slow*, London: Penguin.

Kao, John (1996). *Jamming: The Art and Discipline of Business Creativity*, New York: Harper Business.

Kline, Nancy (2002). *Time to Think*, London: Cassells.

Koestler, Arthur (1964). *The Act of Creation*, London: Hutchinson.

Kotler, Phillip (2010). *Principles of Marketing*, London: Pearson Press.

Laloux, Frederic (2014). *Reinventing Organisations*, Brussels: Nelson Parker.

Lee, Rupert (2002). *The Eureka Moment*, London: The British Library.

Lehrer, Jonah (2010). *How We Decide*, Boston, MA: Mariner.

Levitin, Daniel (2015). *The Organized Mind: Thinking Straight in the Age of Information Overload*, London: Penguin.

Leybourne, S.A., and Kennedy, M. (2015). 'Learning to Improvise, or Improvising to Learn: Knowledge Generation and "Innovative Practice" Project Environments', *Knowledge & Process Management*, Vol. 22.

March, J.G., and Simon, H.A. (1958). *Organisations*, New York: Wiley.

Martellucci, Jacopo (2015). 'Surgery and Jazz: The Art of Improvisation in the Evidence-based Medicine Era', *Annals of Surgery*, Vol. 261, No. 3, 440–442.

McGrath, R., and MacMillan, I. (2009). 'How to Rethink Your Business during Uncertainty', *MIT Sloan Management Review*, Vol. 50, No. 3, 25–30.

Michalko, Michael (2011). *Creative Thinkering: Putting Your Imagination to Work*, Novarto, CA: New World Library.

Miller, Arthur I. (2000). *Insights of Genius*, Cambridge, MA: The MIT Press.

Mintzberg, H., and Waters, J.A. (1985). 'Of Strategies, Deliberate and Emergent', *Strategic Management Journal*, Vol. 6, No. 3, 257–272.

Morgan, Gareth (1993). *Imagination: The Art of Creative Management*, London: Sage.

O'Reilly III, C.A., and Tushman, M.L. (2004). 'The Ambidextrous Organisation', *Harvard Business Review*, Vol. 82, No. 4, 74–81.

Osborn, Alex (1993). *Applied Imagination: Principles and Procedures of Creative Problem-Solving*, London: Creative Education Foundation.

Peters, Tom (1989). *Thriving on Chaos: Handbook for a Management Revolution*, New York: Harper Business.

Peters, Tom (2010). *The Little Big Things: 163 Ways to Pursue Excellence at Work*, New York: Harper Business.

Pink, Daniel (2008). *A Whole New Mind: Why Right-Brainers Will Rule the Future*, New York: Marshall Cavendish.

Porter, Michael (1993). *Competitive Advantage*, New York: Free Press.

Redfield, James (1994). *The Celestine Prophecy: An Adventure*, London: Bantam.

Robinson, Sir Ken (2011). *Out of Our Minds: Learning to be Creative*, London: Capstone.

Rogers, Everett M. (1962). *Diffusion of Innovations*, Glencoe, IL: Free Press.

Schein, E.H. (1985). *Organisational Culture and Leadership*, San Francisco, CA: Jossey-Bass.

Schwab, Klaus (2016). *The Fourth Industrial Revolution*, London: Penguin.

Semler, Ricardo (2001). *Maverick! The Success Story behind the World's Most Unusual Workplace*, London: Random House Business.

Senge, Peter (1990). *The Fifth Discipline*, London: Random Century.

Senge, Peter, Kleiner, Art, Roberts, Charlotte, Boss, Richard, and Smith, Bryan (1994). *The Fifth Discipline Fieldbook*, London: Nicholas Brealey Publishing.

Sertl, Jennifer (2010). *Strategy, Leadership and the Soul: Resilience, Responsiveness and Reflection in a Global Economy*, New York: Triarchy Press.

Smit, Tim (2011). *Eden*, London: Corgi Books.

Syed, Matthew (2012). *Bounce: The Myth of Talent and the Power of Practice*, London: Fourth Estate.

Taleb, Nassim Nicholas (2008). *The Black Swan: The Impact of the Highly Improbable*, London: Penguin.

Taleb, Nassim Nicholas (2012). *Antifragile*, London: Penguin.

Trompenaars, Fons, and Hampden-Turner, Charles (2001). *21 Leaders for the 21st Century: How Innovative Leaders Manage in the Digital Age*, London: Capstone.

VanGundy, Arthur B. (1988). *Techniques of Structured Problem Solving*, Netherlands: Springer.

Wadhwa, Vivek, and Salkever, Alex (2017). *The Driver in the Driverless Car*, London: McGraw-Hill.

Weber, M. (1978). *Economy and Society: An Outline of Interpretive Sociology*, Los Angeles: University of California Press.

Weick, K.E., and Sutcliffe, K.M. (2007). *Managing the Unexpected: Resilient Performance in an Age of Uncertainty*, San Francisco, CA: Jossey-Bass.

INDEX